Psychology for Language Teachers

CAMBRIDGE LANGUAGE TEACHING LIBRARY

A series of authoritative books on the subjects of central importance for all language teachers

In this series:

Approaches and Methods in Language Teaching *by Jack Richards and Theodore S. Rodgers*
Appropriate Methodology and Social Context *by Adrian Holliday*
Collaborative Language Learning and Teaching *edited by David Nunan*
Communicating Naturally in a Second Language *by Wilga M. Rivers*
Communicative Language Teaching *by William Littlewood*
Communicative Methodology in Language Teaching *by Christopher Brumfit*
The Context of Language Teaching *by Jack C. Richards*
Course Design *by Fraida Dubin and Elite Olshtain*
Culture Bound *edited by Joyce Merrill Valdes*
Designing Tasks for the Communicative Classroom *by David Nunan*
Developing Reading Skills *by Françoise Grellet*
Discourse Analysis for Language Teachers *by Michael McCarthy*
Discourse and Language Education *by Evelyn Hatch*
English for Academic Purposes *by R. R. Jordan*
English for Specific Purposes *by Tom Hutchinson and Alan Waters*
Focus on the Language Classroom *by Dick Allwright and Kathleen Bailey*
Foreign and Second Language Learning *by William Littlewood*
The Language Teaching Matrix *by Jack C. Richards*
Learner-centredness as Language Education *by Ian Tudor*
Principles of Course Design for Language Teaching *by Janice Yalden*
Psychology for Language Teachers *by Marion Williams and Robert Burden*
Research Methods in Language Learning *by David Nunan*
Second Language Teacher Education *edited by Jack C. Richards and David Nunan*
Self-Instruction in Language Learning *by Leslie Dickinson*
Society and The Language Classroom *edited by Hywel Coleman*
Strategic Interaction *by Robert J. Di Pietro*
Teaching and Learning Languages *by Earl W. Stevick*
Teaching and Spoken Language *by Gillian Brown and George Yule*
Understanding Research in Second Language Learning *by James Dean Brown*
Video in Language Teaching *by Jack Lonergan*
Vocabulary, Semantics, and Language Education *by Evelyn Hatch and Cheryl Brown*
Voices From the Language Classroom *edited by Kathleen M. Bailey and David Nunan*

Psychology for Language Teachers: a Social Constructivist Approach

Marion Williams and Robert L. Burden

CAMBRIDGE
UNIVERSITY PRESS

PUBLISHED BY THE PRESS SYNDICATE OF THE UNIVERSITY OF CAMBRIDGE
The Pitt Building, Trumpington Street, Cambridge CB2 1RP, United Kingdom

CAMBRIDGE UNIVERSITY PRESS
The Edinburgh Building, Cambridge CB2 2RU, United Kingdom
40 West 20th Street, New York, NY 10011–4211, USA
10 Stamford Road, Oakleigh, Melbourne 3166, Australia

First published 1997
Reprinted 1997

Printed in the United Kingdom at the University Press, Cambridge

Typeset in Sabon 10/12 pt

A catalogue record for this book is available from the British Library

Library of Congress cataloguing in publication data applied for.

ISBN 0 521 49528 8 Hardback
ISBN 0 521 49880 5 Paperback

WD

Contents

Contents

Thanks

We would like to thank the following people for their invaluable assistance in the preparation of this book; Janet Welburn – for typing; Luba Atherton – for help with the index; Rita Chapman, Chris Ireland, Susan Lawrence and Norhayati Zamhari – for proof reading; Teresa Tyldesley – for help with typing; Alun Rees – for indefatigable encouragement; our students – for constant encouragement over many years to put the book together, and most importantly, Pauline and Andrew for their patient support.

Acknowledgements

The authors and publishers are grateful to the following copyright owners for permission to reproduce copyright material. Every endeavour has been made to contact copyright owners and apologies are expressed for any omission.

Figure 1, p.11 from *Look, Listen and Learn* by L. G. Alexander, figure 2, p.12 from *Kernel Lessons Intermediate* by R. O'Neill, R. Kingsbury and T. Yeadon, figure 26, p.170 from *Process and Experience in the Language Classroom* by M. Legutke and H. Thomas, reprinted by permission of Addison Wesley Longman Ltd; Collins Cobuild for Figure 3, p.14 from *Collins Cobuild English Course* by J. and D. Willis; Cambridge University Press for Figure 6, p.80 from *True to Life Pre-intermediate* by R. Gairns and S. Redman; Professor Reuven Feuerstein for Figures 7, p.82, 28, p.181, 29, p.182, 31, p.185; Patricia Warren for Figure 8, p.85; Consulting Psychologists Press, Inc. for figure 10, p.92; Figure 17, p.118 from Dörnyei, Z. *Motivation and Motivating in the Foreign Language Classroom.* MODERN LANGUAGE JOURNAL, Volume 78, Number 4 (Winter 1994): 515–584. Reprinted by permission of the University of Wisconsin Press. Section on 'arousal' p.127 from *The Dynamics of Intrinsic Motivation* by M. Csikszentmihalyi and J. Nakamura in Research on Motivation Education, vol 3, *Goals and Cognition*, edited by C. Ames and R. E. Ames, published by the Academic Press. Routledge for figure 22, p.146 from *Learning Strategies* by J. Nisbet and J. Schucksmith; Prentice Hall International for list of learner strategies from *Learner Strategies in Language Learning* edited by A. Wenden and J. Rubin, p.150.

Introduction

Why a book on psychology for language teachers?

This book is the result of several years of collaboration between two colleagues from very different professional backgrounds; one of us comes from the field of applied linguistics while the other is an educational psychologist. Several years ago we began to explore, somewhat tentatively, a number of different areas of educational psychology and to consider the possible implications of these for language teachers. The initial results of this work generated for us a tremendous feeling of excitement and we began to realise its potential value to teachers of foreign languages. Out of this preliminary exploration grew an increasing number of lectures, seminars and conference papers as we tried out our ideas with professionals in different parts of the world.

To our surprise, the sense of discovery that this work had generated grew. The more we worked together with different groups of teachers around the world, the more our ideas took on new shapes and new meanings. After a while we found that we had aroused the interest of an increasing audience, many of whom encouraged us to put down our developing ideas in the form of a book.

Spurred on by the interest and encouragement of the teachers with whom we worked in various teaching contexts, we began to commit our ideas to paper. Thus this book was conceived, heralding the beginning of a lengthy process of incubation which was at times stormy, but always professionally stimulating and increasingly exciting.

As we wrote, our ideas continued to be reshaped, so that at the end of each chapter we felt the need to return to the previously completed chapters to revise and renew what we had written. This we have come to see as entirely appropriate, because it is an illustration in practice of exactly what we are writing about, the process of construction and reconstruction of meaning.

The literature on language teaching provides comprehensive accounts of different language teaching methodologies and is rich with ideas and techniques for teaching a language. However, what has become increasingly clear to us is the fundamental importance to teachers of an understanding of

1

what is involved in the process of learning to inform and underpin our teaching of the language. Teachers' own conceptions of what is meant by learning, and what affects learning will influence everything that they do in the classroom. At the same time, in order to make informed decisions in their day-to-day teaching, teachers need to be consciously aware of what their beliefs about learning and teaching are. These two principles underlie much of the content and format of this book.

What this book is about

This is a book *about* psychology *for* language teachers. It is not a book about language teaching per se; there are numerous volumes on this topic already on the market. Nor is it a book of tips for teachers, or another book about second language acquisition. It is a text that is principally about psychology. It aims to provide language teachers with an introduction to a number of key issues and recent developments in psychology that will help them to understand better the ways in which their learners learn and which will provide a fund of knowledge from which to draw to inform their classroom practices. We shall, where appropriate, provide examples to illustrate the application of the ideas presented to foreign-language classrooms. However, at the same time we would not want to be prescriptive about how to put these theories into practice as what is most appropriate will differ from one situation to another, from one teacher to another and from one learner to another. It would also contradict one of our fundamental beliefs that teachers will make their own sense of the ideas and theories with which they are presented in ways that are personal to them.

This book is different from many books on educational psychology which generally aim to provide a comprehensive survey of different psychological theories. Instead we take one particular psychological approach which we apply to a number of different issues in learning and teaching, such as motivation or task design. In many respects this approach owes a great deal to the humanist tradition in its emphasis upon the whole person and on the affective aspects of learning. However, because of the particular value that we place on recent cognitive theories, our approach is essentially *constructivist*. As we shall explain in detail later in the book, we understand by this that each individual constructs his or her own reality and therefore learns different things in very different ways even when provided with what seem to be very similar learning experiences.

At the same time, we have to face up to the fact that learning does not occur in a vacuum. We therefore need a framework within which our particular psychological perspective can operate effectively. The framework we have chosen is that of *social interactionism*, which we believe encompasses the key elements of learning and education. As we see it, babies are born into social worlds, come to develop a concept of self as a result of their social interactions with others, and increasingly employ language to make sense of that social world and to help them play an effective part within it. Thus, an understanding of the social factors which play a part in our increasing competence as language users is essential for all language teachers.

There are a number of different areas that are currently of interest to language teachers which are directly related to and draw upon the field of psychology. An example is the area of learner training, which looks at how learners can be helped to acquire appropriate strategies for learning languages. This in turn involves an understanding of the cognitive and metacognitive strategies that learners bring to any learning task. Another example is the complex issue of motivation: what motivates learners to learn a language. A deeper understanding of recent views about why people are motivated to learn and of theories of intrinsic and extrinsic motivation can assist the language teacher to a deeper understanding of the motivation of his or her own learners.

This book, then, aims to provide language teachers with a background to a number of topics in educational psychology which will assist them in their day-to-day practice in teaching a language. In addition to this, the book also aims to equip teachers with a means of viewing the teaching and learning situations within which they work in an informed and analytical way.

Who this book is for

This book is intended for teachers of a foreign language at primary, secondary or tertiary levels. The principles discussed are applicable to teachers of English as a foreign language, modern language teachers, or those involved in teaching any language whether in the UK or overseas. It is intended that it should be usable by teachers from a range of teaching contexts and cultural backgrounds.

The book will also be of interest to teacher trainers and anyone involved in teaching psychological aspects of language learning and teaching. Those involved in the management of teaching or teacher training organisations, such as head teachers or inspectors, whether in the UK or overseas, should also find this book of value. It will provide a source of information about such issues as establishing in the school an environment which is conducive to learning, the relationships between teachers and learners, and, most importantly, will help the reader to formulate his or her own view of what the process of educating is all about.

In addition, it is hoped that anyone involved in the education of children who is interested in language might find this book of interest. Whilst we believe that the issues which we raise are of particular relevance to language teachers, it seems very clear to us also that their implications stretch far wider.

Overview of the book

Chapters 1 and 2 provide a brief introduction to the discipline of educational psychology and set the context in which this subject has grown. Important influences on the development of psychological ideas and theories related to the process of education will be described, and the relevance of these ideas to teaching and learning a foreign language will be discussed.

Following this, we present the interactionist perspective that will be adopted in this book. Four key aspects of the teaching/learning situation are identified; the *teacher*, the *learner*, the *task* and the *learning context*. These are seen as interacting with each other in a dynamic way. The rest of the book is organised around these four themes.

Chapters 3 and 4 focus on what the *teacher* brings to the teaching/learning situation. In Chapter 3 teachers' views and perceptions of learning are discussed, while Chapter 4 considers what teachers can do to promote and facilitate learning in their learners. Chapters 5 to 7 consider what the *learner* brings to the teaching/learning situation. In these three chapters various themes that are pertinent to learners are discussed: the learner as an individual, motivation and how learners deal with the process of learning. Chapter 8 looks at *tasks*: the place of the task as the manifestation of teachers' beliefs and the interface between teacher and learners. Chapter 9 then deals with the broader issue of the *context* in which the learning takes place. Finally, Chapter 10 pulls together the issues discussed in the book.

1 An introduction to educational psychology: behaviourism and cognitive psychology

1.1 Introduction

The process of education is one of the most important and complex of all human endeavours. A popular notion is that education is something carried out by one person, a teacher, standing in front of a class and transmitting information to a group of learners who are all willing and able to absorb it. This view, however, simplifies what is a highly complex process involving an intricate interplay between the learning process itself, the teacher's intentions and actions, the individual personalities of the learners, their culture and background, the learning environment and a host of other variables. The successful educator must be one who understands the complexities of the teaching-learning process and can draw upon this knowledge to act in ways which empower learners both within and beyond the classroom situation.

This is as true for the language teacher as for the teacher of any other subject. As we explained in the introduction, this book aims to provide a coherent psychological framework that will help language teachers to make connections between these different aspects of the learning process and to make informed decisions about what to do in their classrooms based on a psychological theory. In order to do so, we shall adopt one particular approach to psychology which we will develop throughout the book so that different aspects of language learning can be viewed from a coherent perspective. The approach we shall take is that of *social constructivism*, which will be explained fully in Chapter 2. In each of the subsequent chapters we shall consider the application of this model to different aspects of the language learning and teaching process. We do acknowledge that helpful insights can also be gained from an examination of other psychological viewpoints. However, these insights will be re-examined within the overarching framework which takes into account the social context of learning experiences and the ways in which individuals make sense of those experiences in such contexts.

Thus, instead of taking the view that different aspects of language teaching are better treated by different psychological approaches (Brown 1994:88–9), for example, the learning of vocabulary uses information-processing, the learning of structures is behaviourist, learner-training is cognitive, we consider that our fundamental philosophy of the educational process must be able to accommodate these different aspects of learning if it is to be coherent.

In the first two chapters of this book we provide an overview of the discipline of educational psychology. Some major schools of thought in psychology are presented as well as the influence that each of these has had on language teaching methodology. The present chapter examines two important approaches to psychology: behaviourism and cognitive psychology. Significant features of each of these approaches that will be of value to language teachers will be highlighted and some of their implications for language classrooms will be drawn.

1.2   Educational psychology

Educational psychology has been defined in many different ways. One such definition offered by Kaplan (1990) describes it as the application of psychology to education by focussing on the development, evaluation and application of theories and principles of learning and instruction that can enhance lifelong learning. Although this is a paraphrase of a widely recognised definition prepared by the American Psychological Association, it is a description which has its limitations as well as its strengths. What we certainly aim to offer in this book is a theoretical framework from which principles of learning and instruction can be drawn and evaluated. We shall also be making a case for the importance of learning throughout the lifespan.

However, what this definition lacks is a recognition that there is a fundamental difference between learning and education. Learning is certainly part of the process of education, but to be truly educative it must give a broader value and meaning to the learner's life. It must be concerned with educating the whole person. To do this it must meet important criteria which will be elucidated further within this book. One consequence of failing to make the distinction between learning and education is that many learning activities which take place in schools are not necessarily educative: they lack a real value to the life of the learner. Teachers may function extremely well as instructors and generate a great deal of learning of a particular nature in their learners, but unless this process is truly educative, then what has been learned is likely to be of limited worth. Within the field of language teaching, for example, many language tasks have little personal interest or relevance to the learners and have limited educational significance beyond the task itself. This is an issue to which we shall return in detail in Chapter 4, when we shall consider how teachers can give value to the activities they set, and in Chapter 8 when we discuss the design of tasks.

We also believe that as part of the process of education, teachers themselves should maintain a continuous process of personal reflection, within which they become aware of the personal and cultural values and beliefs that underpin their own and other people's actions. Only by raising their awareness in this way can teachers come to understand fully their own implicit educational theories and the ways in which such theories influence their professional practice. It should help them to understand also why and how their teaching may or may not lead to worthwhile learning. The importance for teachers of engaging in personal reflection on their practice is discussed further in Chapter 3.

1.3   Approaches to educational psychology

Just as in all other areas of knowledge, educational psychology theory has passed through a number of changes and fashions in its comparatively brief history. Some of these fashions have had a greater impact upon educational practice than others, and it is clear that one or two have had a particular influence over approaches to language teaching. An understanding of how these theories emerged and connected or conflicted with each other should enable the reader to evaluate their respective contributions to language teaching and to place the perspective taken in this book within a meaningful context.

Back in the late nineteenth century, the fledgling discipline of psychology was particularly keen to establish itself as a science on a par with the natural sciences. This led to the adoption of the so-called 'scientific method' as a means of gathering data about human behaviour. It also led to a conflict between those who saw the legitimate area of study as what went on in the human psyche (thoughts and emotions) and those who saw the only way forward as a concentration upon observable behaviour. An examination of the history of psychology makes it clear that the followers of each of these different approaches held sway in different countries such that it was impossible to refer to a 'world view' of psychology.

In the rest of this chapter we shall examine two major psychological approaches. We start with the positivist school and one of its main offshoots, behaviourism, and the influence this has had on language teaching. We then discuss cognitive psychology and the way different developments in this field have left their mark on language teaching.

1.4   The positivist school

Psychology as a discipline of study grew directly out of philosophy. However, many of the pioneers of this fledgling subject in the last decades of the nineteenth century saw the path to acceptance and respectability as lying with the natural sciences. Thus, in seeking to bring scientific rigour to its methods of enquiry, early psychologists abandoned their focus on the human mind in their attempts to understand and predict human behaviour. Instead, they sought to find the principles of human learning by investigating the behaviour of animals lower down the biological hierarchy of the animal kingdom, under rigorously defined conditions. This led to an adherence to an experimental methodology which is part of a philosophical form of enquiry known as 'logical positivism'. Basically, this approach begins with the premise that knowledge and facts exist within the real world and can be discovered by setting up experiments in which conditions are carefully controlled and where hypotheses are set up and tested.

It led in turn to the dominance of a view of psychology which could accept only empirical data as evidence that a phenomenon was occurring, and which rejected anything which could not be seen and/or measured as unscientific. Thus, for many years the predominant view in Western psychology was that efforts should be concentrated upon trying to understand how organisms lower down the hierarchy learned to perform simple tasks; for example, how rats learned their way through mazes to obtain food. It was assumed that the lessons learned from this could then be fairly easily applied to higher-order human learning. The thoughts and feelings of humans were considered to be inaccessible to proper scientific investigation within this paradigm, and, therefore, were not investigated.

1.4.1 Behaviourism

Behaviourism is an approach to psychology that has its roots within positivism, and which has had a profound influence on language teaching throughout the world. This approach arose out of the ideas of early learning theorists who attempted to explain all learning in terms of some form of *conditioning*. The most well-known example is that of the Russian Pavlov who demonstrated with dogs and other animals that a response (e.g. salivation) generated by one stimulus (e.g. food) could be produced by introducing a second stimulus (e.g. a bell) at the same time. This came to be known as S–R (Stimulus–Response) theory or *classical conditioning*.

It was postulated that all human behaviour could be explained in terms of the way in which simple S–R connections were built up. In the USA for example, J. B. Watson was able to demonstrate how easy it is for phobias to arise out of a normally innocuous stimulus (e.g. a white rabbit) or an event becoming associated with something unpleasant that occurred at the same time (e.g. a loud noise).

Part of the problem with early behaviourist theories was that they concentrated almost exclusively upon the nature of the incoming stimuli and the way that these could be altered to provoke different kinds of responses. However, this proved to be of limited value in accounting for the enormous range of human actions. Russian psychologists, most notably Luria and his followers, Vygotsky and Leontiev, came to acknowledge the importance of language within this process, although the political ideology under which they worked restricted the way in which they were able to develop and express their ideas. On the other side of the world, in the USA, meanwhile, a different route was taken by behaviourists, who began to focus much more on the nature and shaping of responses in the S–R chain, and the conditions under which stimulus–response relationships were formed.

1.4.2 B. F. Skinner

The founder of modern behaviourism is generally considered to be B. F. Skinner, who constructed a system of principles (he preferred not to call it a theory) to account for human behaviour in strictly observable terms (Skinner 1957, 1987). He also began with the premise that learning was the result of environmental rather than genetic factors. Skinner extended the possible application of principles of conditioning by introducing the notion of *operants*, i.e. the range of behaviours that organisms performed or were capable of performing. He also emphasised the importance of *reinforcement*. Behaviourist theory thus came to explain learning in terms of *operant conditioning*: an individual responds to a stimulus by behaving in a particular way. Whatever happens subsequently will affect the likelihood of that behaviour recurring. If the behaviour is reinforced (i.e. rewarded or punished) then the likelihood of that behaviour occurring on a subsequent occasion will be increased or decreased. In this way any range of behaviours could be gradually, and even rapidly, increased by reinforcing the behaviour required. In his early writing Skinner (1957) even argued that language development could be explained in this way, although this claim has been soundly refuted since then.

In subsequently turning his attention to education or, more specifically, instruction, Skinner argued that this could be improved considerably by the adoption of four simple procedures. He suggested that:

- teachers should make explicitly clear what is to be taught;
- tasks should be broken down into small, sequential steps;

- students should be encouraged to work at their own pace by means of individualised learning programmes;
- learning should be 'programmed' by incorporating the above procedures and providing immediate positive reinforcement based as nearly as possible on 100 per cent success.

Behaviourist views of learning were taken up widely by language teachers, and were a powerful influence on the development of the audio-lingual approach to language teaching. When this theory is applied to language learning, language is seen as a behaviour to be taught. Learners are given language tasks in small, sequential steps. A small part of the foreign language, such as a structural pattern, is presented as a *stimulus*, to which the learner *responds*, for example, by repetition or substitution. This is followed by *reinforcement* by the teacher, based on 100 per cent success. Learning a language is seen as acquiring a set of appropriate mechanical habits, and errors are frowned upon as reinforcing 'bad habits'. The role of the teacher is to develop in learners good language habits, which is done mainly by pattern drills, memorisation of dialogues or choral repetition of structural patterns. Explanation of rules is generally given when the language item has been well practised and the appropriate habit acquired.

An example can be found in Figure 1 below which shows an exercise from L. G. Alexander's (1968) coursebook for children, *Look, Listen and Learn*.

The exercise is designed to teach the structures *there's a . . .* and *there's some . . .* In this task the learners are required merely to repeat the stimulus sentences after the teacher, which they can do correctly without understanding the meaning of the utterances.

A second example is taken from a popular coursebook for adults, *Kernel Lessons Intermediate* (O'Neill *et al.* 1975). See Figure 2. This exercise uses a substitution drill where the teacher gives a prompt (e.g. 'the theatre at weekends') and the learners are required to complete the sentence (e.g. 'He often goes to the theatre at weekends'). Again, the exercise can be completed with fairly limited understanding of the meanings of the words.

It can be seen that audiolingualism does have a number of limitations. First, the role of the learners is a fairly passive one; they are merely directed to respond correctly to stimuli. There is little active engagement in analysing the language, or developing their own strategies to learn more effectively or initiating discussions or negotiating meanings. Second, there is little concern for what goes on inside the learners' heads, or the cognitive processes involved in learning something. Recent work in the area of learning strategies has shown us that conscious use of strategies can significantly enhance learning. This is a point that will be taken up in Chapter 7. Third,

- **Repetition Drill**: Books open.

  Chorus and Group Repetition.
  Ask the pupils to repeat the following statements
  after you first in chorus then in groups:

  TEACHER: *Look at the 1st picture.*
  There is a plate on the table. *All*
  together!
  Look at the 2nd picture.
  There is some tea in the pot. *All*
  together!

  The remaining items are as follows:

  3rd: a cup behind the pot.
  4th: some coffee in the cup.
  5th: a sweet in the packet.
  6th: some sugar in the bowl.
  7th: a refrigerator in the kitchen.
  8th: some lemonade in the bottle.
  9th: some milk in the jug.
  10th: some water in the glass.
  11th: a lollipop on the table.
  12th: a spoon near the plate.

Figure 1   *From* Look, Listen and Learn *(Alexander 1968:159)*

as we have seen, audiolingual drills can be carried out with little attention to the meaning that the language conveys. Fourth, there is no room for the actual process of interaction and negotiation of meanings which is an important feature of communicating in a language. Fifth, the making of mistakes is an important part of learning. However, audiolingualism, with its emphasis on correct responses, does not allow for learning from mistakes.

In spite of its shortcomings, a structural or audiolingual approach has nevertheless dominated language teaching around the world. There are a number of possible practical reasons for this. In many countries teachers are not provided with a professional training; in some contexts the prerequisite for teaching is a primary education. It can be quicker and easier to teach teachers to use the steps involved in an audiolingual approach: presentation, practice, repetition and drills. Teachers can also follow the steps provided in their coursebook in a fairly mechanical way. Teachers who lack confidence tend to be less frightened of these techniques, whereas allowing language to develop through meaningful interaction in the classroom can be considerably more daunting, and requires teachers with some professional

1. Invention Exercise

MODEL:

He She	often never always	does that

PROMPT: football on Saturdays
RESPONSE: He always plays football on Saturdays
or: He never watches football on Saturdays

Prompts:
a) the theatre at weekends
b) jazz
c) tea without sugar
d) to work by bus
e) French magazines
f) to the seaside in winter
g) brown bread
h) detective stories
i) coffee with cream
j) Turkish cigarettes

Figure 2   *From* Kernel Lessons Intermediate *(O'Neill* et al. *1975:6)*

knowledge. An audiolingual methodology can also be used by teachers whose own knowledge of the target language is limited.

However, one of the major reasons for the dominance of audiolingualism may well have been that it is underpinned by a coherent psychological perspective, i.e. behaviourism, whereas more communicative approaches have lacked a coherent theory of learning. In this book we intend to show that social constructivism can go some way towards providing us with such a theory.

A behaviourist view does, however, have some positive points that should not be dismissed lightly. For example, the emphasis placed by Skinner and his followers (Skinner 1968, 1974; Poteet 1973; Wheldall and Merrett 1987) on the important part played by parents and teachers in setting appropriate learning conditions and ensuring particular kinds of behavioural consequences should not be ignored. (This in fact is in keeping with a social interactionist view of learning.) Moreover, the notion of reinforcement as a powerful influence in shaping human behaviour does have a great deal to commend it though, as we shall see in Chapter 6, the whole issue of rewards and feedback is extremely complex.

Concern has been expressed by many psychologists and educators about the ethics of behaviour modification (Pring 1984), in that it can be seen as a form of manipulation or 'brainwashing' rather than 'education'. This view has naturally been disputed by the behaviourists (Fontana 1988). This is an important issue to which we shall return when considering the meaning of 'education', and how language tasks can be truly educational.

Perhaps the strongest indictment of behaviourism has been that it is only concerned with observable behaviour. In choosing to concentrate only on that which is observable, behaviourism denies the importance of a fundamental element in the learning process, the sense that learners themselves seek to make of their worlds, and the cognitive or mental processes that they bring to the task of learning. In learning a language, it is clear that learners make use of a wide repertoire of mental strategies to sort out the system that operates in the language with which they are presented. In order to explore this aspect of learning further, we now turn to the field of cognitive psychology.

1.5   Cognitive psychology

In contrast to behaviourism, cognitive psychology is concerned with the way in which the human mind thinks and learns. Cognitive psychologists are therefore interested in the mental processes that are involved in learning. This includes such aspects as how people build up and draw upon their memories and the ways in which they become involved in the process of learning.

In recent years cognitive psychology has had a considerable influence on language teaching methodology. In a cognitive approach, the learner is seen as an active participant in the learning process, using various mental strategies in order to sort out the system of the language to be learned.

Figure 3 shows an example from *Cobuild English Course*, Book 1. This exercise contrasts sharply with those in Figures 1 and 2 above. Here the learners are required to use their minds to observe, think, categorise and hypothesise, and in this way to gradually work out how the language operates.

In direct contrast to the behaviourist approach, the cognitive school of psychologists perhaps best epitomises George Miller's famous description of psychology as 'the science of mental life'. However, the ways in which human thought has been investigated have themselves varied considerably. At one extreme are *information theorists* who have drawn the analogy of the brain as a highly complex computer and who seek to explain its workings in terms of rules and models of how different aspects of learning take place. Examples of this approach can be seen in work on artificial intelligence systems and, particularly, in models of memory and reading processes.

29 **Language study**

Words ending in s

Look at the transcripts below of David and Bridget talking about their families (sections 26b and 19).

How many words are there ending in **s** or **'s**?
Does the **s** or **'s** always mean the same?

Some words always end in **s**, for example, **his**.

What about this one?

I've got one brother and he's got two daughters.

Put the words ending in **s** or **'s** into 4 categories.

Bridget's family

DF: If we look at, erm, your mother Sheila. Has she got any brothers and sisters?

BG: Yes, she's got one sister.

DF: No brothers?

BG: No.

DF: Okay. What about your father?

BG: He's got three sisters.

DF: Oh, and no brothers?

BG: No.

David's family

BG: Now it's my turn. Your father's called John? and your mother's called Pat? –

DF: That's right.

BG: and your brother's married – to . . . Jane?

DF: Jane. Good.

BG: Jane. And they've got two daughters called . . . Emma and – Sarah.

Now look at the text in section 24. Find thirteen more words that end in **s** and put them into categories.

Figure 3 *From* Collins Cobuild English Course *(Willis and Willis 1988:15)*

At the other extreme is the so-called *constructivist* movement, growing mainly out of the work of the Swiss developmental psychologist, Jean Piaget, but also encompassing George Kelly's *personal construct psychology*. Psychologists taking this approach have been mainly concerned with ways in which individuals come to make their own sense of the world.

Yet another aspect of cognitive psychology, which should not be over-looked in our present context, is the rich and varied literature on human intelligence. Here a distinction can be drawn between theories which seek to describe and explain what we mean by intelligence or, more helpfully, intelligent behaviour, and attempts to measure it by such methods as IQ testing. Somewhat surprisingly, standard approaches to measurement are not always built upon sound theories.

Each of these different approaches to cognition will now be described in greater detail.

1.5.1 Information processing

The first approach to cognitive psychology that we shall consider is *information processing*. As its name implies, cognitive psychologists who take this approach to learning are mainly concerned with the way in which people take in information, process it and act upon it. Thus it can be seen that such factors as attention, perception and memory become the focus of the work of information processing theorists. Most usually they construct *models* (Atkinson and Shiffrin 1968) or *scripts* (Schank and Abelson 1977) to try to account for the way in which the human mind works. In doing so, they claim to be able to predict the kind of mental processes that will be necessary for effective learning to take place and to identify precisely how and where any malfunctioning is occurring when a person is displaying learning difficulties. Analogies can readily be drawn between this kind of approach and the workings of any other system such as the human body, a motorcar engine or a computer. As such, it is essentially mechanistic and not at all concerned with meanings or emotions. Much of the work on learner strategies in language learning, which includes memory strategies, has drawn on such information processing models.

Attention is one area where an information processing approach has provided valuable insights into the workings of the human mind. It is clear to any experienced teacher that some learners have considerable difficulty in paying attention to their work and that invariably this will have a negative effect on their learning. But why do people differ so much in this respect and what can the teacher do about it? One view (Klatzky 1980) suggests that attention should be seen as a process of filtering out an overwhelming range of incoming stimuli and selecting out only those stimuli which are important for further processing. Another view (Best 1986) conceptualises attention as a cognitive resource which can be drawn upon as a means of concentrating our mental efforts. This resource will be needed most when a learning task is new or when it is just beyond the present capabilities of the learner, but as one becomes more skilful as, for example, in the case of reading or driving, there is less need to call upon one's full attention.

Research by developmental psychologists has shown that children's ability to focus their attention, to select what is important for them to attend to and to adapt their attention to the demands of the situation improves with age (Flavell 1985; Wittrock 1986). However, it is also clear that different kinds of stimuli will be more effective in gaining attention and keeping it.

Learning a foreign language can be a very confusing experience, especially in the early stages. Audiolingual approaches tend to stress the importance of a controlled structural input. More communicative approaches, on the other hand, depend on the use of language for a real purpose. If the latter approach is to be favoured, care must be taken to help individual learners to focus their attention on certain key aspects of what they are hearing or trying to communicate rather than attempting to cope with everything at once. In particular, the ability to select relevant from irrelevant information and focus their attention on how this can be remembered and used distinguishes efficient from inefficient learners.

1.5.2 *Memory*

Another area to which information processing theorists have devoted considerable attention is that of memory. Perhaps the best known model of memory is that of Atkinson and Shiffrin (1968).

This model describes the memory process in terms of a *sensory register* where stimuli are initially recorded for a brief amount of time before being passed into *short-term* (or *working*) *memory* if attention is given to them. The term *working memory* is used to refer to whatever one has in mind at any particular time, which tends to be of a short duration, lasting no longer than thirty seconds. Because of the small capacity of most people's working memory, which is usually considered to be about seven items at any one time, it is necessary to find ways of breaking down complex material into related 'chunks' before consigning these to the *long-term memory* store. The most common way of doing this is by *rehearsal*, which may take the form of simple repetition or more elaborate means which involve the association of meaning to what is to be remembered.

As far as the language teacher is concerned, there are a number of practical implications emerging from such models. Memory is particularly important in learning a language. One of the main problems language learners face is memorising vocabulary items. However, there is nothing to be gained from overloading learners' short-term memory or in expecting a great deal to be retained from any one session without some form of rehearsal. The teaching of ways of remembering things, including mnemonic strategies and involving more than one of the senses is, therefore, likely to more than justify the time involved. Oxford (1990) provides an analysis of different memory strategies used in language learning. These will be discussed in more detail in Chapter 6.

An intriguing and apparently highly successful application of memory research to foreign language learning has been the use of the *linkword* method (Gruneberg 1987; Gruneberg and Jacobs 1991). This technique involves linking words in both the first and second language to construct a picture in the mind. Gruneberg suggests, for example, that the French word *nappe* can be remembered by an English speaker who conjures up a picture of having a *nap* on a *tablecloth*. Merry (1980) found that this method was a particularly effective way of teaching French vocabulary to eleven- and twelve-year-old English children. Studies by Raugh and Atkinson (1975) demonstrated also that both Spanish and Russian vocabulary learning was enhanced when adults were taught to use the linkword technique.

Another helpful strategy for teachers to aid their learners' memorisation of information is the employment of what the cognitive psychologist David Ausubel (1968) calls *advance organisers*. By this he means some kind of topical introduction to a lesson that orientates learners to the subject matter and relates new learning to what the learners already know. Such introductions need to be more general and at a higher level of abstraction than the material that is to be learned.

Ausubel has a significant place in the history of educational psychology because he not only emphasised the importance of cognitive processes, but also set the concept of meaning at the heart of such processes. Thus, the principal function of advance organisers is to act as a bridge between what learners already know and what they need to know. This means that it can be both helpful and important when introducing a new topic or set of ideas to begin by talking about what will follow from these ideas even before the ideas themselves are grasped.

1.5.3 Intelligence and intelligence testing

Nowhere are the strengths and weaknesses of taking a cognitive approach to educational issues more apparent than in the way that the concept of intelligence has been defined, measured and employed. Intelligence is a topic about which a great deal has been written, but about which most teachers continue to feel confused. If asked to define what was meant by intelligence, most people would probably refer to some form of inborn, general ability which enables some of us to learn better or faster than others. Such a view would tend to assume that intelligence is fixed at birth and unlikely to change after about the age of five. This is the kind of perspective which underpins selection procedures such as streaming in schools and the segregation of some children into special schools, because it also holds that intelligence is the main factor in predicting success or failure in school. Put simply, this view states that people who are born more intelligent are much more likely to succeed at school or in any learning task than those who are born less intelligent. This often leads to the logically unjustifiable conclusion that anyone failing in school or having difficulty in learning must, therefore, lack intelligence.

Since early views of intelligence arose out of the work of pioneers of the *eugenics* movement who were committed to the improvement of the human race by genetic engineering, it is easy to see how these ideas took hold. They were taken up by *psychometricians* who sought ways to measure the so-called 'g' (or general intelligence) factor and even gave rise to misguided notions that some races were intellectually superior to others. This belief in the unchanging nature of intelligence has led to the development of intelligence (IQ) tests and their use for the purposes of prediction or placement and even as diagnostic tools to explain learning failure.

Such views of fixed intelligence dominated the development in the 1950s of language aptitude tests, notably Carroll and Sapon's *Modern Language Aptitude Test* or MLAT (1959). These tests were based on the premise that people possess a fixed amount of ability at language learning, and that this ability can be measured. Thus it was believed that aptitude tests could predict someone's success at learning a foreign language. While there is evidence to show that these tests do have some predictive value, they are, however, open to exactly the same kind of criticism as are IQ tests. What we shall argue is that if we view aptitude or intelligence as fixed, then we are placing limitations on the way in which we view learners and consequently the way we treat them.

A recent development of this traditional view of intelligence which may be of particular interest to language teachers stems from the work of the Harvard psychologist Howard Gardner. In his persuasively written book *Frames of Mind* (1983), Gardner argues that instead of viewing intelligence as a unitary faculty, we should consider instead the possibility of different kinds of *intelligences*. He suggests that at least seven are clearly identifiable, one of which is linguistic intelligence.

Gardner argues that there are vast individual differences between children from the moment that they first begin to use language, but also that different languages require different kinds of brain functioning. Thus, in the phonologically based writing systems of the West, auditory processing is important in developing literacy skills. In the Orient, however, where pictograms play an important part in written language, then visual processing becomes more important. Gardner also cites a number of examples in support of his contention that people from different cultural backgrounds use different kinds of linguistic intelligence to learn. Thus, an erudite Iatu male will be likely to have a phenomenal verbal memory for names, whereas among some Mexican tribes the flexible use of language is so prized that they may have up to four hundred different terms referring to language use (Gardner 1983:73–98).

Despite the persuasiveness of Gardner's writing, the practising teacher is forced to return to some fundamental questions. If differences do exist from birth in general or even specific kinds of intelligence, what are the implications for me as an educator and a foreign-language teacher? Is intelligence something that people have more or less of and which can't be added to or improved after a certain age? Do people with different levels of measured intelligence require different methods of teaching? If so, what should these methods involve?

The British educational psychologist Philip Vernon provided a helpful, but unjustly neglected, perspective on the issue of whether and how intelligence could be measured. Vernon (1964) suggested that instead of conceptualising intelligence as a unitary concept, it would be more helpful to think in terms of Intelligence A, Intelligence B and Intelligence C. Intelligence A represents the intelligence with which we are born. For genetic reasons this will vary from individual to individual, except in the case of identical twins. However, because we are all affected by our environments from the moment of conception, this genetic intellectual endowment can never be measured. Intelligence B refers to the intelligence we display in all aspects of our everyday lives which is continually changing and very much context-bound. This kind of intelligence will be gauged by the appropriateness of a person's actions in any given situation. Intelligence C represents what is measured by IQ tests. As such, it can only be a tiny sample of all the possible kinds of intelligent behaviour that a person can demonstrate and is totally dependent upon the *validity* of the particular IQ test employed, i.e. how good that test is at predicting the speed and efficiency of learning at school or elsewhere.

Conventional IQ tests have been found to be quite (but not very) good at predicting academic success, including success at learning languages. However, as we shall demonstrate throughout this book, the kind of intelligence that they represent has been overrated as a central factor in learning and can even act as a barrier to teachers' understanding of the learning process.

One reason for the confusion that surrounds the notion of intelligence and its measurement is that it has been traditionally used as a common noun, representing some sort of entity that people have more or less of. In fact, 'intelligence' is what psychologists call a *hypothetical construct*, a term of convenience to account for something that doesn't really exist. In many ways, such constructs can be very helpful in enabling us to make sense of unexplained behaviour, but in others they can be extremely misleading, particularly if they cease to be hypothetical and are treated as if they really exist. It is far less dangerous and more helpful to treat intelligence as a descriptive term – an adjective or adverb. Thus, we can refer to someone acting more or less intelligently or demonstrating intelligent behaviour in a particular circumstance.

This is another area where information processing models have been particularly helpful. In particular, the cognitive psychologist, Robert Sternberg, has reconceptualised intelligence in terms of people's purposeful adaptation to the real world. He argues that what may be intelligent behaviour in one country or cultural context might be viewed as unintelligent in another. The kind of behaviour that would be interpreted as intelligent in an academic private school might serve no recognisably intelligent function in a slum area of a city and vice versa.

Sternberg (1985) proposed a *triarchic* theory of intelligence which, as its name suggests, contains three major sets of components. *Metacomponents* (or executive skills) are the cognitive skills employed in planning and decision making. These include the recognition that a problem exists, awareness of various possible strategies to solve it, allocation of time and monitoring of one's attempts to find a solution. *Performance* components include the basic operations involved in actually solving any given task, such as encoding information, inferential thinking and drawing comparisons. *Knowledge acquisition* components are the processes used in acquiring new knowledge, such as selecting relevant rather than irrelevant information, integrating the new knowledge in a meaningful way and relating it to what is already known.

Since the main emphasis in this approach is placed upon the conception of intelligent behaviour as the appropriate use of cognitive skills and strategies within specific contexts, it frees us from conceiving of it as something that is static and fixed. It also enables us to see that people *can become more intelligent* and that schools can (and should) play a part in this. This view of course has powerful implications for language teachers. If we hold such a view, we then believe that we can help *all* learners to become better at language learning. We free ourselves from the concept of learners possessing a fixed amount of aptitude for language, and see everyone capable of succeeding, given appropriate teaching. One of the challenges for the language teacher is to help learners to develop the strategies needed to learn a language more effectively, a principle which is embodied in the current work on learner training in English as a foreign language (EFL). It also follows that learning how to think effectively should be an important aspect of education, which needs to be taught independently and through subject domains. This important principle will be taken up again in Chapter 8 where we shall focus on ways in which language teaching can involve teaching learners how to become more effective thinkers.

1.5.4 Constructivism

Helpful though information processing approaches can be, as we indicated earlier, they place little or no emphasis upon the ways in which individuals seek to bring a sense of personal meaning to their worlds. To understand this kind of cognitive approach we need to look towards the *constructivist* movement. Jean Piaget has been the dominant figure in cognitive developmental psychology partly because he wrote so extensively about it over many years. At the same time, this has made it extremely difficult for any one person to become completely familiar with all of Piaget's volumes of writings (e.g. Piaget 1966; Piaget 1972; Piaget 1974). Excellent summaries and critical reviews are provided by Flavell (1963), Elkind (1970), Brown and Desforges (1979) and Sutherland (1992). Alternative explanations of the reasons children responded in a particular way to the mini-experiments that Piaget constructed are offered in two influential books by Margaret Donaldson (1978, 1992).

Piaget

One of the most enduring aspects of Piaget's work has been his emphasis upon the *constructive* nature of the learning process. In contrast to more traditional views which see learning as the accumulation of facts or the development of skills, the main underlying assumption of constructivism is that individuals are actively involved right from birth in constructing *personal meaning*, that is their own personal understanding, from their experiences. In other words, everyone makes their own sense of the world and the experiences that surround them. In this way the learner is brought into central focus in learning theory.

Piaget himself was mainly interested in the way in which people came to know things as they developed from infancy to adulthood. Thus, his theory is one which is 'action-based', more concerned with the process of learning than what is learned. It suggests that we 'come to know' things as a direct result of our personal experiences, but that we make sense of those experiences at different stages of our lives.

Piaget's theory is based on learners passing through a series of stages. For the young infant, the most important way of exploring the environment is considered by Piaget to be through the basic senses. This he calls the *sensorimotor* stage of learning. Gradually through the development of organised actions and thoughts, the child comes to perceive and deal with the world in more sophisticated ways. The next stage is the *intuitive* or *pre-operational* stage, which is usually considered to last between the ages of two and seven. This is when the child's thoughts become more flexible and when memory and imagination begin to play a part. Piaget uses the term *operation* to refer to internalised actions, i.e. the way in which actions become part of children's imaginations. In these early years such operations are beginning to take place, but they are as yet quite crude and fairly inflexible.

After about the age of seven, the child is seen as entering the *concrete-operational* stage when the realisation begins to dawn that operations can be reversed, e.g. that ice that melts into water can be frozen again into ice. This enables children to go beyond the information given, but is still dependent upon concrete (rather than abstract) examples.

Finally, there is a move into *formal operational* thinking when abstract reasoning becomes increasingly possible. Piaget considered this should not happen before the adolescent years and will tend to vary across subject areas, e.g. because I am able to think at a high level of abstraction mathematically, this will not necessarily reflect my ability to think scientifically.

Piaget's stages do have a message for the language teacher. When teaching young learners, we should not expect them to have reached the stage of abstract reasoning, and, therefore, should not expect them to apply this to sorting out the rules of the language. It is more important at this stage to provide experiences in the target language which are related to aspects of the child's own world.

The fact that subsequent research studies have tended not to support Piaget's sequence or age-delineation of stages of cognitive development (see Sutherland 1992 for a good summary of such studies), should not blind us to the fact that people learn in different ways and that many people continue to find it difficult throughout their lives to cope with abstract reasoning. However, one of the most important factors that determine whether learners are able to think at an abstract level, as Margaret Donaldson and her co-workers have shown, is the development and use of language.

Piaget saw cognitive development as essentially a process of *maturation*, within which genetics and experience interact. The developing mind is viewed as constantly seeking *equilibration*, i.e. a balance between what is known and what is currently being experienced. This is accomplished by the complementary processes of *assimilation* and *accommodation*. Put simply, assimilation is the process by which incoming information is changed or modified in our minds so that we can fit it in with what we already know. Accommodation, on the other hand, is the process by which we modify what we already know to take into account new information. Working in conjunction, these two processes contribute to what Piaget terms the central process of cognitive *adaptation*. This is an essential aspect of learning, and one that is particularly relevant to the learning of the grammar of a new language.

As we mentioned earlier, there is a great deal of published material by and about Piaget and his theory of cognitive development. We have merely chosen to highlight one or two central aspects here which we believe to be of particular significance to the language teacher.

First, we can see how important it is to take account of the learner as an individual, actively involved in constructing meaning. When learners learn a new language, they are, in these terms, actively involved in making their own sense of the language input that surrounds them as well as the tasks presented to them. Thus, it is important for teachers to help and encourage learners in this process, rather than seeing them as passive receivers of the language.

Second, the development of thinking and its relationship to language and experience become a central focus of learning. It becomes clear, for example, that language teaching based mainly on memorisation will not lead to deeper understanding. The relationship between the development of language and the development of thinking will be considered in Chapter 8.

Third, care should be taken to match the requirements of any task to the cognitive level of which the learner is capable. Language tasks set by teachers should be neither too abstract for those who are not yet conceptually capable of functioning at this level, nor too simple in that the conceptual level is below the level of the learner's competence.

Fourth, we can see the application of Piaget's notions of assimilation and accommodation to learning a new language. When we receive new input of the language, for example by listening to a conversation, we need to modify what we already know about the language (accommodation) so as to 'fit' the new information into our existing knowledge (assimilation). In this way our knowledge of how the system of the new language operates gradually develops. This is entirely in keeping with *interlanguage theory* in the field of second language acquisition, which holds that a learner's knowledge of the language is gradually re-shaped as it more closely approximates to the target language.

As a cognitive developmental psychologist, Piaget was not unduly concerned about the implications of his theory for educators. It would be unfair, therefore, to criticise him for the limited applicability of this theory. However, there are two fairly common interpretations which can be seen as having had an inhibiting effect on many teachers. First, it became popular in some teacher-training establishments to interpret Piaget's views on maturation and personal experience as indicating that there is no place for direct instruction in teaching. Certainly, Piaget made little reference in his early work to the significance of parent or teacher intervention, although in some of his later writings he acknowledged this omission.

While this kind of interpretation had the positive effect of encouraging teachers to place more emphasis upon their classrooms as environments in which experiential learning could take place, it also meant that many teachers of young children, in particular, became insecure as to what an appropriate role might be for them beyond this. This feeling has carried over into language teaching, where many teachers have expressed similar concerns. If learners learn by interacting with the language environment (the language input), then what is the role of the teacher beyond providing suitable input to allow learning to take place? This question is taken up in Chapter 4 where we consider the importance of the teacher's role in promoting learning. At the same time, Piaget's emphasis upon *individual* development caused him to overlook the significance of the social environment for learning. The importance of the social context in which learning takes place will be taken up in the next chapter, and again in Chapter 9.

Finally, it is clear that Piaget originally underestimated the fundamental part played by language in the development of thought. In fact, in his early work he argued that language follows behind the development of thought, providing a means of encapsulating 'pure' thought in symbolic form (Sutherland 1992). However, this is not a view which has been borne out by research investigations.

Jerome Bruner

An important advocate of Piaget's ideas has been Jerome Bruner, Professor of Psychology and founder of the Centre for Cognitive Studies at Harvard University, particularly regarding their implications for the *discovery* approach to learning described below (Bruner 1960, 1966). For Bruner, the process of education is at least as important as its product and he was greatly influenced in his early educational writings by Piaget's description of how children's thinking developed. To Bruner, the development of conceptual understanding and of cognitive skills and strategies is a central aim of education, rather than the acquisition of factual information. Through Bruner, this view came to represent the cognitive approach to education.

One particularly significant aspect of Bruner's ideas is that they take a broad view of the education of the whole person. He saw as one of the central elements of this the need to *learn how to learn*, which he considered to be the key to transferring what was learned from one situation to another (1960:4). The challenge that Bruner posed to educators to identify the 'optimum conditions' for learning, in this broad sense, to take place, has generated some of the most exciting developments in both education and psychology over the subsequent decades. It is a theme to which we shall be returning constantly throughout this book.

Bruner also recognised that learning in schools must have a purpose, and he posed the following questions as a means of deciding what that purpose should be and what should be included in any curriculum:

> We might ask, as a criterion for any subject taught in primary school,
> whether, when fully developed, it is worth an adult's knowing, and
> whether having known it as a child makes a person a better adult. If the
> answer to both questions is negative or ambiguous, then the material is
> cluttering the curriculum.
>
> (1960:52)

He argues, therefore, that the first object of any act of learning is that it
should serve us in the future; it should not only take us somewhere, but
should also allow us later to go further more easily. The limitation of such
a view, of course, is that it does not represent the value of learning something for its own sake and neglects the relevance of any learning activity to
the learner in the here and now.

Because Bruner, unlike Piaget, was a committed educationist, he tried to
relate his ideas on cognitive development to what takes place in classrooms.
He therefore offered advice on such topics as the structure of the curriculum
as well as on ways in which learners could be motivated and helped to
remember what they had learned. One of his most famous dictums is that
'the foundations of any subject may be taught to anybody at any age in some
form' (Bruner 1960:12), which itself gave rise to the notion of the *spiral*
curriculum. The point here is that teachers should first introduce the basic
ideas that give life and form to any topic or subject area, and then revisit and
build upon these repeatedly. This is a notion that has been extensively used
in language syllabuses.

For Bruner the most general objective of education is the cultivation of
excellence, which can only be achieved by challenging learners to exercise
their full powers to become completely absorbed in problems and thereby
discover the pleasure of full and effective functioning. As we shall see in
Chapters 4 and 6, this notion of challenge has been taken up enthusiastically
by psychologists working in other areas, and is highly pertinent to language
teachers.

Bruner claimed that by encouraging young learners to discover for themselves the solutions to educational problems that were set for them in a way
that was not artificially sectionalised into 'subjects', they could come to
understand even the most complicated topics and relate their understanding
in a meaningful way to a coherent knowledge of the world. He even went so
far as to devise a whole curriculum, Man A Course of Study (MACOS),
based upon these principles. Although this curriculum package was only
taken up in a limited way, Bruner's influence upon Western educators has
been profound, as was demonstrated, for example, by the British Schools
Council Humanities Project developed in the 1960s by Lawrence Stenhouse
(Stenhouse 1975).

Bruner emphasised the importance of achieving the right balance between the degree of structure imposed on a lesson and the amount of flexibility that is built in to allow learners to discover principles, concepts and facts for themselves. He stressed also the importance of encouraging guesswork and intuitive thinking in learners. This will only occur if learners feel self-confident and able to take risks, which in itself will be fostered by a sense of curiosity. In order to encourage this process, Bruner recognises that teachers need to be able to ask the right kind of questions.

> Given particular subject matter or a particular concept, it is easy to ask trivial questions or to lead a child to ask trivial questions. It is also easy to ask impossibly difficult questions. The trick is to find the medium questions that can be answered and that take you somewhere.

> (1960:40)

Bruner's notion of purposefulness to help learners reach a coherent knowledge of the world, has a message for us regarding the design of tasks for language learning, a point we shall develop in Chapter 8. Similarly, his notion of achieving a balance between a solid structure and flexibility for discovery also has implications for the language teacher. In Bruner's terms, we need to seek a balance between, on the one hand teaching aspects of the target language and skills in the language, and on the other hand developing the learners' ability to analyse the language, to make guesses as to how rules operate, to take risks in trying out the language, and to learn from their errors.

An original thinker in his own right, Bruner extended aspects of Piagetian theory to suggesting that three different modes of thinking needed to be taken into account by educators. These he termed the *enactive*, the *iconic* and the *symbolic* modes of thought. These three categories are considered by Bruner to represent the essential ways in which children make sense of their experiences: through their actions, by means of visual imagery and by using language. At the enactive level, learning takes place by means of direct manipulation of objects and materials. At the iconic level, objects are represented by visual images one step removed from the real thing. Illustrations are recognised for what they represent, but can also be created independently. At the symbolic level, symbols can be manipulated in place of objects or mental images. Language comes to play an increasingly important part as a means of representing the world.

Although Bruner's three categories of representation are presented as developing in sequence, rather like Piaget's stages, they increasingly overlap rather than substitute each other. Teachers need to be aware of the ways in which learning can be enhanced by using these three modes. At the enactive level, we can see the importance of the use of drama, play, total physical response and the handling of real objects. The iconic mode would be brought into play through the use of pictures, or words in colour. At the same time, learners begin to use the symbolic mode as they use the target language, including the paralanguage, to express ideas in context.

It should be apparent that Bruner cannot be considered a purely cognitive psychologist. In his writings about education in particular he places great emphasis upon the interaction of the learner with curriculum materials and with the teacher and significant others. There is a strong case, therefore, for classifying Bruner as a social constructivist even though we have included him here as an important cognitive psychologist. In fact, Bruner has a foot in both camps. He can also be viewed as a key figure in establishing a bridge between cognitive psychology and pedagogy.

George Kelly

George Kelly has been one of the unjustly neglected pioneers of the constructivist movement, even though his *personal-construct theory* has profound implications for teachers, teacher trainers and educational psychologists (Kelly 1955). Kelly began with the premise of 'man-as-scientist' constantly seeking to make sense of his world. People carry out their own personal experiments, construct hypotheses and actively seek to confirm or disconfirm them. In this way they build up theories about the kind of place that the world is and the kind of people that live in it. These personal theories or *constructs* are rather like templates which people place over their impressions of any new events or persons with which they come into contact, in order to establish some kind of reasonable 'fit'. To Kelly, learning involves learners making their own sense of information or events. Learners are actively involved in constructing their own personal understanding of things, and this understanding will be different for different people.

Kelly was dismissive of what he called the 'push-pull' theories of psychodynamics and behaviourism. Instead, he argued that people were active participants in deciding how to act and that they made such decisions on the basis of what made sense to them personally. Each person's individual construction of the world will depend upon their previous experiences, which will also influence how they anticipate what will happen in the future.

As a clinical psychologist and psychotherapist, Kelly wrote very little about education, but his ideas have been taken up by a small group of educational psychologists (most notably, Pope and Keen 1981, Thomas and Harri-Augstein 1985 and Salmon 1988), who have set out clearly some important implications of taking a personal construct approach to teaching and learning.

First, a clear distinction is made between meaningful and meaningless learning activities. Worthwhile learning does not entail the reception of ready-made facts, but must involve the building of new personal meanings and understanding. Only by developing our own understanding of the world is it possible for us to change and develop. To translate this into language learning, language is not learned by the mere memorisation of discrete items of grammar, discourse, function or other aspects of language. Rather, learners are involved in an active process of making sense, of creating their own understanding of the world of language that surrounds them. A meaningful activity, in Kelly's sense, is one that encourages this process of making sense, of fitting or mapping the new onto the old to create a new understanding.

Second, as Salmon (1988:22) points out, though each of us inhabits a unique experiential world, if it is to be a social world, we must find ways of reaching a common understanding together with others. The human enterprise depends on a shared reality. Teachers and learners are just as much involved in learning about each other and trying to achieve some kind of shared understanding of what is happening in their classrooms. More-over, 'the teaching-learning encounter is, essentially a meeting between the personal constructions, the subjective realities of teacher and pupil. This means that we cannot understand school learning without acknowledging *both* sorts of reality' (Salmon 1988:14).

Third, it is also important for teachers to realise that although a syllabus or curriculum may be set down precisely for them, it inevitably becomes shaped by them into something personal which reflects their own belief systems, their thoughts and feelings about both the content of their lessons and their learners, and their view of the world in general. In addition to this, the curriculum that they actually deliver becomes itself interpreted in different ways by their learners, so that the whole learning experience becomes a shared enterprise. Emotions must, therefore, be considered as an integral part of learning, as also must the particular life contexts of those who are involved in the teaching-learning process.

In this book we shall adopt an essentially constructivist stance, which we see as operating within an *interactionist* perspective. In other words, learners make their own sense of their world, but they do so within a *social context*, and through *social interactions*. This perspective will be explained in the next chapter. We shall be returning to personal construct theory in Chapter 3 when we consider the perspectives that teachers and learners bring to education and schooling, in Chapter 5 when we discuss the individual learner, and in Chapters 7 and 8 when we look at the way learners make sense of learning tasks. However, one further point is worth making here. Personal construct psychology never offers solutions, but provides instead possible alternative ways of looking at situations which may lead to their reconstruction. This is well summarised by Salmon:

In learning, we cannot ever achieve final answers; rather we find new questions, we discover other possibilities which we might try out. Knowledge is ultimately governed by constructive alternativism; everything can always be reconstrued.

(1988:22)

1.6   Conclusion

In this chapter we began our overview of educational psychology by presenting two major schools of thought. We first considered the positivist school, and discussed the influence of behaviourism on education in general and language teaching methodology in particular. We saw the way in which behaviourism was influential in structural and audiolingual approaches to language teaching around the world. This was followed by a survey of the cognitive school of psychology. We first looked at the rather more mechanistic information-processing approaches and related these to the areas of attention and memory. We then considered the difference between fixed and more dynamic views of intelligence, and discussed how a more dynamic view enables language teachers to see that all learners are capable of learning a language. Finally, we discussed an approach that we shall use repeatedly throughout this book, namely constructivism, which we shall use to explain the ways in which learners make their own personal sense of learning tasks, their environment, the teacher and the actual process of learning.

In the next chapter we shall look at two more major approaches to psychology, humanism and social interactionism, and the way in which these can shed more light on the process of language learning.

2 Further schools of thought in psychology: humanism and social interactionism

2.1 Introduction

In this chapter we continue our overview of approaches to educational psychology and present two more major schools of thought: humanism and social interactionism. Although humanism in particular has been highly influential in both educational psychology and language teaching, social interactionism has as yet had more limited impact. A major purpose of this book is to relate aspects of both approaches to language teaching.

In the final part of this chapter we present a social constructivist model which will form the framework for the rest of the book. This is based on a constructivist view of learning which is discussed in Chapter 1; that is, we believe in the centrality of learners constructing their own knowledge and understanding. We see this constructivist viewpoint as operating within a social interactionist framework; that is, the learning occurs through social interactions within a social environment. Humanism provides an added dimension here in that it emphasises the development of the whole person rather than focussing solely upon the development and employment of cognitive skills.

2.2 Humanistic approaches

Humanistic approaches emphasise the importance of the inner world of the learner and place the individual's thoughts, feelings and emotions at the forefront of all human development. These are aspects of the learning process that are often unjustly neglected, yet they are vitally important if we are to understand human learning in its totality. We will therefore begin by considering some major aspects of humanism, before linking such a view with social interactionism.

The most well-known proponent of the psychic viewpoint was Sigmund Freud whose theories about human emotional development have had a powerful influence on the development of clinical psychology and psychiatry across the world, but less apparent influence on educational psychology. A notable exception, however, has been the work of Erik Erikson, who made an outstanding attempt to draw together Freud's views on human psychosexual development into a theory based on stages of development throughout a human's life with important implications for personal, social and emotional development.

2.2.1 Erik Erikson

The basis for Erikson's ideas, which he sets out brilliantly in his classic text *Childhood and Society* (1963), is that human psychological development depends on the way in which individuals pass through predetermined maturational stages and upon the challenges that are set by society at particular times in their lives. Erikson calls this the fundamental *epigenetic principle*. He suggests that every individual proceeds through eight stages from birth to old age, each of which poses a particular kind of challenge or crisis. If this challenge is handled well with the help of other significant people in their lives, then individuals can move relatively smoothly onto the next stage and will be in a stronger position to meet future challenges. However, if challenges are inadequately dealt with, for whatever reason, they will continue to reappear throughout a person's life, making it more and more difficult to deal with subsequent stages and challenges appropriately.

Early infancy is seen as a stage where basic trust in the world as a predictable, caring place is established by parents or other caretakers. The challenge here is whether the child can learn to *trust* others and thereby her/himself or whether, as a result of early experiences, a sense of basic *mistrust* becomes internalised. By the age or two or three the challenge becomes one of establishing *autonomy* as opposed to shame or *doubt*. It has been argued that this is the key stage in a person's life where the foundations of a feeling of self-competence are set and where appropriate actions by caregivers can help to establish a basic attitude of 'I can do it' (Hamachek 1988). By the time children reach about four years of age, they can begin to formulate a plan of action and carry it through. Parental encouragement of this will foster a sense of *initiative*, but punishment for exploratory activity is more likely to generate feelings of *guilt*, which will inhibit future initiative.

Freudian theory epitomised the early school years as a 'latency' period during which not very much was happening in psychic development. Erikson, however, describes this stage as one in which the child will establish a sense of *industry* as basic educational skills and learning competence are developed, or a sense of *inferiority* if learning experiences are beset with failure. Competitive situations in which children are constantly being compared with each other are more likely to generate feelings of inferiority than are situations where the emphasis is upon individualised or co-operative learning. It is, therefore, important that those who teach a language to younger learners are aware of the need to foster a spirit of co-operation rather than competition, and of the development of this sense of industry.

Adolescence is seen by Erikson as a period within which the search for *identity* provides the key challenge. If this strong sense of personal identity is not established, then the outcome may be role confusion, aimlessness and anti-social behaviour. Adolescents with a strong sense of self identity have been described as less susceptible to peer pressure, having a high level of self-acceptance, optimistic and firm in their belief that they are in control of their own destinies (Erikson 1968; Hamachek 1988). Thus, an important function for teachers in secondary schools is to foster this sense of personal identity by encouraging learners to make decisions for themselves and helping them to express their individuality in constructive ways. Some helpful reflections on the construction of a curriculum based on these principles is offered by Dreyer (1994).

Learning does not end when a young person leaves school. For the young adult the primary challenge becomes one of attaining *intimacy*, but how well this is accomplished will depend very much on how well each of the previous life challenges have been met. Someone who has developed a strong sense of personal identity which is based upon feelings of trust in others as well as personal autonomy, initiative and industry should be in a good position to establish intimate relationships. However, a person who is still struggling with feelings of inadequacy related to unresolved crises from one of the previous life stages is far more likely to have problems in establishing such relationships. For those who are unable to make close intimate relationships, the outcome may well be a sense of personal isolation and even alienation from society. It is this alienation that is so often demonstrated by disruptive and disaffected youth. The interested reader can find a helpful in-depth discussion of these issues in Marcia *et al.*'s 'state of the art' handbook (1993).

A significant problem faced by many people in middle age is a sense of stagnation, often leading to the well-known 'mid-life crisis'. The challenge here is to maintain a sense of *generativity*, to continue to see oneself as a person who is capable of generating new interests and insights and who continues to have something to offer to others. This is related to how far young people's creative instincts have been encouraged to flourish during their early years and later school careers. There is a great danger that an overemphasis upon examination success and purely logical thinking can stifle this creative endeavour. Thus we can see a strong theoretical justification for the use of music, art, stories, games and drama, all familiar techniques with language teachers.

Beyond this, old age, the last psychosocial state, revolves around the conflict between *integrity* and *despair*. If all the previous stages have been passed through in a way that builds a foundation for subsequent stages, then old people should be able to look back on a life of self-fulfilment and personal accomplishment, and look forward to the inevitability of death without fear. Alternatively, a life of unresolved conflicts and perceived missed opportunities will leave a person with a profound sense of failure and even despair.

Erikson's theory is important to educators for a number of reasons. Firstly, it provides a 'life-span' view of psychology which helps us to recognise learning and development as lifelong, rather than restricted to a particular phase of one's life. At the same time, by focussing on important tasks at different stages of a person's life, it enables us to see that real-life learning involves challenges which often require a particular kind of help from others who are in the position of providing this help, if we are to meet them successfully. It also presents learning as a cumulative process whereby our resolution of one set of life tasks will have a profound influence upon how we deal with subsequent tasks. In addition, education is viewed as involving the whole person, the emotions and feelings; it does not involve merely transmitting pieces of knowledge.

2.2.2 Abraham Maslow

As we shall see later in Chapter 6 on motivation, human behaviour has been explained by some psychologists (including Freud) in terms of meeting basic needs. We experience certain drives to meet these needs, and we are driven to act in particular ways in order to reduce these drives. Perhaps the best known exponent of this idea was Abraham Maslow (1968, 1970), who suggested a hierarchy of needs which is usually presented in the form of a pyramid as in Figure 4.

Maslow argued for two distinct categories of needs, *deficiency* (or *maintenance*) needs, and *being* (or *growth*) needs. The first four layers represent deficiency needs. These are directly related to a person's psychological or biological balance, and include such physiological requirements as food, water, sleep and the absence of pain; they also include the needs for security, belonging, and self-esteem. Maslow considered that if these needs were not met, or their fulfilment was disrupted in some way, then it would become difficult, or even impossible for a person to fulfil needs further up the hierarchy. Thus, children who are hungry or in pain (the basic psychological needs) will find their lives dominated by this and will be unable to concentrate on, say, meeting their aesthetic needs. Similarly, children who feel insecure, or who have low self-esteem, are unlikely to be able to give their full attention to learning in class.

Being needs are represented by the top three levels in Maslow's system. These are related to the fulfilment of individual potential, in terms of

Figure 4 *Maslow's hierarchy of human needs*

cognitive and aesthetic development and the attainment of self-actualisation (realising one's full potential). Few people ever realise their full potential or achieve 'self-actualisation', the highest point in the needs hierarchy, because their lower order needs tend to remain unsatisfied. Moreover, being needs are considered to require a particular kind of nurturing environment in which people can express themselves and explore. There is also an apparent contradiction between the two sets of needs. Whereas deficiency needs require a safe, secure environment which is aimed at producing a state of equilibrium, being needs can drive the individual into potentially dangerous territory, where a degree of tension and stress can be most productive.

Attractive as it may sound, it should be recognised that the evidence offers only partial support for the notion of a hierarchy of needs. Writers such as Frank (1964), Levi (1979) and others have written movingly and eloquently about how in times of severe physical pain and deprivation during the Holocaust, it was the drive to meet so-called 'being needs' which enabled many people to survive and overcome their appalling conditions. Rather than envisaging these essential components of human development as hierarchical, therefore, it might be more helpful to view them as constantly interacting in a less static, more dynamic way. As we shall reveal at greater length later, we see a more interactive perspective such as this as both more helpful in understanding human development and the teaching/learning process, and more in line with recent views of science.

For all their theoretical limitations, Maslow's ideas about human need fulfilment do have significant things to say to the teacher. They help us to recognise that children may be having difficulties with learning in school because their basic needs are not being met at home or in the classroom.

They point to the importance of establishing a secure environment where learners feel that they belong and where they can build up self-respect by receiving respect from others. Maslow also helps us to see that learners should be encouraged to think (cognitive needs) and not be penalised for being different and creative (aesthetic needs). Classroom tasks should be challenging and encourage curiosity in order to help learners realise their full potential. There is an important lesson here for those who seek to impose a rigid structure on the content and process of education (on what should be taught and how), as was the case with the early drafts of the National Curriculum in the UK. At the end of the day, Maslow, like Erikson, sees one of the primary functions of education as enabling learners to develop as individuals in their own right and thereby achieve self-actualisation.

Erikson and Maslow can be seen as two pioneers of what has come to be called the *humanist* school of educational psychology. Another great figure in this particular movement has been Carl Rogers, whom many see as the founder of counselling psychology.

2.2.3 Carl Rogers

Rogers (1969) identified a number of key elements of the humanistic approach to education. Beginning with the premise that human beings have a natural potential for learning, he suggested that significant learning will only take place when the subject matter is perceived to be of personal relevance to the learner and when it involves active participation by the learner, i.e. experiential learning. Learning which is self-initiated and which involves feelings as well as cognition is most likely to be lasting and pervasive.

Moreover, when there is a perceived threat to the learner's self-image, resistance to learning is likely to occur. Independence, creativity and self-reliance are most likely to flourish in learning situations where external criticism is kept to a minimum and where self-evaluation is encouraged. The most socially useful kind of learning to prepare learners to cope with the demands of the modern world is learning about the process of learning itself, a continuing openness to experience and a preparedness to become involved in the process of change.

> The only man who is educated is the man who has learned how to adapt and change; the man who has realised that no knowledge is secure; that only the process of seeking knowledge gives a basis for security.

> (Rogers 1969:104)

Rogers suggests that this kind of learning best takes place in an atmosphere of 'unconditional positive regard'. This can best be established when teachers come to see their learners as clients with specific needs to be met.

Within such a relationship it is essential that the teacher conveys warmth and empathy towards the learner in order to establish a relationship of trust.

Adopting a humanistic approach to teaching also brings back into focus our question of what makes any learning experience truly educational. From this perspective, learning experiences are seen to be of limited educational value unless they have an impact upon the human condition. This offers a counterbalance to the kind of criticism which is sometimes levied against formal educational systems, i.e. that they treat people as objects and act towards them as if they were interchangeable units, thereby leading to alienation and a decreasing sense of self-worth. As Pine and Boy express it,

> Our best preparation for an evolving society is helping children face the future with confidence in their own abilities and with a faith that they are worthwhile and important members of whatever culture they might find themselves in.
>
> (Pine and Boy 1977:47)

2.2.4 Implications of the humanist approach

Hamachek (1977) provides some useful examples of the kind of educational implications that follow from taking a humanistic approach. First, every learning experience should be seen within the context of helping learners to develop a sense of personal identity and relating that to realistic future goals, i.e. learning should be *personalised* as far as possible. This is in keeping with the view that one important task for the teacher is *differentiation*, i.e. identifying and seeking to meet the individual learner's needs within the context of the classroom group.

Second, in order to become self-actualising, learners should be helped and encouraged to make choices for themselves in what and how they learn. This again is in sharp contrast to the view that the curriculum content for every child of a similar age should be set in 'tablets of stone', so that any informed outsider could predict what was happening in any classroom at one particular time. From a humanist perspective, such a scenario would be seen as representing *indoctrination* rather than education.

Third, it is important for teachers to empathise with their learners by getting to know them as individuals and seeking to understand the ways in which they make sense of the world, rather than always seeking to impose their own viewpoints.

> Humanistic education starts with the idea that students are different, and it strives to help students become more like themselves and less like each other.
>
> (Hamachek 1977: 149)

Rogers (1982) has a number of helpful suggestions to make about the implications of taking such an approach. First, as has been stated earlier, it is important to provide optimum conditions for individualised and group learning of an authentic nature to take place. This will be taken up in detail in Chapter 8. Within this there is a need to foster both a sense of freedom and a counterbalancing sense of responsibility, a point which is often missed by those who misunderstand the full implications of humanistic teaching. Thus, from a humanistic perspective, a learning experience of personal consequence occurs when the learner assumes the responsibility of evaluating the degree to which he or she is personally moving toward knowledge instead of looking to an external source for such evaluation.

2.2.5   Humanism in ELT

Humanistic approaches have had a considerable influence on English language teaching (ELT) methodology. Stevick (1976) saw a need for a humanistic approach to language teaching as a response to what he saw as 'alienations', which were accountable for failure in modern language teaching: alienation of learners from materials, from themselves, from the class and from the teacher.

A number of different language teaching methodologies have arisen from taking a humanistic approach, the main ones being the *silent way*, *suggestopaedia*, and *community language learning*. These three methodologies have a number of things in common. First, they are based more firmly on psychology than on linguistics. Second, they all consider affective aspects of learning and language as important. Third, they are all concerned with treating the learner as a whole person, and with whole-person involvement in the learning process. Fourth, they see the importance of a learning environment which minimises anxiety and enhances personal security.

Clear summaries of these approaches are given in Richards and Rodgers (1986), and in Stevick (1980). They will, therefore, not be discussed in detail here. The silent way originated from Gattengo (1972), and involves the teacher remaining as silent as possible while the learners are involved in learning. This method initially centres around the use of cuisenaire rods of various lengths and colours which the teacher uses to elicit language from the learners, while still remaining firmly in control of the process and content of the lesson. Community language learning was developed by Curran (1972), based on principles of counselling. In this method, the learners sit in a circle, as a community, and decide what they want to say. The 'knower', who remains outside the circle, whispers the translation into the speaker's ear, and the speaker then repeats the utterance in the target language. Suggestopaedia (Lozanov 1979) is founded on the principle that people are capable of learning more if their minds are clear of other things, and also free of anxiety. It is based on relaxation at a deep level and on the use of classical music to help learning.

However, rather than seeing what humanism has to offer to ELT as one or other of these 'fringe' methods, we see the value of humanism in language learning as informing and enhancing the teacher's practices in a variety of ways, no matter what methodology the teacher is following.

To summarise the points made so far, humanism has a number of messages for the language teacher:

- create a sense of belonging;
- make the subject relevant to the learner;
- involve the whole person;
- encourage a knowledge of self;
- develop personal identity;
- encourage self-esteem;
- involve the feelings and emotions;
- minimise criticism;
- encourage creativity;
- develop a knowledge of the process of learning;
- encourage self-initiation;
- allow for choice;
- encourage self-evaluation.

These maxims link well with a communicative classroom, and can be a powerful influence on the design and execution of purposeful tasks for language learning (discussed in Chapter 8).

One important outcome of the humanistic approach to learning has been the growing recognition of how vital each individual's search for personal meaning becomes in the learning process. Thus, another task for the teacher is to help learners establish a strong sense of personal values. As we have seen, this aspect of learning also receives particular emphasis within the personal construct psychology of George Kelly (Bannister and Fransella 1986).

2.3   Social interactionism

We have seen that cognitive approaches to psychology emphasise the learner's cognitive involvement in learning. Such approaches have had a significant impact on language teaching methodology, moving us towards methods involving the learners being actively engaged in making sense of their language input, and more cognitive approaches to grammar teaching. However, an understanding of the workings of the human mind is not in itself adequate to explain what goes on when we learn something.

We have seen too that humanistic approaches provide us with powerful educational messages regarding whole-person involvement in learning, and that such approaches have strong links with constructivism, as both are concerned with the individual's search for personal meaning.

In this section we present a psychological approach that we consider provides a framework which encompasses the insights provided by cognitive and humanistic perspectives, and to which we feel committed as educationists, that of social interactionism. We shall describe the main ideas of two of the most well-known psychologists of this school of thought, the Russian, Vygotsky, and the Israeli, Feuerstein, and consider the application of their views to language teaching.

The application of social interactionist views to language teaching has been discussed surprisingly little. This is all the more surprising when we consider the social nature of language itself. Most books on language learning include a section on such psychological schools of thought as behaviourism, humanism and cognitive psychology. However, the implications for the language teacher of taking a social interactionist perspective have only recently begun to emerge. Some helpful considerations of a Vygotskian perspective on second language learning are provided in Foley 1991, Schinke-Llano 1993, John-Steiner 1988, Appel and Lantolf 1994, Donato and McCormick 1994, Aljaafreh and Lantolf 1994, and De Guerrero and Villamil 1994. However, the powerful views of the Israeli psychologist, Reuven Feuerstein, have not yet been tapped by language teachers.

Both Vygotsky and Feuerstein in their own way took issue with the Piagetian view that from the time of their birth children learn independently by exploring their environment, and with the behaviourist view that adults are entirely responsible for shaping children's learning by the judicious use of rewards and punishments. For social interactionists, children are born into a social world, and learning occurs through interaction with other people. From the time we are born we interact with others in our day-to-day lives, and through these interactions we make our own sense of the world. Thus we can begin to see in social interactionism a much-needed theoretical underpinning to a communicative approach to language teaching, where it is maintained that we learn a language through using the language to interact meaningfully with other people.

2.3.1 Lev Vygotsky

In the 1960s the first Western translations of some of the prolific writings of the remarkable Russian psychologist, Lev Vygotsky, were published. Two of the most influential of these were *Thought and Language* (Vygotsky 1962) and *Mind in Society* (Vygotsky 1978). Because of the context within which Vygotsky lived during the aftermath of the Russian Revolution, the expression and application of his ideas were restricted. The prevailing political ideology of the time was anti-intellectual and favoured a behaviourist approach which ran counter to his developing theories. His work was suppressed and has only become widely available in translation in the last thirty years. Vygotsky emphasised the importance of language in interacting with people; not just speech, but signs and symbols as well. It is by means of language that culture is transmitted, thinking develops and learning occurs.

Vygotsky's approach was essentially *holistic* in that he rejected the view that what is to be learned can be broken down into small subcomponents and taught as discrete items and skills. Instead he argued that *meaning* should constitute the central aspect of any unit of study. Moreover, any unit of study should be presented in all its complexity, rather than skills and knowledge being presented in isolation.

Central to the psychology of both Vygotsky and Feuerstein is the concept of *mediation*. This is a term used by psychologists of the social interactionist school to refer to the part played by other significant people in the learners' lives, who enhance their learning by selecting and shaping the learning experiences presented to them. Basically, the secret of effective learning lies in the nature of the social interaction between two or more people with different levels of skill and knowledge. The role of the one with most knowledge, usually a parent or teacher, but often a peer, is to find ways of helping the other to learn. Particularly, this involves helping learners to move into and through the next layer of knowledge or understanding. This important person in the child's learning is known as a *mediator*.

Vygotsky's most widely known concept is probably the *zone of proximal development*, which is the term used to refer to the layer of skill or knowledge which is just beyond that with which the learner is currently capable of coping. (See Rogoff and Wertsch 1984 and Cole 1985 for a fuller description of this concept.) Working together with another person, either an adult or a more competent peer at a level that is just above a learner's present capabilities is the best way for the learner to move into the next layer. The concepts of mediation and zone of proximal development are important ones in social interactionist theories, and they will be discussed in detail in Chapter 4 where the implications for language teachers are considered.

2.3.2 Reuven Feuerstein

At about the same time as Vygotsky's works were beginning to be published in the West, the work of the great Israeli psychologist and educator, Reuven Feuerstein, was beginning to take shape. As he is one of the key figures in the social interactionist movement and his ideas form one of the central themes of this book, we shall briefly introduce Feuerstein at this point. His ideas will be revisited in Chapters 4 and 8.

In contrast to Vygotsky's mainly theoretical writings, the work of Feuerstein arose directly from a practical need, and is, therefore, firmly grounded in its implications for classroom teaching and learning. It is for this reason that we have decided to place such an important emphasis upon Feuerstein's ideas throughout this book.

Reuven Feuerstein was one of the founder members of the State of Israel after the Second World War, and one of those responsible for the education of immigrant Jewish children from all over the world. As a result of the Holocaust, many of these children had experienced dreadful traumatic experiences in their early lives which had severely impaired their ability to learn. At the same time, other children were arriving in Israel from apparently primitive communities in North Africa and elsewhere where Western approaches to learning had not necessarily been encouraged. The result was that, for a variety of reasons, a large proportion of immigrant children appeared to be mentally retarded and incapable of learning at school. Feuerstein firmly believed that this was not true, so he and a group of co-workers began to devise ways of assessing the true potential of such children which differed significantly from usual tests, and to construct methods of providing them with the skills and strategies to overcome their learning difficulties, and to become effective learners.

Central to Feuerstein's theory is the firm belief that anyone can become a fully effective learner. Another main component of his theory is the notion of *structural cognitive modifiability*, which is the belief that people's cognitive structures are infinitely modifiable, i.e. no one ever achieves the full extent of their learning potential, but people can continue to develop their cognitive capacity throughout their lives. The effect of this will be cumulative. It is worth noting that this view runs counter to more traditional notions of the critical periods and fixed intelligence as central factors in learning as was discussed in Chapter 1.

One of the most well-known aspects of his work is a programme for teaching people to learn how to learn known as *Instrumental Enrichment* (IE). This is built upon his notion of a *cognitive map*, which is a representation of the key factors involved in performing any mental act. These aspects are introduced in greater depth and developed further in Chapter 8.

Another notable aspect of Feuerstein's work is his introduction of the

concept of *dynamic assessment,* which is a way of assessing the true
potential of children that differs significantly from conventional tests. Here
the essentially interactive nature of learning is extended to the process of
assessment. Rather than viewing assessment as a process carried out by one
person, such as a teacher, on another, a learner, it is seen as a two-way
process involving interaction between both parties. The role of the assessor
therefore becomes one of entering into a dialogue with the person being
assessed to find out their current level of performance on any task and
sharing with them possible ways in which that performance might be
improved on a subsequent occasion. Thus, assessment and learning are seen
as inextricably linked and not separate processes.

Like Vygotsky, Feuerstein considers the role of the mediator as a key
factor in effective learning. He identifies the significant part played by the
teacher in selecting and shaping learning experiences and also children's
responses to them. However, he differs from the behaviourists in his
emphasis upon the ultimate goal of preparing learners to learn both
independently and co-operatively. He also sees that mediators play a fundamental role in transmitting culture. Feuerstein and his co-workers spent
many years in identifying the nature of mediated learning experiences, and
from this developed a coherent theory of mediation which we outline in
detail in Chapter 4.

Thus we can see that Feuerstein and Vygotsky quite independently broke
new ground in emphasising the social context in which learning takes place,
and in providing us with the concept of mediation as a key element in this
process. Vygotsky also focussed on the use of language in all its aspects as
a tool in both bringing meaning to and obtaining meaning from learning
activities. Moreover, he pointed out the advantages of collaborative work
set at a level just beyond the learner's current level of competence. In
addition, both psychologists provide us with ways of helping learners to
learn how to learn. We can see, therefore, that social interactionist theories
can provide us with a rich source of ideas which can inform our language
teaching practices. These ideas will be elaborated and drawn on extensively
in this book.

2.4 A social constructivist model

In Chapters 1 and 2 we have highlighted some significant features of
different approaches to educational psychology which we consider to be
of particular value to the language teacher. We are now in a position to
present a coherent framework in which different aspects of the teaching/
learning process can be better understood and which will help to guide
language teachers in their professional practice.

We saw how cognitive approaches emphasise the importance of what the learner brings to any learning situation as an active meaning-maker and problem-solver. Thus, the learner plays a central role in our model. Our examination of humanistic approaches leads us to emphasise also the development of the whole person in educational settings and to suggest that language teaching/learning can and should be seen in this light.

Social interactionism emphasises the dynamic nature of the interplay between teachers, learners and tasks, and provides a view of learning as arising from interactions with others. This interactive view is one that also informs our model. Since learning never takes place in isolation, we also recognise the importance of the learning environment or context within which the learning takes place, which we shall discuss in detail in Chapter 9.

We have identified four key sets of factors which influence the learning process – *teachers*, *learners*, *tasks* and *contexts*. However, none of these factors exists in isolation. They all interact as part of a dynamic, ongoing process. This is illustrated diagrammatically in Figure 5.

Teachers select tasks which reflect their beliefs about teaching and learning. Learners interpret tasks in ways that are meaningful and personal to them as individuals. The task is therefore the interface between the

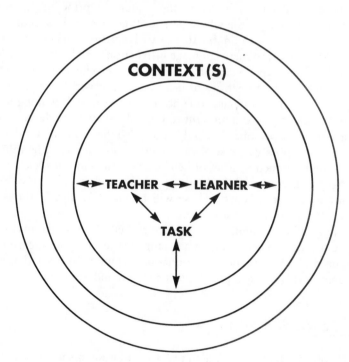

Figure 5   *A social constructivist model of the teaching-learning process*

teacher and learners. Teachers and learners also interact with each other; the way that teachers behave in classrooms reflects their values and beliefs, and the way in which learners react to teachers will be affected by the individual characteristics of the learners and the feelings that the teacher conveys to them. These three elements: teacher, task and learner are in this way a dynamic equilibrium.

In addition to this, the context in which the learning takes place will play an important part in shaping what happens within it. This includes the emotional environment, for example, trust and belonging; the physical environment; the whole school ethos; the wider social environment; the political environment and the cultural setting. This can be represented as a set of concentric circles, influencing each other, with the participants, of course, playing an ongoing part in shaping those environments.

It is worth noting that a change in any one part of the model will influence other parts. So, for example, if the teacher changes, or the context alters in some way, or the tasks (perhaps the coursebook) change, or the learners change, the whole balance will be affected.

In the following chapters we shall examine each of these in some depth and relate recent theory and research in that area to the specific needs of the foreign language teacher. However, one of our key principles throughout will be that of educating the whole person. If educational psychology is to have anything really meaningful to say to language teachers, it is about education as opposed to mere language instruction, and how to transform a language learning experience into a truly educational one. Education is concerned not just with theories of instruction, but with learning to learn, developing skills and strategies to continue to learn, with making learning experiences meaningful and relevant to the individual, with developing and growing as a whole person. We would argue also that it has a moral purpose which must incorporate a sense of values. Education can never be value-free. It must be underpinned by a set of beliefs about the kind of society that we are trying to construct and the kinds of explicit and implicit messages that will best convey those beliefs. These will be manifest also in the ways in which we interact with our students.

We believe, like Candlin, in his preface to Legutke and Thomas (1991), that there has never been a time when language teaching and learning was more in need of a systematic educational underpinning to its activities. It is the purpose of this book to provide just such an underpinning.

2.5   Conclusion

In this chapter we have provided an overview of humanism and social interactionism, and considered the implications of each of these schools of thought for language teaching. We then presented a social-constructivist model of the teaching-learning process in which four key elements, the learner(s), the teacher, the task and the context interact with and affect each other.

In subsequent chapters we take each of these elements in turn and discuss research and practice related to each, while not losing sight of our over-arching theme, that of educating the whole person. In the final chapter of the book we shall pull the four elements together once again to form some general propositions or principles about the whole process of teaching a language.

3 What do teachers bring to the teaching-learning process?

3.1 Introduction

In Chapter 2 we presented the four key elements of our model of the teaching-learning process. The perspective we have taken is based on a particular view of knowledge. This is one which sees knowledge as essentially constructed by individuals rather than transmitted from one person to another, but which recognises also that such constructions always occur within specific contexts, mainly as a result of social interactions.

We see this not as a linear sequence of events but as a dynamic process whereby those with more knowledge, known as mediators, influence and are influenced by those with less knowledge, as occurs in parent-child or teacher-learner relationships. This is often achieved by setting various tasks and responding to the ways in which the learner attempts those tasks. In addition, the environment within which this occurs will itself influence and be influenced by the teaching-learning process and its outcomes.

Although we recognise the inherent contradiction in separating out each of these elements and treating them as somehow distinct from each other, we feel that such a separation, albeit artificial, is necessary in order to enable readers to make their own sense of what each part contributes to the dynamic whole. In the present chapter, therefore, we shall focus on what individual teachers bring of themselves to the teaching-learning process. This will be followed in Chapter 4 by a specific focus on the notion of teacher-as-mediator.

3.2 Studies in effective teaching

In the first two chapters we examined a number of different ways in which people have tried to explain how learning occurs. Similarly, there have been many different attempts to account for effective teaching. Once again, some of these fall within a positivist paradigm; that is, they are mainly concerned with *measuring* characteristics of teachers, with *correlating* information, and with drawing general conclusions from the results obtained. These are sometimes referred to as *process-product* studies in that one of their major concerns has been to identify what kind of action on the part of teachers is most likely to bring about a desired result (e.g. good exam grades). We shall first examine some of these studies of what makes a 'good' teacher, before considering an alternative perspective.

In his book *The Essence of Good Teaching* (1984), Seymour Ericksen describes a study in which the views of learners and administrators about teachers were analysed. The conclusion reached was that 'an outstanding teacher should be an inspiring instructor who is concerned about students, an active scholar who is respected by discipline peers, and an efficient organised professional who is accessible to students and colleagues' (Ericksen 1984:3).

This is just one of many studies in which various personal characteristics of good teachers have been sought (see Brophy and Good 1986; Bennett 1987; Helmke *et al.* 1986). Such studies generally produce lists of characteristics like those in the study cited by Ericksen, or describe desirable ways of behaving, as in Merrett and Wheldall's positive teaching mode (Merrett and Wheldall 1990; Wheldall and Merrett 1984). Rosenshine (1971) and Rosenshine and Furst (1973) review a number of 'process-product' studies, in which various forms of teacher behaviour were connected with measurable learning outcomes such as test results. From this they identified nine key factors contributing to effective teaching:

- clarity of presentation;
- teacher enthusiasm;
- variety of activities during lessons;
- achievement-oriented behaviour in classrooms;
- opportunity to learn criterion material;
- acknowledgement and stimulation of student ideas;
- (lack of) criticism;
- use of structuring comments at the beginning and during lessons;
- guiding of student answers.

Although some attempts have been made to translate these and similar findings into guidelines for action (e.g. Perrott 1982), on the whole they have proved surprisingly unhelpful to most teachers seeking to improve their professional practice. This is partly because such factors are themselves open to a variety of interpretations (e.g. What exactly is meant by 'enthusiasm'?), but also because in the real world good teachers come in all shapes and sizes, with a wide range of different personalities, beliefs and ways of working.

They also come from different backgrounds and belong to different cultures. We would, therefore, expect them to work in different ways that suit their own personalities and situations. In Bennett's original (1976) study of effective teachers, for example, one of the most highly rated teachers demonstrated very few of the descriptors of how an effective teacher should behave.

In another study of effective teaching, Brown and McIntyre (1992) report a study of the opinions of seventy-five 12- to 13-year-olds in one city comprehensive school in the UK as to what made a good teacher. Ten categories were identified as representing elements of good teaching:

- creating a relaxed and enjoyable atmosphere in the classroom;
- retaining control in the classroom;
- presenting work in an interesting and motivating way;
- providing conditions so pupils understand the work;
- making clear what pupils are to do and achieve;
- judging what can be expected of a pupil;
- helping pupils with difficulties;
- encouraging pupils to raise their expectations of themselves;
- developing personal, mature relationships with pupils;
- demonstrating personal talents or knowledge.

At the conclusion of their study, however, these authors found themselves faced with the dilemma that although they could identify such elements of what they termed professional 'craft' knowledge amongst teachers, they could draw no simple conclusions or generalisations about how this highly complex knowledge could be transformed into guidelines for action.

If, therefore, it seems fruitless to attempt to shape oneself into the model of a good language teacher, as indicated by research, what other routes appear to be open? A radical alternative involves an inner exploration of oneself rather than a search for the outward characteristics of the perfect teacher. Such an alternative is provided by a constructivist approach to teachers and teaching. We explained what is meant by a constructivist approach to learning in Chapter 2. We shall now discuss briefly the broader issue of what is meant by a constructivist view of education, before moving on to consider what light constructivism sheds on what it means to be a good teacher. We choose to introduce the notion of a constructivist view of education here for two reasons. First, as we shall suggest later in this chapter, one of the many facets that teachers bring to the teaching-learning process is a view of what education is all about, and this belief, whether implicit or explicit, will influence their actions in the classroom. Second, we wish to introduce at this early stage a number of the main issues and themes that will be taken up later in this book, such as the distinction between learning and education and the importance of learning to think and solve problems.

3.3   A constructivist view of education

The generally acknowledged 'father' of constructivism, Ernst von Glasersfeld argues that education is essentially a 'political' enterprise with two main purposes – to empower learners to think for themselves, and to perpetuate in the next generation ways of acting and thinking that are judged the best by the present generation (von Glasersfeld 1995). He argues, moreover, that all knowledge is instrumental, that is, it is used for particular purposes and is meaningless in isolation. Because of this, learners need to know the reasons why they are required to act in particular ways.

> The first thing required, therefore, is that students be given the reasons why particular ways of acting and thinking are considered desirable. This entails explanations of the specific contexts in which the knowledge to be acquired is believed to work.
>
> (von Glasersfeld op. cit.:177)

In von Glasersfeld's view, a constructivist approach to education is best put into practice by presenting issues, concepts and tasks in the form of problems to be explored in dialogue rather than as information to be ingested and reproduced. This is best performed by what he terms the teacher's *orienting function*.

> The teacher cannot tell students what concepts to construct or how to construct them, but by judicious use of language they can be prevented from constructing in directions which the teacher considers futile but which, as he knows from experience, are likely to be tried.
>
> (op. cit.:184)

This, of course, presents a dilemma in itself because by acting in such a preventative way the teacher may restrict the very development of genuinely creative critical reflection that brings about new insights and even scientific breakthroughs.

From Socrates onwards, the problem-setting/solving approach to teaching has had a number of powerful advocates, including John Dewey, Maria Montessori and Paulo Friere, without ever coming to play the dominant role in pedagogy that it would seem to warrant. In recent years, however, there has been a resurgence of interest in this approach, as exemplified by Harvard Project Zero (Kornhaber and Gardner 1991) in the US, Cognitive Education through Science Education (CASE) in the UK (Adey and Shayer 1994), Matthew Lipman's Philosophy for Children programme (Lipman *et al.* 1980) and Feuerstein's Instrumental Enrichment (Feuerstein *et al.* 1980). Many examples of this kind of approach are provided in the proceedings of a conference organised by the Centre for Educational Research and Innovation of the OECD in Paris in 1989 (Maclure and Davies 1991).

There has, however, been a considerable amount of interest in the use of problem-solving tasks in teaching a foreign language for a number of years (e.g. Nunan 1989; Prabhu 1987). This is a theme that we shall develop in Chapter 8 where we discuss how task-based approaches to language teaching could involve tasks which foster thinking and problem-solving.

As we shall suggest in Chapter 6, moreover, a central component in motivation to learn is the individual learner's feelings of competence and self-efficacy, which can best be gained by working out one's own solutions to problems.

In this respect, for von Glasersfeld nothing succeeds like success:

> The motivation to master new problems is most likely to spring from having enjoyed the satisfaction of finding solutions to problems in the past . . . The insight **why** a result is right, understanding the logic in the way it was produced, gives the student a feeling of ability and competence that is far more empowering than any external reinforcement . . . If students do not think their own way through problems and acquire the confidence that they can solve them, they can hardly be expected to be motivated to tackle more.

> (op. cit.:181)

He adds one further rider:

> Problem solving is undoubtedly a powerful educational tool. However, I would suggest that its power greatly increases if the students come to see it as *fun*.

> (op. cit.:183)

In a persuasive paper Thomas and Harri-Augstein (1985) argue that all approaches to teaching, whatever their differences, can best be seen as an organised attempt to help people bring some kind of meaning to their lives. The difference between these approaches lies in the value that is placed on different states of knowing. For the personal construct psychologist, teaching is seen as primarily concerned with facilitating the process by which significant, viable, personal meanings are achieved.

> For education to be an enriching experience the meanings that emerge must become **personal**, and they must be significant and important in some part of the person's life. Meanings must also be **viable**; that is they must prove useful and effective in mediating one's transactions; transactions with stored knowledge, with people and with the world around.
>
> (Thomas and Harri-Augstein 1985:257)

Looked at in this way, the essence of effective teaching and learning becomes understanding how meaning becomes attributed, and conducting conversations that elaborate, relate and extend personal meaning.

In this section we have discussed some of the key themes that emerge from taking a constructivist perspective on education. We see that from such a viewpoint, education becomes concerned with helping people to make their own meanings. We see also that presenting learners with problem-solving activities becomes an important part of putting such an approach into practice. This discussion sets the scene to consider next what constructivism has to offer us when examining what makes a good teacher.

3.4   A constructivist view of teaching

Constructivism holds that, basically, there is never any one right way to teach. In considering what a constructivist approach offers to teachers, von Glasersfeld asserts:

> Constructivism cannot tell teachers new things to do, but it may suggest why certain attitudes and procedures are counter-productive, and it may point out opportunities for teachers to use their own spontaneous imagination.
>
> (1995: 177)

Teaching, like learning, must be concerned with teachers making sense of, or meaning from, the situations in which they find themselves.

Researchers have used a variety of different methods in their attempts to understand the meaning that teachers make of their work, ranging from investigating the thinking and planning that teachers do outside the classroom (Clark and Peterson 1986), through ethnographic studies of their routines, rules and patterns of teaching, to autobiographical accounts of the understanding teachers bring to their work (Ashton-Warner 1980; Connelly and Clandinin 1990). A fascinating example of the latter approach is offered by Louden (1991). This study follows the progress of a newly qualified teacher in her struggle to establish professional competence. Louden summarises this struggle in the following way:

> From a practitioner's perspective . . . teaching is a struggle to discover and maintain a settled practice, a set of routines and patterns of action which resolve the problems posed by particular subjects and groups of children. These patterns, content and resolutions to familiar classroom problems are shaped by each teacher's biography and professional experience. The meaning of these patterns of action only becomes clear when they are set in the context of a teacher's personal and professional history, her hopes and dreams for teaching, and the school in which she works.
>
> (Louden 1991:xi)

For Louden, the fatal flaw that pervades most attempts to improve teaching is a failure to understand this point. If teacher improvement projects are ever to be successful, they should always begin with the question 'How does this change relate to these teachers' understandings of their work?' What this in turn will lead us to do is to pay close attention to the meaning that teachers make of the physical environment of their classrooms, the syllabus or particular teaching practices, and to act in accordance with our understanding of these meanings.

Louden also introduces us to the notion of teachers' *horizons* of understanding which are constantly in the process of formation but which are constructed within *traditions*, larger frames of reference which provide shared ways of making sense. When confronted by new problems and challenges, a teacher struggles to resolve them in ways that are consistent with the understanding she brings to the problem and this process leads in turn to new horizons of understanding about teaching. Thus a language teacher's horizons will be shaped in part by her own personal experiences, but also by traditional ways in which other language teachers throughout history have made sense of what it means to be a language teacher. However, understanding is not merely the recreation of someone else's meaning, but is in principle incomplete and continues to grow with every new experience. It always involves the creation of meaning from those experiences in the light of the meaning-maker's preconceptions and the tradition of interpretation within which he or she acts.

Perhaps the most helpful interpretation of a constructivist approach to teaching is offered by Salmon (1988) in a book which is both powerful and deceptively simple. Although she does not object to traditional studies of teacher effectiveness, teaching for Salmon involves far more than this. She describes it 'not as the passing on of a parcel of objective knowledge, but as the attempt to share what you yourself find personally meaningful' (Salmon 1988:37). She argues as a consequence that teachers are indivisible from what they teach.

The differences between teachers, therefore, are not simply a question of whether they are good or bad, competent or incompetent, because every teacher is unique. As teachers we do not just act as gateways to knowledge because we ourselves represent and even embody the curriculum. We convey not just what we know, but our position towards it, the personal ramifications and implications which it has for us. At the same time, teachers experience an *engagement* with their learners out of which further constructions emerge. Both teacher and learners reshape their ways of understanding, their knowledge structures and the meanings that they attribute to events and ideas as a result of this interactive process. They also continually reconstruct their views of each other. Because in teaching we are essentially inviting our learners to take up, at least provisionally, our own personal stance towards the curriculum, we are bound to be affected by their response to this invitation and to construe their actions and attitudes accordingly, just as they do ours.

In contrast to a skills-based approach with its emphasis upon how to perform effectively, which seeks to find commonalities between good teachers, a constructivist approach to teaching emphasises the fact that no two teachers and no two teaching situations are ever the same. For the constructivist, both the content of any lesson and the way in which it is offered are part of the person of each individual teacher. The need here, therefore, is for teachers to become more self-aware with regard to their beliefs and the ways in which they make sense of the world, particularly with regard to their views about education and how those views themselves come to be shaped. At the same time, they need to be aware also that they themselves are being construed by their learners and that their words, their actions and their interactions form part of every individual learner's own construction of knowledge. It is apparent, therefore, that an important component of a constructivist approach to education is for teachers to become aware of what their own beliefs and views of the world are, which leads us into the notion of the reflective practitioner.

3.5   The teacher as reflective practitioner

If teachers are to be effective in whatever approach they decide to take, it seems reasonable to expect them to act consistently in accordance with their expressed (or 'espoused') beliefs. Unfortunately, according to Chris Argyris and Donald Schön (1974, 1978) this hardly ever occurs in any profession. They argue that there is almost always a discrepancy between what professionals say they believe (their 'espoused' theories) and the ways in which they act (their 'theories-in-action'). These authors provide an impressive array of case studies from a wide variety of professions in support of this contention.

In teaching, if the discrepancy, where it exists, between a teacher's expressed beliefs and the ways in which that teacher acts professionally is a large one, then learners are likely to receive confused and confusing messages. In an effort to improve teachers' self-awareness in this respect, some educational theorists have fostered the notion of *critical reflection* (Boud, Keogh and Walker 1985). The intention here is to enable teachers to become *reflective practitioners* (Schön 1983), thereby they subject their everyday professional practice to ongoing critical reflection and make clear their own particular world view by means of such consideration.

Schön (op. cit.) draws the distinction between reflection-*in*-action and reflection-*on*-action. He contends that each individual's knowledge is mainly tacit and implied by the ways in which they act, such that 'our knowing is *in* our action' (Schön 1983:49). We do not necessarily have to think about how to act appropriately as teachers in any situation before we do so. When we 'think on our feet' or make spontaneous decisions about how to act, then we can be seen as reflecting-in-action, which in turn gives rise to the application of 'theories-in-action'. It is such theories, according to Schön, rather than externally imposed knowledge or theories from elsewhere, which underpin each professional's own unique way of working.

The task of the reflective practitioner is to make this tacit or implicit knowledge explicit by reflection *on* action, by constantly generating questions and checking our emerging theories with both personal past experience and with the reflections of others. This is one of the main thrusts of the movement towards teachers as action researchers (Kemmis 1985).

Schön outlines some ways in which teachers-as-reflective-practitioners act. Firstly, the curriculum must be seen as an inventory of themes of understanding and skill to be addressed rather than a set of materials to be learned. Each student has to be treated as an individual, 'a universe of one' (Schön, op. cit.:333).

> A reflective teacher needs a kind of educational technology which does more than extend her capacity to administer drill and practice. Most interesting to her is an educational technology which helps students to become aware of their own intuititve understandings, to fall into cognitive confusions and explore new directions of understanding and action.
>
> (Schön op. cit.: 333)

We shall expand the idea of learners as individuals in Chapter 5. At the same time, any school supportive of reflective teaching would find it necessary to consider the kind of structure within which learning takes place and the very nature of knowledge itself.

> An institution congenial to reflective practice would require a learning system within which individuals could surface conflicts and dilemmas and subject them to public enquiry, a learning system conducive to the continual criticism and restructuring of organisational principles and values.
>
> (Schön op. cit.:336)

In considering the implications of taking such an approach, Smyth suggests that critical reflection can be fostered by asking a number of guiding questions:

- What do my practices say about my assumptions, values and beliefs about teaching?
- Where did these ideas come from?
- What social practices are expressed in these ideas?
- What views of power do they embody?
- Whose interests seem to be served by my practices?
- What is it that acts to constrain my views of what is possible in teaching?

(Smyth 1991:116)

Smyth goes on to make the telling point that reflective practitioners and non-reflective practitioners are not two fundamentally irreconcilable groups, but are, rather, professionals working at different points in different ways to achieve common goals. However, we find ourselves ultimately in agreement with Ruddock's point (1984:6) that 'Not to examine one's practice is irresponsible; to regard teaching as an experiment and to monitor one's performance is a responsible professional act.'

Critical reflection is not necessarily negative in its orientation, but it does imply at the very least that teachers should be aware of their belief systems and constantly monitoring how far their actions reflect those beliefs or are in keeping with them. However, in contrast to the radical constructivist approach of von Glasersfeld with its emphasis upon the individual, social constructivism suggests that this is most helpfully a shared process within which both teachers and learners are engaged in a multilevel process of action, monitoring, reflection, feedback and further action. Thus, to be an effective teacher in our own terms we need to look both inwards and outwards. We need to develop our awareness of others' viewpoints, in this case different perspectives on teaching, and to look to our own beliefs, standards and values. We then need to construct a particular identity of the kind of teacher that we want to be and to seek to reproduce this in our day-to-day activities, in our actions and in our interactions in the teaching-learning arena.

The construction of an 'ideal-self-as-teacher' is inevitably multifaceted. For the remainder of this chapter we will focus on just two of these facets by way of example, but also because we consider them to be of central importance. These are teachers' beliefs about learning and learners and about themselves as functioning individuals within the role of teacher. Before we do this, however, we need to consider further the whole issue of teachers' beliefs.

3.6   Teachers' beliefs

There is a growing body of evidence to indicate that teachers are highly influenced by their beliefs, which in turn are closely linked to their values, to their views of the world and to their conceptions of their place within it. One comprehensive review of the literature on teachers' beliefs concluded that these had a greater influence than teachers' knowledge on the way they planned their lessons, on the kinds of decisions they made and on their general classroom practice (Pajares 1992). Beliefs were also found to be far more influential than knowledge in determining how individuals organise and define tasks and problems, and were better predictors of how teachers behaved in the classroom.

Beliefs are notoriously difficult to define and evaluate, but there do appear to be a number of helpful statements that we can make about them. They tend to be culturally bound, to be formed early in life and to be resistant to change. Beliefs about teaching, for example, appear to be well established by the time a student gets to college (Weinstein 1989). They are closely related to what we think we know but provide an affective filter which screens, redefines, distorts, or reshapes subsequent thinking and information processing (Nespor 1987). Our beliefs about one particular area or subject will not only be interconnected, but will also be related to other more central aspects of our personal belief systems, e.g. our attitudes and values about the world and our place within it. Because they are difficult to measure, we usually have to infer people's beliefs from the ways in which they behave rather than from what they say they believe (Agyris and Schön 1974).

We have stressed earlier the importance of teachers reflecting upon their own actions in order to make explicit their often implicit belief systems and to help them clarify what is personally meaningful and significant to them in their professional roles. Teachers' beliefs about what learning is will affect everything that they do in the classroom, whether these beliefs are implicit or explicit. Even if a teacher acts spontaneously, or from habit without thinking about the action, such actions are nevertheless prompted by a deep-rooted belief that may never have been articulated or made explicit. Thus teachers' deep-rooted beliefs about how languages are learned will pervade their classroom actions more than a particular methodology they are told to adopt or coursebook they follow. If the teacher-as-educator is one who is constantly re-evaluating in the light of new knowledge his or her beliefs about language, or about how language is learned, or about education as a whole, then it is crucial that teachers first understand and articulate their own theoretical perspectives.

Beliefs about learners

Teachers may hold any one or a combination of beliefs about those whom they teach. The sociologist Roland Meighan has suggested that there are at least seven different ways in which teachers can and do construe learners and that such constructions reflect individual teachers' views of the world and also have a profound influence on their classroom practice (Meighan and Meighan 1990).

Meighan suggests that learners may be construed metaphorically as:

- resisters;
- receptacles;
- raw material;
- clients;
- partners;
- individual explorers;
- democratic explorers.

He sees these constructs in terms of a continuum which reflects the nature of the teacher-learner power relationship. Thus the first three constructs are heavily teacher dominated while the latter constructs involve increasingly active learner participation.

The notion of learners as *resisters* sees learners as people who do not want to learn but only do so because they are made to. Such a view has given rise to the commonly associated assumption that force or punishment is the most appropriate way of overcoming such resistance in the classroom. Even at its most benign, the assumption that children do not start with what Bruner calls 'the will to learn' will lead to a view that *instruction* is the natural function of the teacher.

An alternative view, of course, is that children begin school full of desire to learn, but gradually, sometimes even rapidly, lose such desire as a result of their learning experiences (Holt 1964). The psychologist and educator William Glasser expressed this point particularly well in his book *Schools Without Failure*: 'Very few children come to school failures, none come labelled as failures. It is school and school alone which pins the label of failure on children' (Glasser 1969:26).

It would of course be naive to think that all learners attending classes to learn a new language are there because they want to be. For a host of possible reasons, language teachers might meet some degree of resistance from some of their learners. However, if learners are viewed narrowly as resisters, teachers may well employ methods involving compulsion rather than seeking ways of helping them to want to learn the language or to see the value in what they are doing. What we would emphasise here is that the use of force or punishment has never been found to be particularly useful in helping learners to master a language or to foster a lifelong love of languages; far more effective ways exist of helping reluctant learners. We shall take up this point further in later chapters.

Perhaps an even more common conception of learners is one in which they are seen as *receptacles* to be filled with knowledge. This is sometimes referred to as 'the jugs and mugs' theory. The teacher is seen as having a large jug of knowledge which is poured into the learner 'mugs' or receptacles, which in turn can only accept a certain amount of that knowledge according to the size of the learner's IQ. Here again we can see that instruction and information-giving become the natural way of working for teachers who begin with such assumptions, particularly if they also view intelligence as something which is fixed at birth and immutable. Freire (1970) describes this as the 'banking' conception of education, where learners are like bank accounts into which deposits are regularly made and drawn upon later for specific purposes such as examinations. Thus, if language teachers view their learners as receptacles, with a specific amount of language aptitude which determines their capacity to absorb language, they will be likely to adopt methods which involve transmission of language items to their learners.

Another common metaphor conceives of learners as *raw material*, like clay to be moulded into a fine work of art or building material to be constructed into a solid and well-designed building. There is much to be said in favour of such an approach insofar as most of us remember being influenced by an inspirational teacher, and this view does in fact form a part of social interactionist theories. However, there are also dangers of manipulating learners and shaping them according to the teacher's wishes.

The notion of *learner as client* places greater emphasis upon the identification of educational need and begins to alter the nature of the relationship between teachers and learners. Much adult foreign language learning begins with such a premise, and this view has been prevalent in teaching English for Specific Purposes (ESP) for some time. The prospective learners are likely to know what they want to learn and how much time and money they are prepared to invest in doing so, while the role of the teacher can be seen as attempting to meet those needs. Interestingly, while this is a common way of working with fee-paying adults in language schools, it is nevertheless still rare to involve school children in deciding what they need to learn, or in evaluating how helpful they find their lessons to be.

An alternative conception is that of *learner as partner*, where the emphasis is shifted from consultation to negotiation and where it is possible in Freire's terms for the teacher to 'take on the role of student amongst students'. The assumption here is not one of equality but one of a sharing relationship within which teachers recognise that they are also learners. The starting point for this kind of teacher is not one of 'I'm in charge!', but one of 'Let's decide together how we can all benefit from our time together'. The underlying notions are of mutual trust and respect leading to growth and development for teachers and all their learners. This approach is best exemplified by humanist teachers such as Carl Rogers. In the language classroom, learners can be treated as partners by involving them in decisions about what activities to carry out, asking them what topics they are interested in or allowing them to select books to read. It is also a view that has underpinned work on the use of process syllabuses in language teaching.

Two further possible conceptions of learners are those of the *learner as individual explorer* and the *learner as democratic explorer*. In the first of these the role of the teacher becomes almost entirely one of *facilitator* working largely from a Piagetian perspective, i.e. the classroom is organised in such a way as to enable the learners to explore for themselves and come to their own conclusions with a minimum of prompting from the teacher. This particular approach became very popular with teachers of young children in the UK following the publication of the Plowden Report (1967). This is a view that has tended to pervade approaches to language teaching based on input and acquisition, i.e. the teacher's role is to provide appropriate comprehensible input, which the learners act on in their own ways, leading to language acquisition.

Democratic exploration takes this process one step further and sees it as the function of any learning group to set its own agenda, decide upon its goals and preferred ways of working, and how, if at all, it wishes to draw upon the particular knowledge and expertise of the teacher. Meighan clearly favours this particular approach, at least in working with mature learners. Although it is difficult to envisage how this could be put into practice with younger learners, perhaps the classic example of an attempt to do so is provided by A. S. Neill's alternative school, Summerhill (Neill 1962, 1967).

Approaches such as community language learning draw a little on this conceptualisation of learners. More particularly, task-based approaches to language learning which involve giving groups of learners tasks to engage in, allow groups the freedom to decide how they wish to work, although it is, of course, generally the teacher who selects the activities.

It should be readily apparent that the social constructivist approach which we favour tends to fit more comfortably with the latter end of Meighan's continuum than with the former, but it is also clear that the extent to which teachers feel able to work with their learners as democratic explorers rather than as, say, clients, often depends on factors outside of their control. In making their belief systems about learners explicit, however, teachers should be able to identify inconsistencies and frustrations in their work and thereby search for ways of bridging the inevitable gap between their espoused theories and their theories in action.

Beliefs about learning

As important as their views about learners are teachers' beliefs about learning, although the two are inextricably linked. In Chapters 1 and 2 we outlined a number of different psychological approaches to learning. We have also made the point that teachers' beliefs about what is involved in learning will influence the way in which they teach.

It is, of course, impossible to contemplate teaching in isolation from learning. The question of what makes a good teacher must ultimately be concerned with what and how and how much learners learn and what exactly that learning is for. This is just as true for the language teacher as it is for any other. We can only be really effective teachers if we are clear in our minds what we mean by learning because only then can we know what kinds of learning outcomes we want our learners to achieve. If our aim is to teach enough language items to pass an examination, then this will have significant implications for the way in which we teach. If, on the other hand, we see learning a new language as a lifelong process with much broader social, cultural and educational implications, then we will take a very different approach to teaching it.

As a result of their comprehensive review of the literature on conceptions of learning, Gow and Kember (1993) suggest that most approaches to learning can be subsumed under one of the following headings:

- a quantitative increase in knowledge;
- memorisation;
- the acquisition of facts, procedures etc. which can be retained and/or used in practice;

- the abstraction of meaning;
- an interpretative process aimed at the understanding of reality;
- some form of personal change.

The first three of these conceptions can be conveniently subsumed under the heading of *reproductive* approaches while the subsequent three can be seen as *meaning-based*. It would, of course, be unwise to view such approaches as mutually exclusive. Most methods used in language teaching appear to belong to several overlapping categories, and most teachers' views would incorporate a mixture of these. However, a few examples can usefully be given to illustrate these categories. 'The quantitative increase in knowledge' might lead to transmission of knowledge about how the language operates or explanation of grammar rules. The learning of vocabulary or verb tenses might belong more to 'memorisation'. Teaching learners skills such as guessing meanings of words from their context are more concerned with the 'learning of procedures which can be used in practice'.

'The abstraction of meaning' is a particularly interesting category, which appears to belong more to communicative approaches to teaching a language and techniques such as task-based listening, reading with information transfer, or tasks requiring meaningful interaction. These particular techniques would also belong to the fifth category, 'an interpretative process aimed at the understanding of reality', provided the language used conveys reality. This issue of 'purposefulness' of language is taken up in Chapter 8.

The final category, 'some form of personal change' will have particular implications for the way in which a language is taught. A belief in this form of learning would lead to the selection of activities that have personal significance or relevance to the learners leading to some personal benefit such as learning to think, learning some social skill or learning about the world. These are all issues that are taken up in future chapters.

We are now in a position to make our own statement as to what we believe learning involves, and which we consider represents central aspects of our own espoused theory.

We believe that worthwhile learning:

- is a complex process;
- produces personal change of some kind;
- involves the creation of new understandings which are personally relevant;
- can take a number of different forms;
- is always influenced by the context in which is occurs;

- results mainly from social interaction;
- often needs to be mediated;
- differs from individual to individual;
- is an emotional as well as a cognitive process;
- is closely related to how people feel about themselves;
- is a lifelong process.

Each of these statements reflects an important aspect of social constructivism with an additional emphasis upon the affective dimension as well as the cognitive. Each will be taken up, therefore, at different points within this book and will be represented as ongoing themes throughout.

Teachers' beliefs about themselves

At this point, therefore, it seems appropriate to turn finally in this chapter to consider how teachers' views of themselves as *persons* and what they believe to be the most appropriate form of social interaction with their learners can influence the learning process. Our view of education has much in common with many aspects of the humanist approach introduced in Chapter 2, particularly as exemplified by statements of the following nature:

> Effective teachers create learning atmospheres which are cognitively and affectively expanding; learning atmospheres which enable the learner to become a more adequate and knowledgeable person.
>
> (Pine and Boy 1977:iii)

It is clear that this kind of approach places great emphasis upon what the teacher as a person brings to the teaching-learning relationship and how the learner can be helped to develop as a whole person by the provision of a supportive learning environment, which allows individuals to develop in their own way.

For the humanistic teacher, teaching is essentially a personal expression of the self. As Pine and Boy express it, 'Pupils feel the personal emotional structure of the teacher long before they feel the impact of the intellectual content offered by that teacher' (op. cit.:3). This obviously has particular implications with regard to teachers' views of themselves since a teacher who lacks self-esteem will find it impossible to build the self-esteem of others. This is equally true when it comes to conveying dignity and respect. Similarly, the teacher who does not accept her learners for who they are makes it difficult for them to accept themselves. Thus, the language teacher needs to convey a sense of self-confidence in using the language whilst at the same time respecting learners' attempts to express themselves and their views in the language.

One further quality which is central to the humanistic approach is that of permissiveness. 'Permissiveness' is defined here in a very special way as 'permission to be oneself', to pursue interests and curiosity in search of meaning in one's life, as well as the freedom to have ideas, beliefs and values.

Humanistic education is sometimes described as *learner-centred teaching*. However, such a definition does not do justice to the full implications of taking this approach to one's teaching. Whilst it is true that humanistic teachers begin with the premise that everything they say or do has, or could have, a significant impact on the personal growth and development of their learners, it is equally true that in every teaching act the teacher defines herself as a person. Humanistic teaching, therefore, is not just learner-centred, but *person-centred*. A teacher's view of teaching mirrors her view of herself and her teaching behaviour reflects her essence as a person.

One natural consequence of taking such an approach is that we have to accept that teaching is an expression of values and attitudes, not just information or knowledge. Another consequence is that teachers must recognise that they themselves are constantly involved in a lifelong process of learning and change. The influence of the developmental theories of such psychologists as Maslow and Erickson, as outlined in Chapter 2, provide the foundation upon which this approach is based.

3.7   Conclusion

In this chapter we have argued that there are no simple answers to the question of what makes a good teacher. Studies which focus exclusively on what good teachers do or even on what learners and others think that teachers do appear to be surprisingly unhelpful to individual teachers wanting to improve their own practices.

A more helpful approach seems to lie within the area of teachers' beliefs; about themselves, about learning and its educational relevance and about learners. At the same time, the consistency with which teachers' actions reflect what they claim to believe would appear to be a vitally important aspect of effective teaching. The notion, therefore, of the teacher-as-reflective practitioner becomes central to our developing perspective.

Constructivism lies at the core of our pedagogical model. Therefore, teachers' constructions of learning and learners need to be made explicit. At the same time, social interactionism emphasises the importance of both the context of learning and the nature of the social and communicative interactions that take place within that context, usually a classroom. A humanist perspective has been offered as one which should help teachers to focus on both the cognitive and affective aspects of such relationships.

In the next chapter, we take the role of the teacher a step further and consider more precisely some practical implications of this kind of model with particular reference to the work of Reuven Feuerstein.

4 What can teachers do to promote learning?

4.1 Introduction

The previous chapter considered ways in which teachers seek to make sense of the learning process and suggested that their beliefs about learning and learners will have a profound influence on their teaching, no matter what syllabus or coursebook they use. However, an understanding of what makes an effective teacher is inevitably more complex than this. As well as an awareness of the degree of match or mismatch between their 'espoused' theories and their 'theories-in-action', teachers need to understand also the many different ways in which their words and actions can influence the learning that occurs in their classrooms. In this chapter we take a different perspective on the teaching process and consider what teachers can do to help their learners become effective and independent.

We only have to reflect on our own learning experiences in school to realise that teachers can affect learning in a range of ways that go far beyond the transmission of knowledge. Some of these ways would be likely to include teaching learners how to learn, boosting their confidence, motivating, displaying a personal interest, enhancing self-esteem and organising an appropriate learning environment.

In Chapter 2 we introduced the concept of *mediation* which has played a central role in all social interactionist theories. For Vygotsky and his followers, mediation refers to the use of 'tools'. Tools in this sense refer to anything that is used in order to help solve a problem or achieve a goal. The most important of these tools is symbolic language (Kozulin 1990). For these theorists, the use of mediational language to help learners move into and through their *zone of proximal development* (ZPD) is of particular significance.

The concept of ZPD was introduced in Chapter 2. It is a notion that has been enthusiastically taken up by some educational psychologists because it has important implications for teachers with regard to what they can do to help children in their learning. It provides a particularly positive message about how to help learners when they are 'stuck' at any stage in their learning. It suggests that the teacher should set tasks that are at a level just beyond that at which the learners are currently capable of functioning, and teach principles that will enable them to make the next step unassisted. Bruner and others have used the term 'laddering' to refer to this process (Bornstein and Bruner 1989).

Despite the attractiveness of the concept of ZPD in its commonsense simplicity, its application in practice is more problematic. Vygotsky himself did not offer much in the way of practical advice as to how ZPD might be helpfully employed in the classroom, and it has been left to others to find effective ways of doing so (e.g. Brown and Campione 1986; Moll 1990). It is also important to establish that the concept of ZPD does not imply that these levels of learning are hierarchically ordered or neatly sequenced. In fact Vygotsky explicitly stated that they are not.

In terms of language learning, ZPD can be seen as complementary to interlanguage theory. As we explained in Chapter 1 (page 23), this theory conceives of each learner's understanding of the language system as being gradually reshaped as it develops and more closely approximates towards the target language system. The ZPD can thus be seen as the next level of understanding in the learner's interlanguage.

Some current views of second language learning tend to take a somewhat non-cognitive approach, seeing language as 'picked up' or acquired by natural processes with which the teacher should not interfere (e.g. Krashen 1981, 1982). What mediation theory tells us, however, is that it is the role of the teacher to help learners to find ways of moving into their next level of understanding of the language.

The extent to which instruction in the classroom does help learners to acquire linguistic rules is a topic that has been hotly debated in language teaching. Opinion is divided between those who maintain that instruction can assist language acquisition, and those who believe it cannot (Long 1980). Some researchers such as Ellis (1984) suggest that it may be that instruction helps only when the learner is ready to acquire the form being taught, that is, when the form is in the learner's ZPD. Pienemann also picks up this concept in his 'teachability hypothesis', where he maintains that instruction can promote acquisition of language if the form to be acquired is close to the next form that would be acquired naturally in the learner's interlanguage (Pienemann 1989).

Two important issues arising from this are how the learner progresses from one level to the next, and what the teacher's role is in facilitating this progression. We shall discuss the first question in Chapter 7 when we consider the strategies people use to learn something. It is the second question that we will address next by examining the theory of mediation of the Israeli psychologist, Reuven Feuerstein.

4.2   Feuerstein's theory of mediation

Feuerstein suggests that right from birth a child's learning is shaped by the intervention of significant adults. He refers to these important figures in the child's learning as *mediators* or *mediating adults*, and the experiences that they provide as *mediated learning experiences*. These adults, at first parents, but later teachers, select and organise stimuli that they consider most appropriate for the child, shape them and present them in the ways considered most suitable to promote learning. They also intervene in shaping the child's early attempts at responding to stimuli, directing and encouraging more appropriate responses whilst explaining why one response is more useful or appropriate than another (Feuerstein *et al.* 1980). Thus, in contrast to Piagetian theory, where it is believed that children develop at their own pace through interaction with the environment, the way in which significant adults interact with children is considered to play a central part in the latter's cognitive development. This enables the child to construct a view of the world and his or her place within it. Cognitive, social and emotional development are seen as inextricably linked, and the establishment of an appropriate climate in the home or classroom within which this can be effectively fostered is as important as the content of what is conveyed.

Where Feuerstein is less clear, however, is with regard to the part played by the child within the interactive process of mediation. It is worth noting here the dominant role played by the powerful adult within Feuerstein's theory. There is certainly room for criticism of the lack of attention he gives to the learner's contribution to the mediating process. What we now know from studies of early childhood development (Bornstein and Bruner 1989) is that within the social context of the family, the actions of children affect those of the parents as well as the other way round. Thus, it is important to see the child as an active participant in the mediation process, and that this process is truly interactive rather than unidirectional.

Feuerstein does not deny the importance of what the individual learner brings to the learning situation and to the development of what he terms 'efficient cognitive functioning' (i.e. effective thinking and problem-solving), and in this he can be seen to be supportive of some aspects of Piagetian theory. However, he emphasises the centrality of mediated learning experiences above all else in cognitive development and learning to learn. At the same time, he differs from a behaviourist viewpoint in his emphasis upon the role played by culture in guiding the effective mediator in his or her actions. Thus, a vital role for both parents and educators is the transmission of culture from one generation to the next, and the term 'culturally deprived' is used by Feuerstein to refer to those who have been denied access to their culture. It should be noted here that this is a very different use of the term 'culturally deprived' to that often employed.

The key question to ask at this point is to what extent the concept of mediator differs from a more narrow view of the teacher as disseminator of information. We see a fundamental difference. First, mediation must be concerned with empowering, with helping learners to acquire the knowledge, skills and strategies they will need in order to progress, to learn more, to tackle problems, to function effectively in a particular culture and a changing society, and to meet new, emerging and unpredictable demands. It is also concerned with helping learners to become autonomous, to take control of their own learning, with the fundamental aim of enabling them to become independent thinkers and problem-solvers. In response to this, readers may well argue that this is, and always has been, the job of a good teacher, in which case, their concept of what a teacher is has already encompassed the notion of mediation. Nevertheless, we see the distinction between the teacher as mediator and teacher as instructor as a useful one for the purpose of our discussion.

Second, it is important to establish that mediation involves interaction between mediator and learner, and that the learner is an active participant in the process. Third, there is an emphasis on *reciprocation*, that is, the importance of the learner reciprocating the intentions of the mediator or teacher. This means that the learner is ready and willing to carry out the task presented, and that there is an agreement as to what should be done and why. Reciprocation can occur at the level of acceptance and willingness to comply, or it may involve a process of negotiation whereby agreement is reached as a result of other mediational activities. Feuerstein calls this the principle of *reciprocity*, one which he sees as often lacking in classrooms. Fourth, it is important to note that learner autonomy involves more than the provision of suitable self-access materials. The mediator needs to help the learners to interact with the materials in various ways until they become truly self-directed.

In the rest of this chapter we shall describe Feuerstein's theory of mediation, and then use this theory to consider some ways in which language teachers can enhance the learning and wider education of their learners.

4.2.1 Key features of mediation

To provide learning experiences which are truly educational, the teacher or other adult can 'mediate' in a number of different ways. Feuerstein identifies twelve features of mediation which we shall now describe. The first three features are considered by Feuerstein to be essential for all learning tasks. The other nine are important and helpful, but they do not necessarily apply to all tasks, and depend to some extent on the situation and culture in which the learning is taking place.

- *Significance*
  The teacher needs to make learners aware of the significance of the learning task so that they can see the value of it to them personally, and in a broader cultural context.
- *Purpose beyond the here and now*
  In addition, learners must be aware of the way in which the learning experience will have wider relevance to them beyond the immediate time and place.
- *Shared intention*
  In presenting a task, the teacher must have a clear intention, which is understood and reciprocated by the learners.

As well as these three essential factors, teachers can enhance the significance and strength of learning experiences if they encourage and develop the following in their learners:

- *A sense of competence*:
  the feeling that they are capable of coping successfully with any particular task with which they are faced;
- *Control of own behaviour*:
  the ability to control and regulate their own learning, thinking and actions;
- *Goal-setting*:
  the ability to set realistic goals and to plan ways of achieving them;
- *Challenge*:
  an internal need to respond to challenges, and to search for new challenges in life;
- *Awareness of change*:
  an understanding that human beings are constantly changing, and the ability to recognise and assess changes in themselves;
- *A belief in positive outcomes*:
  a belief that even when faced with an apparently intractable problem, there is always the possibility of finding a solution;
- *Sharing*:
  co-operation among learners, together with the recognition that some problems are better solved co-operatively;
- *Individuality*:
  a recognition of their own individuality and uniqueness;
- *A sense of belonging*:
  a feeling of belonging to a community and a culture.

We shall now consider the relevance of each of these features of mediation in more detail, and discuss their possible implications for the language teacher. They are presented here in a slightly different order than is the case in most of Feuerstein's writings, but one that we feel will make the issues clearer to the reader.

The first three features

- significance
- purpose beyond the here and now
- shared intention

In order to understand these first three features of mediation, the reader may find it helpful to consider a series of questions:

- What are my reasons for selecting a particular activity for my learners?
- What significance (or value) does that activity hold for these learners personally or in a wider cultural sense?
- How can I help the learners to perceive this value?
- How might the activity lead to learning that will be useful to the learners in the future?
- How can I help the learners to understand this?
- How can I introduce the activity to the learners in a manner that conveys clearly what I want them to do and why?
- How can I ensure that the learners are ready, willing and able to attempt the task?

The first question is an overarching one that all teachers should ask themselves before setting a task for their learners. The second and third questions are concerned with the first key feature of mediation, *significance*. Any learning task must have value or personal meaning to the learners. In mediating in this way, the teacher's role is to help learners to perceive how the activity is of value to them. If learners do not find personal significance in a task, then it lacks the necessary vitality or relevance.

Feuerstein also emphasises in his writing the importance of the transmission of culture from one generation to the next as a key element in making a task significant. However, for the language teacher, this inevitably raises further questions about the teaching of the culture of the target language.

Closely linked to this is the second feature of mediation, *purpose beyond the here and now*. This is addressed by the fourth and fifth questions above. Feuerstein refers to this characteristic as *transcendence*. A learning experience, he argues, should produce learning which is more than just the behaviour required by the task itself. The learner should learn something of more general value than the actual item taught by the task. For example, in learning vocabulary, learners might learn a strategy that will help them to learn further items of vocabulary more easily. In analysing a piece of language to learn about grammatical rules, they could learn analytical strategies that will help them to work out other grammatical rules. The teacher, therefore, needs to be aware of the more general learning value of a task, and to convey this to the learners.

A simple activity to help learners to think about the significance and purpose of a learning task is to ask them to complete the following form after each task that they do.

ACTIVITY	WHY I DID IT

Once we are clear in our minds what it is that we want our learners to do and why, we need to consider the third feature of mediation, *shared intention*. (This is referred to by Feuerstein in his writings as *intentionality* and *reciprocity*.) In presenting learners with any learning task, teachers should convey to them precisely what they want them to do by providing a clear set of instructions. At the same time it is essential to ensure that learners understand exactly what is required of them, and that they are both able and willing to attempt it, so that they will approach the task in a focussed and *self-directed* way. This produces in the learner what Feuerstein calls a 'state of vigilance' and a sharpness of purpose and perception.

This does not necessarily imply that reciprocity is a one-way process with every decision being made by the teacher. Since the ultimate purpose is to encourage autonomous learning, negotiation becomes an increasingly important aspect of this process. The developmental stage of the learners also plays an important part. Young children will initially need more direction from their teachers and need to be helped gradually to take on more responsibility for their learning as they become more self-directed. Adults, on the other hand, are more likely to have fairly clear ideas about what they want to learn and would, therefore, play a more central role from the start in negotiating learning activities.

As far as language teachers are concerned, they should be clear in their own minds why specific tasks have been selected and careful to convey exactly what is required of the learners. As foreign language teachers know, this is particularly difficult in the target language, and yet the language of classroom instructions provides learners with valuable and realistic input of the language. One challenge to the language teacher, therefore, is to find ways of conveying clear intentions through the target language, and, equally importantly, of checking that these intentions are understood and reciprocated. Common ways of doing this are demonstrating while explaining, asking learners to repeat instructions, or asking a group to demonstrate while the teacher explains what to do.

Factors concerned with taking control of learning

- a sense of competence
- control of behaviour
- goal-setting
- challenge
- awareness of change
- a belief in positive outcomes

In this section we shall consider the next six features of mediation, all of which are concerned with different ways with helping learners to take control of their learning. The first is *a sense of competence*. Successful learners tend on the whole to be those who feel competent and capable of learning. In order to foster such feelings teachers should see one of their primary functions as encouraging a positive self-image, self-esteem, self-confidence; a feeling of 'I can', or 'I am capable of doing this'.

This is a factor that is familiar and particularly pertinent to language teachers, who often find themselves dealing with individuals who lack confidence in themselves as language learners, who have a negative self-image as regards speaking other languages, and who are afraid to express themselves in the foreign language.

The importance of the learner's self-image has been confirmed in a vast number of studies. Although it is difficult to prove cause-effect relationships, what is clear is that there is a strong relationship between having a positive self-image and performing well on learning tasks. The nature of this relationship will be explored more fully in Chapter 5 but it is emphasised here to highlight the significant role the teacher plays in enhancing this aspect of motivation.

Feuerstein argues that it is the teacher who is often to blame for poor motivation, for feelings of incompetence, for fear of failure and for feelings of inadequacy. Once learners perceive themselves as incompetent, it will be extremely difficult to change this self-image, which can lead to under-achievement, apparent lack of ability, and erratic behaviour in tackling tasks. Thus, instilling a positive (but, we would add, also realistic, and not over-positive) self-image is a key function of the teacher-as-mediator. These are issues that will be discussed in depth in Chapter 6 when we consider motivation.

This notion of competence has considerable implications for the teacher of a foreign language. If learning is to be successful, it is crucial that teachers establish in their classrooms a climate where confidence is built up, where mistakes can be made without fear, where learners can use the language without embarrassment, where all contributions are valued, and where activities lead to feelings of success, not failure.

The feature we have just described is concerned with *feeling* competent. However, feelings of competence are necessary but not sufficient for learning to be effective; learners also need to *become* competent, that is, they need to learn the necessary skills and strategies in order to take control of their own learning. The next feature of mediation, *control of behaviour*, is concerned with helping learners to do this.

From a developmental perspective, it is important that teachers teach children to take a logical and systematic approach to solving problems; learning a foreign language is in these terms a vast problem to be solved. This means learning how to break a problem down, to gather and assess information, to process the information, and to express results logically. In this way individuals can learn to take control of and responsibility for their own learning, so that they not only become more effective learners, but also independent ones. If this has not been done in schools, then it is even more important for it to be taken up later. Those who are unable to take control of their own behaviour in approaching a learning task are likely to act impulsively which will prevent them from tackling problems systematically and logically.

In learning a language, many learners do not feel that they are in control of their learning, that they possess the necessary skills to take on such a task, or that they can manage and take control of the process in a competent and self-directed way. Thus we can see the importance of this aspect of mediation in language classrooms. It also provides us with a strong theoretical underpinning to the notion of learner training (Ellis and Sinclair 1989; Dickinson 1987; Ellis 1991). Briefly, learner training means teaching learners *how* to learn languages, so that they are equipped with strategies to learn on their own, or to learn in class as effectively as possible. This will be discussed in more detail in Chapter 7 when we consider how the learner actually deals with the business of learning a language. However, it is worth emphasising that there is still considerable scope for developing activities that teach learners the skills and strategies they need to learn a language, for example, analysing new pieces of language, processing input in order to work out rules, or ways of remembering new items of vocabulary. In addition, the current interest in language awareness is concerned with developing in learners the skills of analysing language. A good example is provided by Bolitho and Tomlinson (1980) in their excellent book *Discover English*, which consists of tasks to develop this ability.

The next three categories of mediation develop further this notion of control. The first is *goal-setting*. Individuals need to be able to set their own goals in life and in their learning, and to plan how they will achieve them. An absence of goals can lead to aimlessness and a lack of any sense of direction. Some people will then tend to look for 'quick-fix' immediate solutions to problems without thinking through the possible long-term consequences. In the classroom, however, it is usually the teacher who sets goals for the learners, and who decides how the learners will achieve them, as well as whether they have achieved them, rather than helping learners to set their own goals and seek realistic ways of achieving them for themselves. Goal-setting is also an important aspect of motivation, and is considered in more detail in Chapter 6.

Recent research has shown that children who set their own goals in any learning activity are more likely to achieve those goals than ones that are set for them (van Werkhoven 1990). There are many ways in which learners of a foreign language can be involved in goal-setting. One is to set their own language learning goals. These can be short-term goals, for example, 'How many words can I learn tonight?' or longer-term ones such as, 'How many English books can I read this term?' Some possible formats are shown below.

a) Long-term goals

By the end of this course/term I want to

My plan to achieve this is

b) Short-term goals

This week I shall

The notion of goal-setting is linked to the next factor, *challenge*. An assumption made by early behaviourists in their attempts to devise programmed-learning machines was that all learning should be based upon a one hundred per cent success rate. Thus, they tried to devise programmes built on such small learning steps that it was impossible to fail. To the surprise of many, these programmes proved to be extremely unpopular and programmed-learning quickly died a death.

The mistake that was made by the behaviourists was their failure to recognise the importance of challenge in learning and in life in general. We saw in Chapter 2 how Erik Erikson believes that the sense of aimlessness displayed by many people approaching mid-life is due to the loss of any sense of challenge or of being stretched. A fascinating set of studies by the Chicago-based psychologists, Csikszentmihalyi and Nakamura, which identified challenge as one of the key elements in producing a sense of 'flow' in people's lives is described in Chapter 6.

If we want learners to become absorbed in the tasks we set them, it is important to provide an appropriate challenge as well as helping the learners to plan appropriate strategies to meet these challenges. This means finding language learning tasks which are sufficiently difficult to provide a challenge, but are not too difficult. It also means encouraging a sense of wanting to grapple with challenges, of feeling that one can always go one step further, rather than the feeling of having reached one's limit. With this in mind, it would be interesting to look at a selection of activities in foreign language coursebooks for children or teenagers and consider which of them provide suitable challenges for learners of the particular age range. As a step towards autonomy, it is important also to help learners to set their own challenges. Thus, when we are helping them to set their own goals, we should ensure that these goals are not always too much within their current capabilities.

No matter how much information a teacher may have about a group or even individual learners, it is virtually impossible to match each learner with the right level of task without involving the learners themselves in the process. Since the ultimate goal of mediated learning experiences is to produce independent learners and problem-solvers, increasing the involvement of the learners in all aspects of the learning process should be encouraged at every opportunity.

If individuals are to learn to take control of their learning, it is important to develop also an *awareness of change*. As people learn and develop, they change in various ways; physically, emotionally, socially and cognitively. This may take the form of an affective change, or a developing ability (an ability to accomplish something that was previously not considered possible). Monitoring and evaluating such changes play an important part in all learning, but are crucial in something so complex as language learning.

Many language teaching programmes are based on learners performing certain tasks and behaviours which the teacher sets and then evaluates. Teachers normally give learners information about their progress in various ways, for example, the use of grades, praise or test results. However, we would see it as equally important to foster the ability to self-evaluate if we are to produce autonomous learners. In order to mediate in this way, the teacher needs to identify ways in which learners can be helped to become more aware of their own progress without needing feedback from the teacher. Some examples are: asking learners to record 'words I have learned this week', 'books I have read this term', 'things I can do in writing', or 'what I have learned this term'. Learners might also be asked to keep a file of their best work over the year and then to assess their own change during the year.

There are many formats for learners to keep personal records. An example is shown below.

ACTIVITY	WHAT I LEARNED	HOW I PERFORMED	DIFFICULTIES I STILL HAVE

Other examples of record-keeping formats are provided by Dickinson (1987).

An important consequence of learning how to monitor one's own progress in learning is that one comes to recognise personal change as continuous, lifelong and within one's own power. The issue then becomes not one of whether or not to change, but what degree of personal influence we choose to exert on that change. Several educators have argued that in preparing young people to cope with a world of rapid and unpredictable change, the recognition of the importance of change as a process in itself becomes one of the central tasks in education. Toffler (1970) and Handy (1989) are just two of the growing number of commentators who argue that our whole education system must change in the direction of teaching people to learn how to learn and become flexible thinkers in order to prepare them to cope with this world of continuous change.

The final feature of mediation that we shall discuss in this category is *a belief in positive outcomes*. In life we are often confronted with problems, and at a basic level we have to decide whether the task with which we are faced is possible or impossible. Deciding that a solution is impossible will automatically prevent us from seeking an appropriate way and trying out alternative paths towards solving a problem. It is important to encourage in learners a firm belief that there is always a solution to any problem, so that they learn to be persistent rather than to give up.

It is clear that this principle is closely related to that of fostering a sense of competence and may even be a precursor of it in that unless we believe something is possible we cannot begin to consider how we might accomplish it. The difference is that we may not necessarily have to feel personally competent at any moment to believe that something can be achieved.

For Feuerstein, this principle formed the basis for a belief system which underpinned the whole of his theory. He argued that unless we begin with the belief that anyone can become a fully effective learner, no matter what their age or disability, we shall always be setting artificial barriers to learning (Feuerstein *et al.* 1991). Certainly, the previous unimaginable learning achievements of people suffering from autism, Down's syndrome and other physiological and emotional problems, recorded by Feuerstein and others, provide strong evidence to support such beliefs (Bachor 1989; Burden 1987; Jonas and Martin 1985).

For language teachers, this belief provides a powerful message to underpin their teaching approach: that no matter how difficult it may appear to be for some people to learn a foreign language, everyone is capable of doing so. There is evidence from all parts of the world that children and adults with little or no education can learn to speak one or two or even more languages if they feel the need to do so. So long as classroom teachers believe that their learners are all capable of succeeding, they will continue to seek effective ways of helping to bring this about.

Factors concerned with fostering social development

- sharing
- individuality
- encouraging a sense of belonging

These three features are all concerned with learning to become an individual and to belong to a community. The first is *encouraging sharing behaviour*. Sharing and working co-operatively are a vital part of our social existence, the absence of which can result in cognitive difficulties and a very idiosyncratic view of the world. Unfortunately, in many classrooms competition is encouraged above everything else. Although we would not advocate the complete removal of all forms of competition from schools and society, it is nevertheless true that co-operation and sharing are ways of interacting which need to be taught, even though the importance of co-operation does of course differ in different cultures. If we see one aspect of our responsibility as educators as preparing our learners to contribute to a world where trust and mutual respect and co-operation are the norm, then we must sow the seeds in our schools and classrooms.

Moreover, there is now accumulating evidence that working in pairs and in groups can have considerable benefit for all learners. Work by Smith *et al.* (1993), Dunne and Bennet (1990) and Thacker and Feest (1991) provides strong evidence in support of group approaches in primary schools. At an adult level, Bligh (1971) in his book *What's the Use of Lectures?*, argues persuasively against traditional didactic teaching in colleges and universities. An excellent book which addresses the many different aspects of learning to work together is *Learning Together and Alone* by Johnson and Johnson (1987).

In language teaching classrooms it has now become common to set up activities where interaction in the target language is essential to complete the task. This is an important aspect of a communicative approach to language teaching. Typical group activities are discussion exercises, information-gap activities such as 'spot the difference', questionnaire completion, group writing, peer editing and testing each other in pairs, all of which develop both language and the ability to work together alongside each other. Thus, an important role for language teachers is to arrange their classes in ways which will encourage sharing behaviour, and to find ways of helping learners to develop this ability through language learning tasks.

A useful idea is to initiate a discussion with the class in the target language about what they consider to be appropriate rules for working in groups, for example, indicating when one wants to speak, allowing other people to finish what they are saying, listening to each other, responding to what people say rather than imposing your views on others. Another is to ask learners to brainstorm ideas for activities to do in class. Recent work on 'process syllabus' in language teaching has involved teachers and learners actually negotiating the content and process of their programme.

At the same time as learning to co-operate, people need to be individuals, to feel they can legitimately think and feel differently from others, to develop and exercise their own personality. This is sometimes referred to as *individuation* (Erikson 1963, 1968), which means a growing awareness of one's own unique place in and contribution to a social world. (See Chapter 2 for a fuller discussion of Erikson's view.) Thus another way in which teachers can mediate is by *encouraging individuality*. However, there is a considerable cultural influence on how this is made manifest of which the language teacher needs to be aware. Within some social contexts the expression of opinions and desires would be more acceptable than in others.

Within Western cultures in particular, the search for 'ego identity', to use a psychoanalytic term, is considered to be one of the primary tasks of the adolescent developmental stage in particular. It can readily be seen how closely related this principle is to the notion of self-concept previously discussed in this chapter. This will be considered in more detail in the next chapter. A fascinating experiment by Denis Lawrence (1973) revealed that children with learning difficulties can be helped more by periods of sympathetic counselling than by traditional remedial methods. Lawrence's subsequent work has been largely geared to finding ways of helping teachers to encourage a sense of individuality or uniqueness in their learners, and thereby promote an inner sense of personal worth.

The language classroom is a place where this sense of individuality can be fostered in various ways through the tasks given, the teacher's actions and the climate created. Learners can be encouraged to express their own individuality through the foreign language. Some examples might be keeping a diary or personal journal, using drama to express oneself, using activities that require the expression of opinions, creative writing, or class discussion.

The final way of mediating is developing a *feeling of belonging*. As well as being individuals, people need to feel that they belong to a community or a culture. This can refer to the classroom culture, or the wider community. For some societies, for example that of the indigenous Hawaiian islanders, this sense of community is so strong that there is a powerful resistance to individualised learning or one person appearing to do better than others (Sugden 1989).

Vale (1990) and Vale with Feunteun (1995) stress the need for what they call *group formation activities* which are performed in the target language, where the aim of the activity is to generate a sense of belonging to the group. In many British schools the development of a so-called *pastoral curriculum* has had the same principle as one of its main aims. Button (1981, 1982) provides excellent examples of activities to generate this sense of belonging in his developmental groupwork programme. Ways of assessing the strength of group identity and whole-school ethos will be described in Chapter 9.

In order to mediate in this way, teachers need to encourage in their own classrooms a sense of belonging to a team or community, which has implications both for the learning group, and also for the school as a whole. It is important to remember that the impetus for a community feeling must come not only from the teacher but from the learners as well. An example might be engaging in a whole-class project like a class newspaper where everyone has a contribution to make and no one is left out.

4.3   Application of mediation theory

In this section we attempt to illustrate Feuerstein's theory of mediation by applying it to some language teaching activities. Before doing so, it is important to state that we are not advocating using each aspect of mediation for every language task given; far from it. Teachers will need to

79

select which areas of mediation to consider for a particular activity with the needs of a specific class and context in mind.

We are, therefore, providing the following examples as illustrations of different ways in which teachers might mediate, not as any form of prescription of what to do. Once teachers become accustomed to mediation, experience shows that finding appropriate ways to mediate will pervade everything that they do in class and become an integral part of their day-to-day work (see also Blagg 1991).

Example 1

Example 1 (see Figure 6) comes from a coursebook for adult pre-intermediate learners. Figure 6 shows a vocabulary exercise involving adjectives that describe people. Used creatively, with appropriate mediation, this exercise becomes rich with possibilities, some of which extend way beyond the language aims of the activity. Some possible ways in which teachers can mediate are shown below.

Value, and purpose beyond the here and now

From a language-learning perspective, the purpose of this exercise is to learn some adjectives which are used to describe oneself and other people. In

---

1 I'm quite hardworking | adjectives |

Complete the grid with suitable opposites and then check your answers with your teacher.

hardworking	x	x	x	x	x	lazy
tidy	x	x	x	x	x	....
....	x	x	x	x	x	easy-going
organised	x	x	x	x	x	....
sensible	x	x	x	x	x	....
efficient	x	x	x	x	x	....

Where would you put yourself on each line of the grid? Put a circle round one x on each line and then compare your answers in groups.

Figure 6 *From* True to Life Pre-intermediate *(Gairns and Redman 1995:22)*

addition, the task has value at another level, as it requires learners to reflect upon aspects of themselves, thereby leading to a better understanding of themselves. In order to mediate these aspects the teacher would need to explain the purpose of the exercise and to help learners to see the value to them at a personal level.

Sense of competence

In choosing where they fit on the grid, all learners can succeed in the task. A teacher wishing to mediate in this way would make it clear to the learners that they are all capable of success.

Goal-setting

Goal-setting could be mediated in a number of ways with this task. One way is to extend the task by asking learners to decide how many more pairs of words they can find. They set themselves a target first, for example, ten pairs, and then evaluate whether they reached their goal and whether it was a realistic one. At another level, learners can be asked to set personal goals for themselves using the words given, for example, to become less lazy or more organised. This could lead to an interesting class discussion if they share these goals with each other.

Change

To mediate change, learners could be asked to reflect, either orally or in writing, on 'What I learned', 'What I can do now' or even 'What I learned about myself'.

Individuality

This task lends itself particularly to mediation of individuality. The teacher would need to make it clear to the learners that whatever they say about themselves is acceptable, that they have a right to their own uniqueness.

Example 2

The second example (see Figure 7) is taken from Feuerstein's Instrumental Enrichment programme. This task is a part of Feuerstein's 'Comparisons' Instrument, designed to teach children how to make comparisons systematically as comparative thinking underpins much higher order thought. Although the task is a part of a thinking skills programme, it is typical of information-gap exercises used in language classes. In Chapter 8 we shall

There are five differences between the two pictures.
Mark each difference you find with an X.

Figure 7 *From Comparisons Instrument of Instrumental Enrichment (Feuerstein et al. 1980)*

develop further the idea of using thinking tasks as language activities; however we shall discuss some possibilities with regard to mediation here.

Value and purpose beyond the here and now

A teacher might select this activity to develop comparative thinking skills as such skills are important in language learning, for example, attending to similarities and differences between languages or cultures, between language structures or between lexis or morphology. The teacher may also have certain linguistic purposes such as particular vocabulary items, or expressions of position such as 'in the picture on the right . . . '. In addition, if the activity is carried out in pairs with each person's picture hidden from their partner, then we generate interaction and negotiation to facilitate language acquisition. In mediating, teachers first need to be clear why they select this activity and then help their learners to see the value to them.

Control of behaviour

In order to succeed in this activity, learners need to approach it in a logical and systematic way rather than acting impulsively. Teachers wishing to mediate control would need to help learners to explore the problem systematically and to discuss their pictures in a logical way. Teachers could ask learners to tell them what strategies they used, and discuss the merits of different ways of solving the problem. They could also discuss the use of discourse strategies such as checking back on information, questioning or listening attentively.

Goal-setting and challenge

Learners could be asked to set themselves a challenge by deciding how many of the five differences they can find in a specified time.

Sharing

Co-operation is essential for the successful completion of this activity. Teachers can mediate sharing by initiating a discussion about co-operative behaviour; listening attentively, taking turns, helping, avoiding aggressive or pushy behaviour and checking back.

4.4   Investigating mediation in language classrooms

There have been few attempts at investigating the mediation that occurs in language classrooms. Warren (1995) designed a questionnaire for teachers to use to evaluate their own mediation in language classes. This can be used by having an observer watch the class and then complete the questionnaire with the teacher. A preferable way of using it is to video the lesson and then watch the video with an observer in order to complete the questionnaire. Some examples of questionnaire items are shown in Figure 8.

A second questionnaire, designed by the authors, seeks to investigate teachers' perceptions of the different features of mediation. This is shown in Figure 9. Part I examines teachers' views of the importance of each aspect of mediation. Part II then asks teachers to assess how often they think they carry out each of these functions.

A Mandarin version of the mediation questionnaire in Figure 9 was piloted by Chin (1990) with 50 primary teachers in Taiwan. The subjects rated shared intention (Q1), feelings of competence (Q4), control of behaviour (Q5) sharing (Q10), individuality (Q11) and a sense of belonging (Q12) as particularly important, each scoring an average of over 9.0. They rated significance (Q2), purpose beyond the here and now (Q3) and awareness of change (Q8) as considerably less important.

This emphasises the point that the way in which people view different aspects of mediation is likely to vary within different cultural contexts.

4.5   Conclusion

In this chapter we have introduced the concept of mediation and examined its use both by Vygotsky and, in particular, by Feuerstein. We have related the different aspects of Feuerstein's mediated learning experience to teaching in general and to language teaching in particular. Although these ideas are only just beginning to be applied in a systematic way to language teaching, there is considerable accumulating evidence from a vast number of studies in general and special education to enable us to conclude that their influence can be both powerful and profound (Burden 1987; Jonas and Martin 1985; Savell *et al.* 1986).

We consider that this chapter is pivotal to the whole book in that it links with and pulls together many of the issues discussed in other sections, for example, motivation, learning strategies and learning environment. Motivation will be discussed in Chapter 6, while the notion of control of learning will be picked up in Chapter 7 where we discuss strategies that learners use to learn a language. In Chapter 9 we consider further what kinds of classroom organisation and classroom ethos best promote learning.

Having discussed the role of the teacher, in the next chapter we move on to a consideration of the part played by the learner in the teaching-learning process.

Significance

2(b) Did the teacher convey purpose, for example:
- Did the learners find some personal value in the task?
- Was there any evidence?

Feeling of Competence

4(c) How did the teacher help the learners to foster a positive self-image and a feeling of confidence?
- by providing a secure environment
- by valuing all responses from the learners
- by encouraging learners to take risks, such as guessing unfamiliar vocabulary, etc.
- by praising appropriately
- by helping learners to learn from their errors
- other ways _____
  _____

Control

5(a) Did the teacher encourage the learners:
- to plan their work?
- not to be impulsive?
- to think before answering?
- to check their own work?
- others _____

Co-operation

6(a) How did the teacher encourage learners:
- to help each other?
- to listen to each other?
- to respect the feelings of others?
- to work together?

Individuality

7(a) Did the teacher select tasks which:
- enabled individuals to express themselves?
- provided opportunities for all the learners to contribute?

7(b) How did the teacher encourage individuality?

Goal-setting

8(b) In what way did the teacher show the learners how to set their own goals?

Awareness of change

10(a) Did the teacher set tasks which allowed learners to
- make self-assessments?
- monitor their progress?
- review their work?
- review the strategies that they used?

Figure 8   *Teacher Mediation Questionnaire (Warren 1995)*

4 What can teachers do to promote learning?

PART I
Please circle the number that best describes your views.

	ESSENTIAL									NOT AT ALL IMPORTANT

How important do you think it is to:

1 make your instructions clear when you give a task to your learners? 10 9 8 7 6 5 4 3 2 1

2 tell your learners *why* they are to do a particular activity? 10 9 8 7 6 5 4 3 2 1

3 explain to your learners how carrying out a learning activity will help them in the future? 10 9 8 7 6 5 4 3 2 1

4 help learners to develop a feeling of confidence in their ability to learn? 10 9 8 7 6 5 4 3 2 1

5 teach learners the strategies they need to learn effectively? 10 9 8 7 6 5 4 3 2 1

6 teach learners how to set their own goals in learning? 10 9 8 7 6 5 4 3 2 1

7 help your learners to set challenges for themselves and to meet those challenges? 10 9 8 7 6 5 4 3 2 1

8 help your learners to monitor changes in themselves? 10 9 8 7 6 5 4 3 2 1

9 help your learners to see that if they keep on trying to solve a problem, they will find a solution? 10 9 8 7 6 5 4 3 2 1

10 teach your learners to work co-operatively? 10 9 8 7 6 5 4 3 2 1

11 help your learners to develop as individuals? 10 9 8 7 6 5 4 3 2 1

12 foster in your learners a sense of belonging to a classroom community? 10 9 8 7 6 5 4 3 2 1

Figure 9 *Mediation questionnaire*

PART II
Please circle the number.

How often do you:

	VERY OFTEN									NEVER

1 make your instructions clear when you give a task to your learners?

10 9 8 7 6 5 4 3 2 1

2 tell your learners *why* they are to do a particular activity?

10 9 8 7 6 5 4 3 2 1

3 explain to your learners how carrying out a learning activity will help them in the future?

10 9 8 7 6 5 4 3 2 1

4 help learners to develop a feeling of confidence in their ability to learn?

10 9 8 7 6 5 4 3 2 1

5 teach learners the strategies they need to learn effectively?

10 9 8 7 6 5 4 3 2 1

6 teach learners how to set their own goals in learning?

10 9 8 7 6 5 4 3 2 1

7 help your learners to set challenges for themselves and to meet those challenges?

10 9 8 7 6 5 4 3 2 1

8 help your learners to monitor changes in themselves?

10 9 8 7 6 5 4 3 2 1

9 help your learners to see that if they keep on trying to solve a problem, they will find a solution?

10 9 8 7 6 5 4 3 2 1

10 teach your learners to work co-operatively?

10 9 8 7 6 5 4 3 2 1

11 help your learners to develop as individuals?

10 9 8 7 6 5 4 3 2 1

12 foster in your learners a sense of belonging to a classroom community?

10 9 8 7 6 5 4 3 2 1

5 The contribution of the individual student to the learning process

5.1 Introduction

In this chapter we consider the part the individual learner plays in the learning process. We start by examining some of the recent work in the area of individual differences in language learning, and point out a number of problems with research that has been carried out in this field. We suggest that an alternative approach to this topic would be a constructivist one, focussing on how individual learners make sense of their learning situations in ways that are personal to them. We then propose three areas that could fruitfully be explored in order to reach a better understanding of individuals; self-concept, locus of control and attribution theory.

A great deal has been written in language teaching books and journals about the importance of considering individual differences in learning a foreign language. In a comprehensive review of the literature on this topic, Oxford and Ehrman (1993) suggest that teachers of a second language need to identify and comprehend significant individual differences in their learners if they are to provide the most effective instruction possible. In many respects this statement reflects commonly accepted wisdom within the language teaching world. Few textbooks on language learning would claim to be comprehensive without reference to this area (see, for example, Ellis 1994; Brown 1994; Lightbown and Spada 1993), and some have even devoted whole books to it (Galbraith and Gardner 1988; Skehan 1989).

It is undoubtedly true that learners bring many individual characteristics to the learning process which will affect both the way in which they learn and the outcomes of that process. However, just what those characteristics are and exactly how they affect the learning process is much more unclear. A moment's thought will probably bring to mind such apparently obvious examples as age, gender, personality, aptitude, intelligence and motivation as characteristics influencing our success in learning a foreign language. Other less obvious but widely researched characteristics relating to language learning have been cognitive styles and strategies, anxiety and preparedness to take risks.

In fact, the very term *individual differences* has been taken from psychology, where an even more vast literature exists on the topic. However, we would argue that there are a number of problems with the approach that has often been taken to work in this area in terms of the selection of particular learner characteristics for investigation, the measurement of those characteristics, and the actual practical application of such measurements. One of the main problems is that the research is often of very little practical value to teachers and other practitioners. Rather than providing insights into how learners differ and how best to help them, the very nature of the research and, in particular, the approach taken to measurement, has somehow lost sight of the individual.

5.2 Some problems with the notion of individual differences

5.2.1 Research methodology

In order to understand our concerns we need to look briefly at the research methodology that has frequently been used in examining individual differences. Interest in this topic arose mainly within a *psychometric* tradition of psychology, that is, one concerned with the scientific measurement of such human traits and abilities. For many psychologists, the road to progress has been seen as developing an increasing accuracy in the measurement of human characteristics such as intelligence, extroversion, risk-taking behaviour and so on. The results of such measurements have then been used to predict individuals' learning capabilities, and action has often been taken as a result of these predictions, for example, streaming learners, or grouping them by ability.

Thus, it seemed to be a perfectly logical step in language learning research to build upon previous work in psychology by attempting to measure individual characteristics and relate these to language learning outcomes. So, for example, there is research to show that the more intelligent people are, the easier it is for them to learn a foreign language, or that learning a language depends to some extent on having an aptitude for languages, or that risk-takers are more successful language learners.

There are literally hundreds of research studies which have investigated the contribution of individual differences to language learning in this way. Summarised briefly, the psychometric approach that has generally been taken to such studies is as follows: (1) a hypothesis is made that a particular characteristic is likely to influence success in language learning; (2) a means of assessing that characteristic is selected or constructed; (3) aspects of that characteristic and success in language learning are both measured, usually with reference to a specific group of learners; (4) the results of the two measures are submitted to statistical analysis and statistically significant relationships are sought; (5) conclusions are drawn about the contribution of the particular characteristic to learning a language.

A standardised test of the particular characteristics may already exist, for example, self-esteem, field dependence/independence or extroversion/introversion. Otherwise, a test is constructed for the purpose, often with a particular focus on language learning, for example, language anxiety (Horwitz and Young 1991). This test is then subjected to appropriate measures of reliability so that it can be standardised.

However, what is often open to question is precisely what the particular test is actually measuring. What is sometimes forgotten in research into individual differences is that the characteristic selected is in fact no more than a researcher's best effort at conceptualising what the particular trait involves. This becomes what psychologists term a *hypothetical construct*, a term introduced in Chapter 1. There is no such thing as 'intelligence' or 'field dependence', or 'motivation', but it can sometimes be convenient to treat such entities as if they do exist so that we can construct tests to measure them. Unfortunately, the outcome of that testing procedure can then come to represent in people's minds the meaning of that construct. For example, for many years the only definition of intelligence that was offered in many psychological textbooks was that 'intelligence is what intelligence tests measure'.

Test constructors often devote considerable time and energy to strengthening the *reliability* and *validity* of their tests so that they can be *standardised*. Reliability is often equated with stability, that is, the test produces similar results on more than one occasion. However, there is a danger that this can lead to a belief that the test is measuring a relatively fixed characteristic, even if no such characteristic actually exists. We would argue instead that individual traits such as intelligence or aptitude or anxiety are more usefully treated as variable, as context specific, and amenable to change. It would follow from this that a test should be expected to produce different results on different occasions.

The validity of a test, on the other hand, is supposed to indicate whether that test actually does measure what it is supposed to measure. Researchers often neatly sidestep this obstacle, however, by comparing one test with another which is supposed to be measuring the same thing. This is known as concurrent validity. Thus, if you constructed your own new test of listening comprehension, you might well test its validity by comparing people's scores on it with their scores on existing tests. Construct validity, on the other hand, indicates how well the test relates to the construct under investigation. However significant this might be found to be, or even if a test has a high rating for validity, it does not necessarily mean that the trait itself actually exists. The point is that it is extremely difficult to construct a test which is truly valid in that it really measures what it is supposed to measure.

Another problem with measurement procedures on standardised tests is that, because of the way the test is constructed, in any given population, scores on the test will be distributed according to a normal distribution curve. Most people will obtain scores around the mean, and a very small percentage (2–3%) will score considerably above or below the mean. Thus the tests can tell us very little about most individuals, whose scores fall somewhere in the middle. What they tell us about is groups of people and average scores, rather than individuals. They can, therefore, give teachers very little information about what to do with individual learners in their classrooms.

5.2.2 *Selection of individual characteristics*

The next problem is how the various individual characteristics described in the literature are selected. Gradman and Hanania (1991) identified 22 different variables referred to in the individual differences literature, whilst Oxford and Erhman (1993) choose to focus on just nine. In his seminal work on the topic, Skehan (1989) examines the research on eight slightly different variables.

The somewhat arbitrary nature of this selection is nowhere more apparent than in the case of *cognitive style*. The most common styles discussed in the literature are *field dependence* and *field independence*. If people are field dependent, their perception is dominated by the whole context, that is, they perceive things in relation to the context, whereas field-independent people perceive items as discrete or unrelated to the surrounding 'field'. Dozens of studies have been carried out investigating the relationship of this variable to successful language learning. Some of them claim to have found that people scoring higher on a test of field independence tend to do better than others at learning a foreign language (d'Anglejan and Renaud 1985). However, the question that remains is what exactly is meant by field dependence or field independence.

The most widely used test of field dependence/independence in language learning studies is the Embedded Figures Test. An example is shown in Figure 10. Subjects are asked to find the 'simple form' shown on the left in the complex figure on the right. If they can do this, they are supposedly field independent. However, it is still unclear as to why success in picking out embedded figures should represent different styles of learning.

Oxford and Ehrman make a valiant attempt to bring some sense to these studies by referring to *global* and *analytic* learning styles. However, whatever field dependence and field independence are, these constructs are being measured by an obscure test of visual perception which is currently little used by professional psychologists, and which appears to bear little relation to learning style. Griffiths and Sheen (1992) provide a strongly critical analysis of the field dependence/independence construct, which is only partially refuted by Chappelle (1992).

SIMPLE FORMS

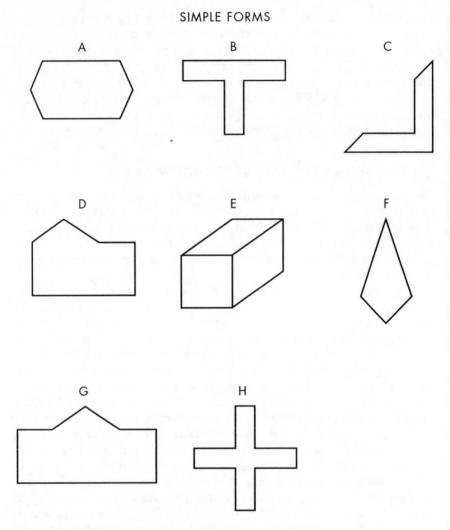

Figure 10 *From* Embedded Figures Test *(Witkin, Oltman, Raskin and Karp 1971)*

5.2 Some problems with the notion of individual differences

SECOND SECTION

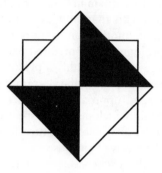

1   Find Simple Form "G"

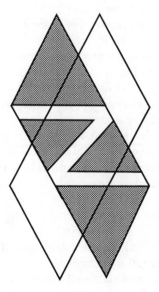

2   Find Simple Form "A"

There are other forms of individual difference which appear to be related to a sounder theoretical rationale. Oxford and Ehrman select motivation as one such variable, but as we explain in Chapter 6, motivation does not refer to a fixed trait or characteristic that individuals possess more or less of. We argue instead that the term 'motivation' is more helpfully used to refer to a state of temporary or prolonged goal-oriented behaviour which individuals actively choose to engage in. How highly a person is motivated to perform a certain task such as learning vocabulary, grammar or any other language related activity, will depend upon a complex set of interacting variables. These variables will certainly include some aspect of individual disposition such as *motivational style*, to which we return in Chapter 6, but will also include the nature and perceived purpose of the task, the actions of the teacher and the nature of the teacher-learner relationship. Motivation is very much context bound, but is also amenable to change.

Another characteristic that has been subject to a considerable amount of investigation is anxiety. Several tests have been constructed to measure this characteristic, e.g. the Foreign Language Classroom Anxiety Scale (Horwitz and Young 1991). However, what studies using such instruments tend to show is that anxiety is also highly situation specific and itself affected by a number of other factors (Horwitz and Young 1990). Moreover, it is clear that behaviour which may be construed as anxious within one culture would not necessarily be so construed in another.

Perhaps the most thoroughly researched area of individual difference in language learning is that of *aptitude*. (See Skehan 1989 for a comprehensive review of this literature.) Most language teachers would readily testify that individual learners differ in the ease with which they learn a foreign language. It seems only reasonable to assume, therefore, that a major contributory factor to this is their ability or language aptitude. If we can measure that aptitude prior to teaching, we should be able to predict the speed at which a learner can learn, and adjust the pace of our teaching accordingly. We can also excuse our lack of success in teaching some learners by pointing to their lack of aptitude for language learning.

For more than three decades, attempts have been made to measure learners' language aptitude by means of such tests as the Modern Language Aptitude Test (Carroll and Sapon 1959) and to use these results in a predictive way. However, the predictive value of the MLAT is not particularly high, nor does it discriminate well between learners at all ability levels, i.e. it is quite good at discriminating between learners who are likely to perform very poorly or very well, but does not discriminate well between the large majority in the middle.

As we explained earlier, this is, in fact, a significant weakness of all such standardised tests. What they tell us is that about two-thirds of any population will score within the average range on that test. Only a small minority will score at either extreme. Thus, they are unable to tell us very much at all about most individuals because of the way they are constructed.

To summarise the points made so far:

- Traditional research on individual differences has been mainly concerned with measuring, labelling and grouping people.

- The purpose of such research is usually not to identify how individuals differ but to group them according to perceived similarities.

- The findings have been of limited practical value because they do not inform us how we can help any individual to become a more effective learner.

- In many instances they do not even help us to improve the functioning of the groups that are identified by the research.

- Research in this area is often based on a theory of learning which views people's behaviour as being heavily influenced by certain traits or attributes which are fixed.

Indeed, the whole area of individual differences is fraught with unanswered questions. In dealing with averages and statistics we appear somehow to have lost track of the individual. This kind of approach does not help us to deal effectively with such issues as how individuals make their own sense of the process of learning a language, or how we as teachers can best help our learners, given that they are all different. We therefore consider a totally different approach is called for. We need an approach which will focus on the unique contribution that each individual brings to the learning situation, and on how the teacher can assist the learner in learning most effectively. We suggest that there are several useful starting points.

- We must start from a theory of learning that is robust and to which as researchers and teachers we subscribe.

- Such a theory should enable us to focus upon the uniqueness of individuals as well as helping us to see what they have in common.

- It should also be a theory of how people change rather than how they stay the same.

- This should give rise to implications for action and intervention.

- It should enable us also to support individuals in taking personal control of their own learning.

- In doing so it must be connected to individuals' views of themselves as learners.

5.3   An alternative approach

In keeping with the perspective taken in this book, we suggest that a more helpful approach to take in seeking to understand individuals is a constructivist one. In Chapter 1 we explained that constructivism attempts to answer the questions: 'What are the ways in which different individuals try to make sense of their worlds?' and 'How do they construct their own personal views or meanings from the world around them?' Every learner will bring a different set of knowledge and experiences to the learning process, and will 'construct', in different ways, their own sense of the situation with which they are faced. Thus, learning is essentially personal and individual; no two people will learn precisely the same thing from any particular learning situation. An individual's understanding of the world is constantly being reshaped as he or she adapts existing knowledge to new information.

Rather than being seen as something that is fixed or static, knowledge is viewed as transitory, provisional and relative. The objective world may be real but is not directly accessible to us. At the same time, we are offered by this the possibility that we are not only changing, but also capable of change.

In Chapter 2 we presented our social constructivist model of the learning process. It is important to re-emphasise here that we see the learner's construction of knowledge as taking place within an interactionist framework; through social interactions and with the help of mediation. What we are concerned with in this chapter is the light that such an approach sheds on the individual's part in the learning process, and the unique way in which each person makes sense of their learning experiences.

If we adopt a constructivist perspective, it becomes apparent that the ways in which individuals view the world and their perceptions of themselves within the world, particularly within a learning situation, will play a major part in their learning and construction of knowledge.

So, instead of asking the question: 'How are learners different from each other and can we measure these differences?', it would be more helpful to seek answers to such questions as: 'How do learners perceive themselves as language learners?', 'What effect do these "personal constructs" have upon the process of learning a new language?', 'How do individuals go about making sense of their learning?', and 'How can we as teachers assist learners in making sense of their learning in ways that are personal to them?'

These questions are highly complex and do not give rise to simple answers. In the rest of this chapter we shall look at three areas that are related to the ways in which individuals perceive themselves. One is *self-concept* which relates to the views people have of themselves. Another is *locus of control*, which is related to how far individuals see themselves as being in control of their own learning. A third is *attribution theory*, which is concerned with identifying the different factors to which individuals attribute their successes and failures in learning.

5.4   The development and importance of self-concept

Self-concept is a global term referring to the amalgamation of all of our perceptions and conceptions about ourselves which give rise to our sense of personal identity. More formally, it has been defined as 'the totality of a complex and dynamic system of learned beliefs which each individual holds to be true about his or her personal existence and which gives consistency to his or her personality' (Purkey and Novak 1984). The multifaceted nature of the self-concept has led many researchers to focus on specific aspects of it such as *self-image* (the particular view that we have of ourselves), *self-esteem* (the evaluative feelings associated with our self-image), and *self-efficacy* (our beliefs about our capabilities in certain areas or related to certain tasks). Thus, an anorexic girl is likely to have a highly complex self-concept, but to have a self-image of being overweight, however slim she may actually be. This will probably lead to her having particularly low self-esteem. She might, nevertheless, see herself as being particularly capable in learning foreign languages and thus have a high degree of self-efficacy in that specific area.

As young children begin to construct a more or less stable view of the world, so they begin to develop also an awareness of themselves as individuals and an understanding of their place within that world. This developing self-concept in turn comes to influence the ways in which they try to make sense of other aspects of their world. The relationship is reciprocal: individuals' views of the world influence their self-concept, while at the same time their self-concepts affect their views of the world. Both of these views will affect their success in learning situations.

One's self-concept is partly determined by one's social relationships. One theory which has been proposed to help to explain how this occurs is known as *social comparison theory* (Kynch *et al.* 1981; Damon and Hart 1982). This theory suggests that learners' conceptions of their own ability as learners will be based, at least in part, on the nature of classroom inter-actions. The basic premise is that we are all predisposed, albeit to differing degrees, to compare ourselves with others and to develop our self-concepts as a result of those comparisons and of the information that we receive about ourselves from others. This is sometimes referred to as 'the looking-glass self' (Cooley 1902). There is evidence to suggest that the more we see other people as being like ourselves, or the more significant a part that people play in our lives, the more likely we are to compare ourselves with them (Suls and Greenwald 1986; Higgins *et al.* 1989).

For young learners, the most influential figures in this respect are likely to be their parents, their teachers and their peers, in that order. During adolescence, peers begin to take on a more central role with regard to one's self-image. After adolescence, specific partners take on this role as well as teachers (Connell and Ilardi 1987; Damon and Hart 1982; Hamachek 1992).

Research into social comparison theory indicates that the extent of the effect of such comparisons is a function of a person's social comparison *orientation* (i.e. we are not all predisposed to compare to the same degree) in combination with the type and amount of information received from others who are perceived as significant. Although this will be occurring in all walks of life, it has particular relevance to the classroom situation because the amount and kind of positive or negative feedback that learners receive in class from both the teacher and their peers will affect their sense of achievement, their motivation to achieve more and the establishment of their self-efficacy in that area.

Research in this field has shown that children are very sensitive observers of teacher behaviour patterns in the classroom (Weinstein 1989). They monitor their own interactions with the teacher and are also very aware of how the teacher interacts with other children, especially those identified as high and low achievers. Children report differences in the frequencies of teacher interactions with different types of learners, with high achievers seen as receiving more positive feedback from the teacher, as well as being given more opportunities to perform, to be challenged and to serve as leaders. By contrast, low achievers are reported to receive more negative feedback, but also more direction and help-giving.

A significant finding of Weinstein's work was that learners' perceptions of teachers' behaviour in class did not necessarily correspond with those teachers' intentions nor with what actually occurred. But it is the learners' perceptions and interpretations which have been found to have the greatest influence on achievement. In a study of junior high school students in Taiwan, Huang (1994) found that learners' perceptions of their own or their classmates' abilities could be accounted for in large part by the social comparison information that they were gleaning from their highly structured classrooms and that it was the (mainly negative) feedback from their teachers which had the most profound effect on those perceptions. In her study, Weinstein (1989) found similarly that children learned how 'smart' they were mainly from teacher feedback in the form of marks, comments, work display and the degree and type of praise and criticism received.

There have been many studies carried out on the relationship between people's views of themselves and their success in a variety of different achievement-related situations (see Burns 1982; Gurney 1986; Lawrence

1973 for comprehensive reviews of much of this work). However, as Wylie (1979) made explicit in her classic text, the self-concept is extremely complex and difficult to measure because of its multifaceted nature.

One very simple but often effective technique for investigating self-concept is the W-A-Y (Who Are You) technique. Simply write the numbers one to twenty on separate lines down a blank page. Then write twenty statements, each beginning with the words 'I am . . . '. You will probably find that the first five or six statements come easily to you but that it becomes progressively more difficult, but also possibly more significant towards the end. Although the W-A-Y can sometimes be very revealing, there is no way of knowing whether it really taps into a person's *core constructs*, nor will it necessarily reveal anything about a person's self-concept with regard to the specific area, in this case language learning, in which we are particularly interested.

Perhaps the most comprehensive attempt to come to terms with the multidimensional nature of people's self-concepts has been made by the Australian researcher Herbert Marsh and his colleagues (Marsh, Parker and Barnes 1985). Marsh and his colleagues have constructed a Self-Description Questionnaire (SDQ) based upon the assumptions that self-concept is multifaceted, hierarchically arranged, and becomes increasingly multifaceted with age (Marsh 1990; Marsh and Shavelson 1985). The SDQ was specifically designed to measure three areas of academic self-concept and four areas of non-academic self-concept arising out of previous research. These include a *general* self-esteem scale, measured by such items as 'Overall, I have a lot to be proud of'; a *mathematics* scale, e.g. 'Mathematics is one of my best subjects'; a *verbal* scale, e.g. 'I get good marks in English'; a *general school* scale, e.g. 'I'm not very interested in any school subjects'; a *physical abilities* scale, e.g. 'I'm good at things like sport, gym and dance'; a *physical appearance* scale, e.g. 'I hate the way I look', scales relating to *relations with the same and opposite sex*, e.g. 'I get on well with girls'; *relations with parents*, e.g. 'It is difficult for me to talk to my parents'; *honesty*, e.g. 'People can count on me to do the right thing'; and *emotional stability*, e.g. 'I get upset easily'. Several factor analytic studies have clearly supported each of these facets of adolescent self-concept in particular. It has also been found that for every grade level from 7 to 12 a significant correlation exists between academic criterion measures and academic, but not non-academic scales of the SDQ (Marsh, Parker and Barnes 1985).

The fact that work with SDQ has found strong evidence for the specificity of self-concept within different academic areas may have implications for foreign language learning, although little research appears to have been carried out in this area as yet. One implication, for example, is that how people perceive themselves as language learners may bear little, if any, relationship to their self-concept in any other academic or non-academic area, although one might predict a significant relationship with verbal self-concept.

Another problem with any investigation into self-concept is that there is almost always an evaluative element involved, particularly when we consider how we feel about ourselves in relation to any particular field of human endeavour. The statement 'I am female' is for most of us non-evaluative, but statements like 'I have a lot to be proud of' or 'I am good at learning languages' are conveying powerful evaluative messages. In many ways it is these evaluative messages that are usually most interesting to us because they represent 'the window to the individual's soul'. Carl Rogers helpfully made the distinction between our *actual* view of ourselves and our *ideal* view. He suggested that the discrepancy between the two represents a measure of our *self-esteem*. The closer our actual self-concept is to our ideal self-concept, the higher our level of self-esteem.

Other researchers short circuited this process by producing self-esteem scales (see Coopersmith 1967; Lawrence 1988; Rosenberg 1965). However, the pitfalls of measurement that we discussed earlier in this chapter become once more apparent here. If we examine the Rosenberg Global Self-esteem Scale, for example, we find ten statements of the kind, 'On the whole I am satisfied with myself' and 'At times I think I am no good at all' to which the respondent is required to indicate agreement or disagreement according to a four-point scale. Thus the range of possible scores for any respondent must lie between 10 and 40. But what exactly does it mean for an individual to obtain a score of 12 or 23? How can such a score help any individual to gain a better understanding of her or himself? What inferences could the teacher draw from such a score? What would be the action implications? We are not denying here the possible utility of such tests for correlational research with large numbers or in helping to discriminate statistically between various groups. We are merely questioning their value in telling us anything about any individual in the real world.

Despite these measurement difficulties, a large body of research has demonstrated consistently the existence of a positive relationship between high self-esteem and academic achievement (see Burns 1982 for a review of some of this literature). There is little doubt that for most people, positive achievement leads to high self-esteem, but the effect of high self-esteem on achievement is more equivocal. What does seem highly likely, however, is that the self-concept may well perform an important inner mediating function in the learning process (Gurney 1986).

A considerable number of studies have sought to enhance children's self-esteem as a means of improving their academic achievement. These approaches offer curriculum packages directly aimed at self-esteem enhancement (Zeeman 1982), interventions aimed specifically at improving academic performance (McCormick and Williams 1974), counselling interventions (Lawrence 1973), and direct instructions to teachers about ways of changing their own behaviour (Ascione and Berg 1983) and that of their learners (Rose 1978).

Although such approaches usually claim at least a moderate degree of success, we can see no reason for selecting any one method in preference to another. Basically, the message to language teachers to be derived from this work is that more successful outcomes are likely to result from teachers gearing their efforts to improving both academic performance and self-esteem at the same time. We would add a word of warning here, however. It seems to us that there is a danger in placing too great an emphasis on the 'feelgood factor' without considering whether high self-esteem is always appropriate. If I happen to think that I'm very good at learning languages and that I have no need to prepare for an important examination when I am, in fact, nowhere near ready, then my positive self-regard is likely to be both unrealistic and detrimental to my chances of passing that examination.

While we are convinced of the importance for every language learner of attaining an appropriate level of self-esteem, since this must be related to developing feelings of competence and self-confidence, we remain unconvinced of the practical value of much of the work in this area. First, it has been subjected to the same problems of measurement that we criticised earlier. Second, the very global nature of such constructs as *self-concept* and *self-esteem* makes it difficult to provide other than general statements about their contribution to successful learning. This has led some psychologists to seek alternative ways of encapsulating the specific nature of the relationship between people's beliefs about themselves as learners and learning outcomes. One particularly promising avenue has been to examine the feelings of control that people have over different aspects of their lives.

5.5   Locus of control

One of the most significant factors in determining people's motivation to act in various ways and in retaining their interest and involvement is their sense of personal *control* over what is happening. This concept is known as *locus of control* or LoC (Findley and Cooper 1983), a term derived from the Social Learning theory of Rotter (1954). Locus of control refers to a person's beliefs about control over life events. Some people feel personally responsible for everything that happens to them in their lives. These people are termed 'internalisers' in LoC theory. Other people feel that events in their lives are all determined by forces beyond their control, e.g. fate, luck or other people. This group are termed 'externalisers'.

Most people, of course, fall somewhere between these two extremes, but it is clear that considerable variation occurs and that many people tend towards one end of the continuum or the other where significant life events are concerned. The situation is somewhat more complicated in that people often vary in how far they feel they have a sense of control over negative as opposed to positive events. Although LoC is considered to be relatively enduring, it would appear to be most clearly established during adolescence, and also open to change by means of structured interventions.

A great deal of research has been carried out in examining locus of control and its relationship with perceived success in life, particularly with regard to academic achievement. From their large scale review of such studies, Findley and Cooper (1983) were able to conclude that more internal beliefs, that is, feeling of being in control of events, are associated with greater academic achievement. This does not necessarily imply causality. The relation tends to be stronger for males than for females and appears to hold across ethnic groups.

However, it is in the approach to learning, perhaps, that the results most pertinent to our purposes here have been found. Those with a high internal locus of control show strong tendencies to seek information and use it appropriately in problem-solving tasks, to be active and assertive and to exhibit a high degree of exploratory behaviour and excitement about learning. They exhibit a great deal of persistence and show a willingness to delay rewards in order to maximise them. Those demonstrating high externality, on the other hand, tend to be relatively passive, compliant, non-exploratory and inattentive. These and other findings are well summarised by Wang (1983).

Why should we consider these findings so important? It appears that learners who believe they can influence their own learning are more likely to succeed in school than those who believe their learning is controlled by other people, and is outside of their control. It is important to re-emphasise here that it is not helpful to view locus of control as a fixed or static characteristic. If we do, we label and categorise learners rather than seeking ways of helping them. If, on the other hand, we see locus of control as changeable, then we can look for ways of helping learners to take control.

Wang reviews a number of studies which demonstrate that particular forms of classroom practice can change individuals' locus of control, particularly when learners are taught to assume responsibility for their own learning. She claims to have identified a number of features of successful programmes which she incorporates into her Adaptive Learning Environments Model (ALEM). A key element of this model is instruction in and opportunities to practise self-management skills. Such skills involve:

- planning and carrying out routine classroom management tasks (e.g. obtaining and returning materials and equipment), rather than expecting the teacher to organise this;

- ways of searching for, ordering and organising information to be learned and remembered;
- breaking complex tasks into meaningful and manageable subparts;
- setting realistic personal learning goals;
- estimating the amount of time and effort that will be required to complete a task.

A study by Arlin and Whitley (1978), in which the opportunities for learner self-management were varied, provided support for such a model. Here a clear relationship was found between learners' perceptions of personal control over learning outcomes and the number of opportunities that those learners had been given to take responsibility for their own learning.

It should be clear that fostering internal beliefs about control over language learning has implications for language teachers. We would suggest that language teachers could help and encourage learners to:

- identify their own attitudes towards language learning, and their strengths and weaknesses both cognitively and socially;
- develop their own individual plans for learning the language;
- take responsibility for carrying out their own plans;
- evaluate realistically their progress and the reasons for their successes and failures;
- participate in the selection of learning activities;
- take responsibility for helping each other in carrying out learning plans.

It can also be seen that these link with a number of aspects of mediation discussed in Chapter 4.

There are, however, problems with the locus of control construct. The fact of the matter is that situations are not always within our control, and, even when they are, there may be rather different forms of internal, and for that matter external, control. Moreover, we may see certain aspects of learning as always well within our control whilst others may vary according to particular circumstances. Even so, the concept of locus of control sheds considerable light on the way learners view their own learning, and how teachers can help learners to make their own sense of this process. We shall now turn to a related concept that is potentially very powerful in helping to explain the orientations of different individuals towards their learning. This is provided by *attribution theory*.

5.6 Attribution theory

In seeking to understand better the ways in which people make sense of events in their lives, the social psychologist Fritz Heider began to develop in the 1940s and 50s what he termed a 'naive' psychology of the layperson (Heider 1944, 1958). A central aspect of Heider's theory was that it was how people *perceived* events rather than the events in themselves that influenced behaviour. When required to give reasons for the outcomes of events or the behaviour of others, Heider suggested that people would tend to refer to a limited range of internal (personal) and external (environmental) factors.

Heider's ideas were taken up by a comparatively small number of writers and researchers, most notably Bernard Weiner (1979, 1980, 1986), who has been particularly concerned with the reasons that people attribute to their perceived successes and failures in academic and other achievement situations. One of Weiner's most helpful contributions to the study of motivation and learning was to draw together aspects of achievement motivation (see Chapter 6, page 113) and locus of control theories in constructing his own influential version of attribution theory.

To make this clearer, if you were to ask people to what they attributed their success or failure on a particular language learning task, they might give a variety of replies. Some possible attributions for success might be:

- I am good at learning languages;
- I know how to do this sort of task;
- I worked hard;
- The task was easy.

Conversely, some attributions for failure might be:

- I'm no good at languages;
- The task was boring;
- I don't like languages;
- I didn't try;
- It was too difficult.

You can then begin to group these attributions under different headings. For example, the statements 'I know how to do this sort of task', 'I am good at learning languages' and 'I'm no good at languages' could be grouped together as 'ability'.

Essentially, Weiner suggested that, on the whole, people tend to refer to four main sets of attributions for their perceived successes and failures in life: (a) ability, (b) effort, (c) luck, (d) the perceived difficulty of the task with which they are faced. Most of the evidence in support of these elements has come from controlled laboratory studies rather than open-ended investigations in naturalistic settings. However, there has been an accumulating body of literature which suggests that these are common elements in most people's attributional systems.

It should be readily apparent that ability and effort are forms of *internal* attribution, that is, they are factors that arise from inside us, while luck and task difficulty refer to *external* factors. Here we can see the extension of the locus of control notions of internality/externality, although Weiner prefers to use the term *locus of causality* (see Chapter 6, page 128), which he refers to as one of the two major attribution *dimensions*. The other dimension against which attribution elements can be gauged is that of *stability*; that is, 'Is the factor stable or can it be changed?' Figure 11 demonstrates how the four most common attributional elements of ability, effort, task difficulty and luck relate to the dimensions of internal/external and stable/unstable.

It should be noted, however, that individuals will vary in the way in which they personally view these attributions. For example, it would be perfectly feasible for a person to see luck as internal and stable, 'I guess I was just born lucky', or ability as unstable, 'I do better on some days than on others according to how I feel'.

Weiner later added a third dimension, that of *controllability*, which made it possible to distinguish between elements that people felt were within their control or not within their control. Thus, most people would be likely to consider that the amount of effort they put into a task is generally within

LOCUS OF CAUSALITY

	internal	external
stable	ability	task difficulty
unstable	effort	luck

STABILITY

Figure 11 *The four main elements of attribution*

their control, but they will probably view their ability to perform well on such tasks as outside their control. The combination of attribution elements and dimensions will differ considerably between individuals with regard to specific events and activities. The important point is that different combinations are likely to lead to different action outcomes. If I believe that I lack the ability to learn a foreign language and I see this as a stable internal factor beyond my control, then I will be unlikely to make much of an effort to improve. However, if I believe that language ability is a form of unstable skill that can be improved by hard work, I shall be more likely to make an effort. Alternatively, if I consider that the tasks I am set by my language teacher are usually too difficult and above my current achievement level, the effort I'm prepared to make may depend upon whether I see myself capable of breaking down those tasks into more manageable subtasks. In this instance, task difficulty is initially seen as an external factor outside of my control which can be internalised and thereby made more controllable by the use of appropriate strategies.

A number of interesting findings are beginning to emerge from research in this area. First, as is implied above, the nature of the event will affect the attributions, i.e. attributions tend to be situation-specific rather than global. Second, it appears to be commonly the case that people develop different attributions to account for success and failure, possibly as a means of protecting their self-esteem. Most people tend towards externalising reasons for failure whilst internalising reasons for success. There appears also to be a gender difference here. It seems that men tend to attribute success to stable internal factors more than do women; women are likely to have lower expectations for themselves and tend to attribute their success more to luck and external causes (Deaux 1985). However, it might just be that women are more modest than men (the so-called 'modesty factor').

We can see that an attributional perspective lies within a constructivist framework. We should not be surprised, therefore, to find that achievement is not universally defined in the same way by different people. Success and failure are not absolutes but relative, defined in different ways by different cultures, groups and individuals (Maehr and Nicholls 1980; Hewstone 1989). In addition, specific emotions appear to be related to certain attributional dimensions, e.g. pride and shame are related to outcomes attributed to perceived internal, controllable elements. For example, I feel pride if I succeed in something because I worked hard. On the other hand, I feel shame if I fail because I did not work hard enough, when I could have worked harder.

One of the most important applications of attribution theory has been 'reattribution training' (Hastings 1994; Craske 1988). This consists of changing people's attributions so that instead of viewing failure as due to stable and uncontrollable factors, they begin to see it as controllable and unstable. In other words, they begin to see that they can have control over their learning outcomes.

5.6.1 Research into attributions in language teaching

So far, research into attributions has been focussed mainly on sport psychology (for example Biddle 1993), and very little has been carried out in the area of language learning. It seems reasonable to assume that attributions for language learning may be very different to those given for successes and failures in sport, and there is scope for a considerable amount of research in this area.

One difficulty with research that has been carried out on attributions in sport is that the results have usually been subjected to a quantitative analysis as described earlier, and statements have been made about groups of people. In an attempt to break away from this mould into a more qualitative analysis of attributions, we carried out a small pilot study with 30 language teachers of mixed nationalities.

Participants were asked to consider situations when they were *unsuccessful* at some aspect of language learning and to reflect on the reasons for their lack of success. They were then asked to respond to the questionnaire shown below. We resisted the temptation to work out averages for each question, seeking instead to find a method that would tell us something about individuals. We therefore plotted 'profiles' of individuals, two of which are shown in Figures 12 and 13 below.

These two profiles indicated that teachers A and B have markedly different attributions for their perceived failures. A, for example, never perceives herself as not very good at learning new languages, whereas B quite often sees herself as not very good.

A further set of questions shown in Figures 14 and 15 below sought to examine whether participants saw different factors as within their control. Again, individual perceptions differed. Teacher C, for example, saw her ability as quite often within her control, while teacher D considered that her ability was not often within her control.

Although such research is still in its infancy, it does provide a methodology for looking at individuals as opposed to groups of people. It gives us considerable scope for arriving at a better understanding of individuals, thereby indicating how we can actually help them in their learning of a language.

5.7 Conclusion

In this chapter we have considered the contribution made by the individual learner to the learning process. We have discussed the reasons why we have

Are your unsuccessful attempts to learn a language because:

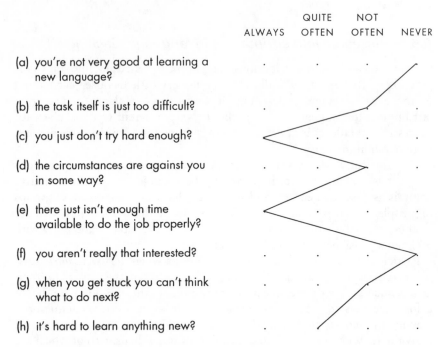

	ALWAYS	QUITE OFTEN	NOT OFTEN	NEVER

(a) you're not very good at learning a new language?

(b) the task itself is just too difficult?

(c) you just don't try hard enough?

(d) the circumstances are against you in some way?

(e) there just isn't enough time available to do the job properly?

(f) you aren't really that interested?

(g) when you get stuck you can't think what to do next?

(h) it's hard to learn anything new?

Figure 12 *Attribution profile of teacher A*

rejected conventional psychological approaches to individual differences. Instead of this, we have suggested that it would be more fruitful to consider individuals' views of themselves as learners, whether they see themselves as in control of events in their lives, and the reasons they attribute to their perceived successes and failures. These aspects are changeable, thus enabling us to support individuals through appropriate interventions and help.

It seems to us that attribution theory is an extremely promising area for research into language learning. If we can begin to seek answers to such questions as: To what do language learners attribute their successes and failures? we might be in a better position to help learners to take control of language learning outcomes.

For the language teacher, an understanding of the individual requires more than a knowledge of differences between learners on certain fixed ability traits. It involves an understanding that everyone has a unique perspective on the world and their place within it. Each of us will approach language learning tasks in a different way as a result of these individual perspectives. Thus, the teacher must seek ways of enabling learners to take

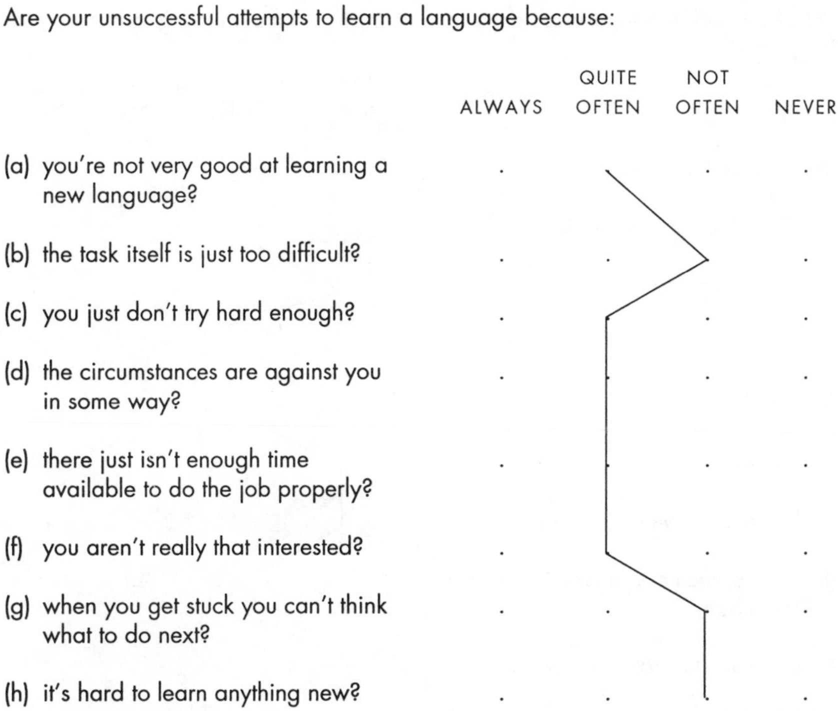

Are your unsuccessful attempts to learn a language because:

	ALWAYS	QUITE OFTEN	NOT OFTEN	NEVER
(a) you're not very good at learning a new language?	.		.	.
(b) the task itself is just too difficult?	.	.		.
(c) you just don't try hard enough?	.		.	.
(d) the circumstances are against you in some way?	.		.	.
(e) there just isn't enough time available to do the job properly?	.		.	.
(f) you aren't really that interested?	.		.	.
(g) when you get stuck you can't think what to do next?	.	.		.
(h) it's hard to learn anything new?	.	.		.

Figure 13   *Attribution profile of teacher B*

control of their learning, to build up an appropriately positive level of self-esteem, to see what happens to them in their lives as within their control, and, therefore, to view their successes and failures as unstable and controllable. By empowering them in this way we can help learners to become truly autonomous.

Having discussed the role of the individual, in the next chapter we move on to a consideration of one particularly important but complex attribute that learners bring to the learning process, that of motivation.

5 The contribution of the individual student to the learning process

Which of the following factors are within your own control in trying to learn a new language?

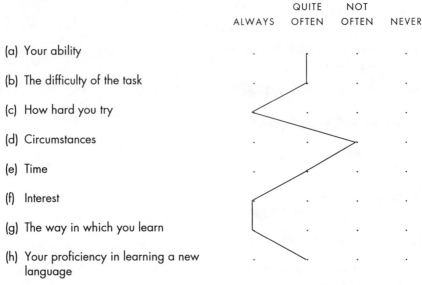

	ALWAYS	QUITE OFTEN	NOT OFTEN	NEVER
(a) Your ability				
(b) The difficulty of the task				
(c) How hard you try				
(d) Circumstances				
(e) Time				
(f) Interest				
(g) The way in which you learn				
(h) Your proficiency in learning a new language				

Figure 14 *Control profile of teacher C*

Which of the following factors are within your own control in trying to learn a new language?

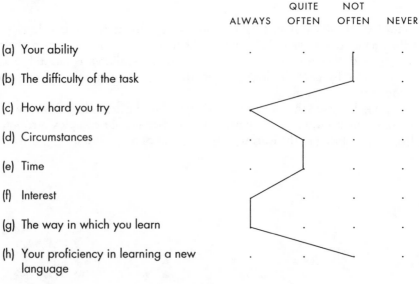

	ALWAYS	QUITE OFTEN	NOT OFTEN	NEVER
(a) Your ability				
(b) The difficulty of the task				
(c) How hard you try				
(d) Circumstances				
(e) Time				
(f) Interest				
(g) The way in which you learn				
(h) Your proficiency in learning a new language				

Figure 15 *Control profile of teacher D*

6 What makes a person want to learn? Motivation in language learning

6.1 Introduction

If asked to identify the most powerful influences on learning, motivation would probably be high on most teachers' lists. It seems only sensible to assume that learning is most likely to occur when we *want* to learn. However, the concept of motivation has passed through a number of different interpretations as theories of psychology have changed, and the term has come to be used in different ways by different people. It is sometimes used as a blanket term to signify that someone has a general disposition to learn, such as when we say 'he is motivated' or 'she has a lot of motivation'. However, it only really makes sense to talk about being motivated *to do something*, i.e. the word 'motivation' is only meaningful in relation to a particular action. More than that, the concept of motivation is composed of many different and overlapping factors such as interest, curiosity, or a desire to achieve. These in turn will differ in different situations and circumstances, and also be subject to various external influences such as parents, teachers and exams. Thus any discussion of motivation is inevitably complicated.

Because of the multifaceted nature of the concept of motivation we shall begin by identifying what we consider to be certain key questions. What do we actually mean by the term motivation? What are the different factors that contribute to a person's motivation and how do they influence each other? How has the conception of motivation changed in recent years? Are different aspects of motivation involved at different stages of the learning process? What is the difference between motivation from within a person and motivation from external forces? Can one affect the other? What can the language teacher do to influence motivation?

This chapter will explore these questions and others in an attempt to bring some clarity to an area which is both confused and confusing. There is now so much written about motivation that it would be impossible to do justice to all of the ideas that pervade the current psychological and language teaching literature. Books of readings edited by Ames and Ames (1984, 1985, 1989) provide an excellent summary of the range of approaches to

111

motivation currently being taken by some psychologists. What we shall do here is to focus upon those ideas and approaches which we find most enlightening and which we consider to have the most helpful implications for language teachers. In particular, we shall focus on what has come to be termed a cognitive approach to motivation where the emphasis is placed upon ways in which individuals make sense of their learning experiences and are seen as being motivated primarily by their conscious thoughts and feelings. We shall examine also the influence of significant other people on an individual's motivation together with some aspects of the learning environment, although this latter factor will be explored in greater depth in Chapter 9.

Because psychological approaches to motivation have changed so markedly in recent years, we shall begin by providing an overview of early psychological views on motivation together with a critique of why many of such views were found wanting. This is followed by a brief survey of motivation in second and foreign language teaching where theories of motivation took a somewhat different direction as they were subject to different influences. We shall follow this with a description of what is meant by a cognitive perspective on motivation, which we then broaden to encompass a social constructivist view. This enables us to construct a definition of motivation which helps us to pull together and provide a framework for explaining much of the recent research in this field. We conclude the chapter by drawing some practical implications from employing this model.

6.2   Early psychological views on motivation

In Chapter 1 we described how positivist approaches to learning gave rise to the concept of classical conditioning and the beginnings of behaviourism. Since most of the early work in this area was based upon the behaviour of animals in laboratories, it was hardly surprising that psychologists tried to explain motivation in terms of how animals behaved in order to meet their basic biological needs, how this behaviour was reinforced when those needs were met and how this reinforcement spread to other events and activities that occurred at the same time. Thus, a hungry dog that hears the sound of a bell whilst salivating at the sight and sound of food would be motivated to seek food when hearing a bell on subsequent occasions. In this way, human motivation to learn any particular thing was accounted for in terms of what biological needs were being met during the early learning years and what kind of reward or reinforcement was provided for early attempts to learn.

It is easy to see how this kind of approach gave rise to modern behaviourism with its emphasis upon the nature and scheduling of reward systems as the most effective way of motivating desired behaviour. Thus, a behaviourist would tend to consider motivation largely in terms of external forces, i.e. what specific conditions give rise to what kind of behaviour and how the consequences of that behaviour affect whether it is more or less likely to happen again. In simple terms, if I give a child a gold star for learning a list of verbs or for reading a certain number of English books, will that child be more or less likely to approach positively the task of learning verbs or reading books on a subsequent occasion, or are there other kinds of reinforcement that might be more successful in inducing the desired behaviour?

An extension and reconceptualisation of these early views centred upon the identification of a whole range of basic human needs. Murray (1938) identified a large number of human needs such as our need to affiliate with other people, our need to dominate others and our need to understand or make sense of our worlds, as well as basic biological needs. Murray envisaged these needs as causing inner tensions which had to be released. Motivation was defined in terms of the 'press', i.e. the urge, to release the tension and satisfy the needs.

For many years such *drive reduction* theories dominated theory and research on motivation. In some respects, as in Maslow's formulation described in Chapter 2, they have provided us with helpful insights into why people behave in the way that they do, or refuse to behave in the way that we may want them to. Similarly, Freud's concept of *unconscious motivation* which suggests that we may often be motivated to behave in ways that we don't even understand ourselves, has been helpfully channelled by Erikson and others into an enlightening theory of human development. However, in all such theories the emphasis is very much upon elements essentially outside of our personal control. They are what George Kelly (1955) called *'push-pull' theories*.

6.2.1 Achievement motivation

An initially more promising reformulation of the drive reduction approach to motivation was the notion of the need to achieve, or *achievement motivation* (Atkinson 1964). The basic premise here is that people differ quite markedly in their need to achieve or to be successful. Atkinson believed that it was possible to assess the differences between individuals' needs to achieve and that this had important implications for their learning histories. For some people, the drive to succeed dominates their lives and pushes them to be high achievers in everything that they do, whereas for others, it really doesn't seem to matter whether they do well or not. However, it is not enough just to know an individual's level of need to achieve, because in any specific situation this will interact with how likely the individual judges the chances of success to be and what value is placed on a successful outcome.

At the same time, a person might be inclined to *avoid* engaging in a particular activity because of a fear of failure. Achievement motivation for any individual can thus be determined by the relative strength of the tendency to approach a task compared with the strength of the tendency to avoid the task. When faced with an examination of English proficiency, a student may be highly motivated to succeed because of the competitive nature of the education system, in order to meet parental expectations or because of the job openings that a successful result would bring. At the same time, he or she might seek to avoid taking the examination because the high level of competition is very stressful and because of concern about letting down the family name and the shame that failure would bring. The level of that learner's motivation to achieve the goal of learning the language to the required examination level will depend on the relative strength of each of these factors.

However, in its earliest form, achievement theory placed little, if any, emphasis upon how people made sense of the tasks with which they were presented. The drive to achieve was viewed as largely unconscious and, in a sense, a simple cancelling out of conflicting forces – a kind of approach/ avoidance ratio. A range of increasingly sophisticated techniques was devised in attempts to measure this drive as accurately as possible, in order to predict the likelihood of people being motivated to perform different activities. It was considered that those who obtained high scores on such measures would need fewer external motivating influences than those who scored poorly. It was also felt that they would prefer more difficult tasks and respond more positively to perceived failure than those lacking in achievement motivation. A great deal of experimental work was carried out to seek evidence in support of these ideas before it was recognised that the whole area of motivation might be somewhat more complex than is implied by achievement theory alone.

6.2.2 Optimal arousal

There are clearly a number of problems associated with drive reduction and achievement theories. One is that they are based on the fundamental principle of *homeostasis*, i.e. they assume that animals and humans prefer not to be in a state of arousal and are constantly seeking to be in a more settled state. An alternative, or at least complementary, view began to emerge in the 1960s as a result of the Canadian psychologist Donald Hebb's classic text *The Organisation of Behavior* (1959). Hebb suggested that both humans and animals seek a level of 'optimal arousal' at which they function best without having to meet any other basic needs. Subsequent work by others such as Berlyne (1960) and Hunt (1965) confirmed that even rats were motivated by curiosity and novelty and not just for edible rewards or to avoid pain.

Thus, we can see that early psychological approaches to motivation have not been entirely satisfactory because they were too simplistic in their attempts to explain highly complex human behaviour; they were based on a principle of homeostasis which does not always apply even to animal behaviour and they presented a view of individuals at the mercy of forces beyond their control. It was only when some psychologists began to differentiate between actions that were perceived as within our conscious control and those outside our control that it became possible to develop an entirely different perspective on motivation – one that drew upon ideas from cognitive psychology. However, before we introduce this perspective we shall consider briefly the direction taken by theories of motivation in foreign and second language learning, which were subject to rather different influences, before people working in this area began to take a more cognitive view.

6.3   Motivation in foreign and second language learning

There is no question that learning a foreign language is different to learning other subjects, mainly because of the social nature of such a venture. Language, after all, belongs to a person's whole social being; it is a part of one's identity, and is used to convey this identity to other people. The learning of a foreign language involves far more than simply learning skills, or a system of rules, or a grammar; it involves an alteration in self-image, the adoption of new social and cultural behaviours and ways of being, and therefore has a significant impact on the social nature of the learner. As Crookall and Oxford (1988: 136) aptly claim, 'Learning a second language is ultimately learning to be another social person.' Similarly, Gardner states that:

> Languages are unlike any other subject taught in a classroom in that they involve the acquisition of skills and behaviour patterns which are characteristic of another community.
>
> (Gardner 1985:146)

Consequently, he argues, success in learning a foreign language will be influenced particularly by attitudes towards the community of speakers of that language.

It is for these reasons that the Social Psychology of Language has developed into an important discipline in its own right, mainly due to the work of sociolinguists such as Howard Giles. The whole field of language is intricately involved with communicating with other people, with social relations between individuals and groups of people, and with social norms of behaviour. It is clear that language learning will also be affected by the whole social situation, context and culture in which the learning takes place. It is not surprising, therefore, to find that a number of models of language learning are social-psychological in nature.

One of the most influential models from this school is Gardner's *socio-educational model* of language learning (Gardner 1985). This model incorporates the learner's *cultural beliefs*, their *attitudes towards the learning situation*, their *integrativeness* and their *motivation*. Gardner emphasises that the primary factor in the model is motivation. He defines motivation as referring to a combination of effort plus desire to achieve the goal of learning the language plus favourable attitudes towards learning the language. Other factors, such as attitude towards the learning situation and integrativeness can influence these attributes.

Motivation is operationally defined by Gardner and his associates in a slightly different way for the purpose of measurement, as consisting of desire to learn the language, motivational intensity, and attitudes towards learning the language. These are measured by the Attitude/Motivation Test Battery or AMTB (Gardner 1985:177–84). This consists of a series of self-report questionnaires containing a battery of questions to measure 19 different subscales which represent different aspects of motivation. Gardner stresses that there is not *one* Attitude/Motivation Test Battery, but that the items should be developed so that they are appropriate to the particular situation under investigation.

Some examples of items from four of the subscales of the AMTB are shown in Figure 16. In this formulation of the AMTB, participants are asked to rank the statements on a scale ranging from strong agreement to strong disagreement. Following this, a number of indices are calculated, representing integrativeness, motivation, attitude towards the learning situation, and finally an overall, composite attitude/motivation index.

Gardner also makes the now well-known distinction between *integrative* and *instrumental orientations* in motivation. Orientation is not the same thing as motivation, but represents reasons for studying the language. An integrative orientation occurs when the learner is studying a language because of a wish to identify with the culture of speakers of that language. An instrumental orientation describes a group of factors concerned with motivation arising from external goals such as passing exams, financial rewards, furthering a career or gaining promotion.

It appears then that an integrative orientation is one of the factors that

Interest in foreign languages
• If I were visiting a foreign country I would like to be able to speak the language of the people.

Attitudes towards learning French
• Learning French is really great.
• I really enjoy learning French.

Motivational intensity
• I really work hard to learn French.
• I make a point of trying to understand all the French I see and hear.

Desire to learn French
• To be honest, I really have little desire to learn French.
• I wish I were fluent in French.

Figure 16   *Attitude/Motivation Test Battery*

contributes towards *integrative motivation*. Ellis (1994:509–10) provides an explanation of what is meant by this term, something that has been unclear from previous literature. He also cites Gardner and MacIntyre's (1992) study where six variables were included in their measure of integrative motivation: attitudes towards French Canadians, interest in foreign languages, integrative orientation, attitudes towards the learning situation, desire to learn French and attitudes towards learning French.

It was originally found that integrative motivation correlates with higher achievement in the language, leading to the suggestion that this is a more important form of motivation. However, other studies have challenged this view. Many writers have also interpreted Gardner's work as implying that integrative motivation is more important than instrumental; this does not, however, represent his position on his research findings (Gardner 1995, personal communication). It may be that while integrative motivation is perhaps more important in a second language context such as learning French in Canada or English in the USA, an instrumental orientation may be important in other situations such as learning English in the Philippines (Gardner and Lambert 1972) or Bombay (Lukmani 1972), or in other contexts where English functions more as a foreign language such as Japan (Niitsuma 1992). However, many studies have found that a number of other factors, such as confidence or friendship may be more important as motivating factors (Ellis 1994).

Gardner's socioeducational model has been highly influential in studies of motivation in foreign and second language learning. Recently, however, a number of writers, apparently thinking along similar lines, have called for a broadening of the theoretical perspective and research base to incorporate cognitive approaches to motivation in education (Dörnyei 1994a and b; Oxford 1994; Oxford and Shearin 1994; Crookes and Schmidt 1991). In responding to these pleas, it is interesting that Gardner and Tremblay (1994a and b) strongly claim that they have always maintained that motivation is a dynamic process where many other variables play a part, and that their model, far from being limiting, can accommodate such broader views.

The 1990s have, therefore, seen a welcome rekindling of interest in motivation in foreign and second language learning with many writers seeking alternative ways of conceptualising motivation and setting new research agendas. This has also given rise to a lively debate between the writers cited above.

In one recent attempt to make sense of the different components involved in second language motivation, Dörnyei (1994a) proposes a three-level categorisation. In Dörnyei's model, the *language level* encompasses various orientations and motives related to aspects of the second language, such as the culture and the community, and the usefulness of the language. These will influence the goals learners set and the choices they make. Dörnyei's *learner level* involves individual characteristics that the learner brings to the learning task. Key features of this level are need for achievement and self-confidence. Finally, the *situation level* includes components related to the course, the teacher and the group dynamics.

Dörnyei's formulation is helpful as it highlights a point that we shall emphasise later in this chapter, that motivation is a multifaceted construct which will be affected by situational factors. It also stresses the importance of what the learner brings to the task of learning including cognitive aspects, which is the area we shall address next. Other researchers have attempted to incorporate more cognitive aspects of motivation into their theorising in different ways. In the next section we shall discuss a cognitive view of motivation before attempting to broaden this concept to include contextual and other factors.

LANGUAGE LEVEL
LEARNER LEVEL
LEARNING SITUATION LEVEL
    (a)   Course-specific motivational components
    (b)   Teacher-specific motivational components
    (c)   Group-specific motivational components

Figure 17 *Components of foreign language learning motivation (Dörnyei, 1994a:280)*

6.4 A cognitive view of motivation

From a cognitive perspective, the factor that is of central importance is that of *choice*; that is, people have choice over the way in which they behave and, therefore, have control over their actions. This is in marked contrast to a behaviourist view which sees our actions as at the mercy of external forces such as rewards. To make an informed choice we need to be aware of the probable outcomes of what we decide to do. This enables us to set goals for ourselves, and we then decide to act in certain ways in order to achieve these goals. Thus, from a cognitive perspective, motivation is concerned with such issues as why people decide to act in certain ways and what factors influence the choices they make. It also involves decisions as to the amount of effort people are prepared to expend in attempting to achieve their goals. The role of the teacher thus becomes one of helping and enabling learners to make suitable decisions.

There is now a considerable body of literature on cognitive approaches to motivation. However, anyone trying to find their way through the different theoretical stances and research reports in this area (see, for example, the three volumes edited by Ames and Ames 1984, 1985, 1989) could be forgiven for thinking that they were being required to select from a range of competing options rather than surveying any kind of coherent theoretical structure. Although there are undoubted links between the ideas of many of the cognitive psychologists writing and researching in this field, these are not always easy to detect because all the writers seem to have developed a particular style and technical language of their own. What is needed, but is not readily available, is a framework within which links between the different theoretical approaches can be made and their practical implications inferred.

A cognitive view of motivation, then, centres around individuals making decisions about their own actions as opposed to being at the mercy of external forces over which they have no control. However, there are limitations to taking a purely cognitive approach as such a view fails to take account of the influence of affective factors, the emotions, or of social and contextual influences. We shall, therefore, attempt to broaden this perspective in the next section.

6.5 A social constructivist perspective

In Chapter 1 we explained what is meant by constructivism and that a constructivist approach to learning belongs within a cognitive framework. In Chapter 2 we presented a social constructivist perspective, and we then applied this perspective in subsequent chapters.

A constructivist view of motivation centres around the premise that each individual is motivated differently. People will make their own sense of the various external influences that surround them in ways that are personal to them, and they will act on their internal disposition and use their personal attributes in unique ways. Therefore, what motivates one person to learn a foreign language and keeps that person going until he or she has achieved a level of proficiency with which he or she is satisfied will differ from individual to individual.

However, an individual's motivation is also subject to social and contextual influences. These will include the whole culture and context and the social situation, as well as significant other people and the individual's interactions with these people. Thus, the approach we are taking, in keeping with the rest of this book, is social constructivist.

6.6   A proposed definition of motivation

We are now in a position to present a definition of motivation, which is essentially cognitive, but fits within a social constructivist framework.
   Motivation may be construed as

- a state of cognitive and emotional arousal,
- which leads to a conscious decision to act, and
- which gives rise to a period of sustained intellectual and/or physical effort
- in order to attain a previously set goal (or goals).

A number of points arise from this definition. To start with, people are aroused in some way. This may involve the element of *desire*, but not necessarily. The initial arousal may be triggered by different causes, perhaps internal ones such as interest or curiosity, or often by external influences such as another person or event. Whatever the cause, the person's interest or enthusiasm is activated, leading them to make a conscious decision to act in certain ways in order to achieve a particular goal (or goals) related to the activity undertaken. As we shall see later, these goals may reside within the activity itself, or the activity may be undertaken because it is a means to other ends. Once the activity has begun, the individual needs to sustain the effort needed to achieve the goal; in other words, to persist. All this is influenced by the context and situation, and will be personal to the individual.

It is clear from this that motivation occurs as a result of a combination of different influences. Some of these are internal, that is, they come from inside the learner, such as an interest in the activity or a wish to succeed. Others are external, for example, the influence of other people. This internal-external distinction is one that has played a significant part in many current theories of motivation. However, it would be a mistake to consider motivation simplistically as something which is either internal or external to the individual as these cannot be easily separated. What we need to know is what external influences are more likely to arouse people's thoughts and emotions, and how they make their own sense of these, or internalise them, in ways that lead them to decide to achieve certain goals.

6.7   A model of motivation

In trying to make sense of the literature on motivation, we have found it helpful to distinguish three stages, which are shown in Figure 18. First, there are reasons for undertaking a particular activity. As discussed above, these will probably involve a mixture of internal and external influences which will be personal to different individuals, who will make their own sense of the various events surrounding them. Second, we consider what is actually involved in deciding to do something: what makes people choose to embark on a particular task and to invest time and energy in it. An individual may have strong reasons for doing something, but not actually decide to do it. Third, people need to sustain the effort required to complete the activity to their own satisfaction. This will, of course, take place within a social context and culture which will influence choices made at each stage.

It is important to emphasise here that motivation is more than simply arousing interest. It also involves sustaining that interest and investing time and energy into putting in the necessary effort to achieve certain goals. We make this point because so often, from a teacher's point of view, motivation is seen as simply sparking an initial interest, for example, presenting an interesting language activity. However, motivating learners entails far more than this.

In simpler terms, the first two stages of our model may be seen as more concerned with *initiating motivation* while the last stage involves *sustaining motivation*. Although it is convenient to discuss these in this way as a linear

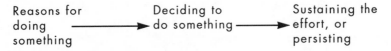

Figure 18   *A three-stage model of motivation*

model, it is of course non-linear. For example, reasons for doing something will affect persistence, the very act of sustaining effort can give rise to further reasons for action. Thus, it is more realistic to perceive the relationship as in Figure 19.

In discussing the literature on motivation it is impossible to fit each theoretical perspective neatly into one or other of these components. Some theories encompass one or two, and some involve all three. In the next part of this chapter, therefore, we shall discuss a number of different perspectives on motivation and attempt to relate them back to this model. We divide this into six sections. We shall first consider the difference between intrinsic and extrinsic motivation. We then discuss the importance of the perceived value of the activity to the learner. This is followed by a consideration of what is meant by arousal. We then discuss a number of theories that are mainly concerned with factors which are internal to the learner. These include locus of control, locus of causality, effectiveness motivation and motivational style. This is followed by a discussion of goal-setting, before we finally consider the role of other people in motivation.

Figure 19 *An interactive model of motivation*

6.8   Intrinsic and extrinsic motivation

In focussing on the reasons why people choose to act in certain ways, it becomes apparent that these reasons for our actions fall into different types. Sometimes we do something because the act of doing it is enjoyable in itself. At other times we engage in an activity not because we are particularly interested in the activity itself, but because performing it will help us to obtain something else that we want. Cognitive psychologists, therefore, came to draw a distinction between intrinsic and extrinsic motivation. Csikszentmihalyi and Nakamura (1989) provide a clear definition of these concepts. Very simply, when the only reason for performing an act is to gain something outside the activity itself, such as passing an exam, or obtaining financial rewards, the motivation is likely to be extrinsic. When the experience of doing something generates interest and enjoyment, and the reason for performing the activity lies within the activity itself, then the motivation is likely to be intrinsic. A general guideline would be to ask: Would I do this even if no reward or punishment followed?

This can be illustrated by considering different actions that we perform in our day-to-day lives, such as going to work, reading a newspaper, driving within a speed limit, listening to music or studying. Some of these are actions that we are intrinsically motivated to do, while others are extrinsically motivated. In reality, of course, this distinction is not watertight, and many of our actions are probably prompted by a mixture of both intrinsic and extrinsic reasons. In considering the relative importance of extrinsic and intrinsic motivation to learning, it is likely that most teachers would agree that both have a part to play, and are in fact linked, but a rather different viewpoint is taken by some cognitive theorists.

The intrinsic/extrinsic distinction has been influential in studies of motivation, and these concepts have been used in various attempts to explain differences in motivation between different learners. Some researchers, most notably Susan Harter (1981), view 'intrinsic' and 'extrinsic' as the opposite ends of a continuum. Harter distinguishes five separate dimensions that are considered to comprise motivation, each of which is defined by an intrinsic and extrinsic pole.

So, for example:

> Does the child work hard to satisfy his or her own interest and curiosity?

is seen as the opposite of

> Does the child do schoolwork to satisfy the teacher and get good marks and grades?
>
> (Harter 1981:304)

123

6 *What makes a person want to learn? Motivation in language learning*

INTRINSIC		EXTRINSIC
preference for challenge	vs	preference for easy work
curiosity/interest	vs	pleasing teacher/getting grades
independent mastery	vs	dependence on teacher in figuring out problems
independent judgement	vs	reliance on teacher's judgement about what to do
internal criteria for success	vs	external criteria for success

Figure 20 *Dimensions of intrinsic and extrinsic motivation (from Harter 1981)*

In these studies, children are given a self-report questionnaire to complete where they are asked to indicate at which end of the pole they see themselves. The problem with this is the assumption that they *are opposites*; there is no allowance for both to be true. Some initial findings from foreign language learners in Japan (Niitsuma 1992), however, suggest that this may not be the case and that respondents could be motivated both intrinsically and extrinsically on the same dimension. It is probably far more realistic to suggest that one form of motivation influences another, or indeed to see all the factors interacting to affect each other.

Harter does acknowledge this possibility in the discussion of her results:

> Although I initially contrasted intrinsic and extrinsic motivation, one can also imagine situations in which intrinsic interest and extrinsic rewards might correlate, as it were, to motivate learning.

> (Harter 1981:310–11)

Closer examination of Harter's five dimensions (see Figure 20) makes it clear that there are at least two distinct phenomena under investigation. On the one hand, there are reasons for wanting to do something, and on the other, what is actually involved in acting in a motivated way. This is similar to our own formulation in Figures 18 and 19.

So, for example, Harter's first two dimensions are more concerned with reasons for acting, while the last two are more concerned with acting in a motivated way, or sustaining the effort. Harter acknowledges this distinction in explaining her results. She sees the first three as truly motivational in that they tap into what the child wants to do. The last two she sees as more concerned with control or judging progress. A child, she concludes, can be relatively intrinsic on the first three while being relatively extrinsic on the last two. It can be seen, therefore, that Harter's concept of motivation is different to the definition presented in this chapter, as the current definition includes the elements of independent judgement and internal criteria as

124

components of sustaining motivation, whereas Harter views these as not truly motivational.

Most of the work in this area suggests that it is important to present tasks which tap into the learners' intrinsic motivation both at the stage of initiating and sustaining motivation. This would include a consideration of interest, curiosity, challenge, and the development of independent mastery and judgement.

6.9   Perceived value of the activity

An overriding principle that seems to have received too little attention in the debate about motivation is the *perceived value of the activity* to the individual performing it. The greater the value that individuals attach to the accomplishment of or involvement in an activity, the more highly motivated they will be both to engage in it initially, and later to put sustained effort into succeeding in the activity. This would appear to be true whether they are influenced by intrinsic or extrinsic reasons.

With regard to intrinsic motivation, however, it is often extremely difficult to predict what kind of activity any particular individual will find worthwhile for its own sake. This is perhaps best illustrated by the enormous range of obsessional interests that capture the hearts and minds of different people. Why should a sports fan devote his life to supporting a particular team and devote all his energies to following the fortunes of that team? Why should one person be motivated to spend all her time and money collecting postage stamps or another to learn to dance whether or not he has any talent? We do not as yet know the answers to such questions, which are likely to be highly complex, but if we can identify those activities that individuals consider important to them personally, it may be possible to use this information to increase their motivation towards other activities.

In a study of the ability of academically retarded children to transfer memorisation strategies from one type of learning task to another, Male (1992) found that, contrary to prevailing views, this could be accomplished by establishing the 'personal authenticity' of the task. Much of the previous research in this area had used tasks (such as remembering nonsense words) which carried little or no personal meaning for the subjects. However, when Male was able to provide an authentic link between the strategies that had been taught and the new task to be performed, her retarded learners became much more motivated to employ those strategies and were able to remember significantly more than before.

The information generated by Male's work has wider implications than generating memory strategies, important as these are. A British survey of some five thousand secondary school students has indicated that by the time of their adolescent years learners differentiate clearly between school subjects that they find interesting and useful, interesting but useless, boring but useful, and boring and useless. In this particular study, learning a foreign language was rated as useful and interesting by about 23% of 15-year-old girls and boys, useful but boring by about 13% of both sexes, but useless and boring by 20% of the girls and 26% of the boys (Schools Council 1968). Although this study was carried out some time ago and is in urgent need of replication, it is clear that if between a quarter and a fifth of all school leavers view learning a foreign language as both boring and useless, then a significant minority are likely to be poorly motivated in this area of the curriculum.

It is worth noting that this aspect of motivation is related to the first two features of mediation discussed in Chapter 4, where we considered the importance of helping learners see value in a learning activity.

6.10   Arousal

It is usual to think of arousal as belonging only to the initial stages of motivation, that is, as concerned with arousing initial interest and turning this interest into a decision to engage in some activity. However, a state of arousal needs also to be maintained to enable someone to put in the necessary effort to complete an activity satisfactorily.

One major component of arousal is *curiosity*. Perhaps the first point to be made here is that human beings are naturally curious. They want to learn about new things and will actively do so. The tragedy of so much of what passes for education in schools is that by the time many children leave school, that spark of curiosity has been dimmed, often irretrievably.

It was the identification of curiosity as a motivating variable by John McVicar Hunt in 1961 that provided a significant landmark in cognitive theory. It held up to question whether humans or even animals always sought to achieve a state of equilibrium, and postulated instead that they might actually have an inclination to explore the unknown just because it was unknown. This, in turn, has led to the suggestion that curiosity can be provoked by making tasks surprising, incongruous or discrepant from existing ideas or beliefs. However, in order to be motivating, it would appear to be important to ensure an optimum level of arousal and complexity (Berlyne 1965). If a task is too complex or incongruous, it is likely to induce confusion and an avoidance response rather than prove appealing.

In recent years the notion of optimal arousal has been excitingly extended and built upon by Csikszentmihalyi and his co-workers who developed the concept of *flow*. These researchers arranged a number of ingenious investigations which involved a wide range of different people from rock climbers to chess players to old men and women living in mountain villages recording what they were doing, thinking and feeling at various random times throughout the day. Out of all the information that was gathered in this way it transpired that when people are involved in any activity in a manner which could be described as highly motivated or aroused, the following conditions are likely to apply:

- all of their minds and bodies are completely involved;
- their concentration is very deep;
- they know what they want to do;
- they know how well they are doing;
- they are not worried about failing;
- time passes very quickly;
- they lose the ordinary sense of self-conscious gnawing worry that characterises much of daily life.

(Csikszentmihalyi and Nakamura 1989)

The term that Csikszentmihalyi coined to describe this sense of total involvement was 'flow experience', which was operationally defined as situations in which people perceive themselves as having a high level of skill and are posed with challenges that stretch those skills. Referring back to our discussion of various aspects of mediation in Chapter 4, we can see that this links with the sense of feeling competent and feeling challenged.

The next group of theories all refer to learners' perceptions of themselves and the way in which these perceptions relate to their motivation. These are locus of causality, locus of control, effectiveness motivation and motivational style. The first three of these can be considered to represent the overarching concept of *agency*.

6.11 Learners' beliefs about themselves

6.11.1 A sense of agency

A number of researchers investigating cognitive approaches to motivation have proposed that the sense people have of whether they cause and are in control of their actions, or whether they perceive that what happens to them is controlled by other people is an important determinant in motivation. These factors are a part of what is known as a *sense of agency*.

Locus of causality

The notion of *locus of causality* was introduced by Richard de Charms to account for whether people see themselves or others as the *cause* of their actions. People who see themselves as largely responsible for originating their own actions are termed *origins* by de Charms, while those who see other people as causing what happens to them are known as *pawns* (de Charms 1984).

In his later work, de Charms takes pains to point out the dangers of over-simplifying this dichotomy in attempting to classify people as either origins or pawns. We are all origins some of the time and pawns some of the time. However, the consequences of feeling that the locus of causality lies basically within oneself (i.e. that one is essentially an origin) are that choice, freedom and ownership of behaviour become issues of personal responsibility. On the other hand, feeling oneself to be a pawn in the hands of others abrogates choice and discourages any sense of personal responsibility for one's actions.

Accepting this 'sense of agency' as an important determinant in motivating people to behave in certain ways leads logically to de Charms' subsequent conclusions that rewarding behaviour may have the opposite effect from that which is intended. If I decide of my own free will to act in a certain way, but then discover that someone else wants me to act in that way so much that they are prepared to reward me for my actions, then my feelings of personal responsibility and freedom of choice may well be diminished. The notion of the hidden cost of reward is taken up in section 6.13.

What we can see here is a link with another important factor in maintaining motivation, our *perception of personal control*.

Locus of control

While locus of causality is concerned with whether people see themselves or other people as the causes of their actions, *locus of control* involves their perception of whether they are subsequently in control of their actions. The ways in which individuals differ in terms of their locus of control and the contribution of this construct to the learning process have already been described in Chapter 5. In the present context we would merely reiterate that the extent to which learners are in control of their own learning of a language will have a pronounced effect upon their motivation to be continually involved in learning that language. In contrast, the construct *learned helplessness* (Seligman 1975), which is discussed later in this section, came to be used as a popular descriptor of learners who feel that they are so lacking in control over what happens to them that they lose all motivation to try to succeed.

Effectiveness motivation

A number of authors have postulated that individuals possess an innate drive towards mastery, which differs from the need to achieve, in that mastery involves succeeding in a task for its own sake, whereas need to achieve entails succeeding in order to be better than other people. Although their terminology differs somewhat, all of these authors are referring to a form of *effectiveness motivation* (White 1959; Harter 1978). Each of these theories incorporates the notion of challenge and relates it to uncertainty of outcome. When we seek to master something, the outcomes are often uncertain; however, there is an optimum level of uncertainty which provides for the most motivating conditions.

A more recent development of these ideas is contained within Bandura's theory of *self-efficacy* (Bandura 1977, 1986). The term *self-efficacy for learning* refers to 'students' beliefs about their capabilities to apply effectively the knowledge and skills they already possess and thereby learn new cognitive skills' (Schunk 1989: 14). This is one way of explaining the common distinction between capability and performance. I may have all the necessary skills to perform a certain task, but unless I believe that I am capable of doing so, I am unlikely to demonstrate those skills in that context. Thus, our self-efficacy will influence our choice of activities that we undertake. It will also affect the amount of effort that we are prepared to expend and our level of persistence.

The notion of self-efficacy was derived from clinical work with phobic patients from a cognitive-behaviourist perspective known as social learning theory (Bandura 1977, 1986). Here it was found that participant modelling and desensitisation procedures used to help overcome fear of snakes were considerably enhanced by patients' growing self-belief in their ability to do so. Subsequent work by Schunk and others in school settings revealed that self-efficacy did indeed appear to be a significant factor in training poor achievers to overcome their difficulties, particularly with regard to effort expenditure and persistence.

It is clear that aptitudes and prior experiences will affect learners' initial beliefs about their capabilities for learning. However, research seems to indicate that the development of self-efficacy is more complex than this. It also shows that learners with high self-efficacy may well perform better on achievement tasks than some apparently more capable peers. Again, there is a connection here with another form of mediated learning experience – the development of a sense of competence. It is clear, however, that a great deal of research still needs to be done in this area, particularly in determining exactly how individuals construe their learning experiences in ways that contribute to their feelings of self-efficacy about any particular set of tasks or activities.

6.11.2 Motivational style

In seeking to make sense of different patterns of responses to perceived success and failure, some cognitive theorists have developed the notion of *motivational style*. One such approach, which draws heavily upon attribution theory, has identified a style known as *learned helplessness*. This concept originated in laboratory work with animals that were placed in situations where they had no control over their environments (Seligman 1975). However, it has proved useful in describing people who see failure as essentially due to a lack of ability, and who feel that they have no control over their actions. In such circumstances, they become demotivated, find it difficult to discriminate between appropriate and inappropriate responses, show symptoms of anxiety and depression (Dweck and Wortman 1982), and give up trying altogether. An opposite group referred to as *mastery oriented*, tend to explain failure in terms of lack of effort and seek clues in their mistakes for ways of improving their subsequent performance.

A different approach to the self-perception of ability has been taken by Covington (1992), who has developed a theory of *self-worth concern*. People with high self-worth concern will seek situations where they enhance their feelings of their worth and avoid situations in which failure would signify low ability, particularly where the expenditure of a great deal of effort is involved. People falling into this category would, therefore, be likely to avoid expending great effort on tasks seen as ego threatening.

In an interesting set of experiments, Craske (1988) developed a technique for discriminating between children who responded poorly to failure situations because of learned helplessness and those suffering from self-worth concern. Having identified a group of children whose performance on arithmetic tasks deteriorated after failure, she then classified them according to their response to being told that a task on which they had failed was very difficult. The children whose performance improved after being given this explanation were considered to be self-worth motivated because low ability was not implied and their self-esteem was not threatened. On the other hand, those children whose performance deteriorated after being given this explanation were considered to be suffering from learned helplessness, as they clearly felt unable to make the necessary effort to improve, even when the subsequent task was easier than the first one.

One of the most interesting implications of Craske's findings is that no one approach to motivating learners is necessarily correct. Moreover, specific suggestions were offered as to ways in which people suffering from learned helplessness could be helped to change their motivational style to one with a more positive orientation. There are, however, a number of as yet unanswered questions with regard to whether individuals apply the same motivational styles in all situations (unlikely) or tend to confine them to specific contexts. An interesting example of this is demonstrated by the high level of mathematical ability demonstrated by Brazilian street children in their natural settings, even though they tend to perform poorly in academic subjects in school (Carraher, Carraher and Schliemann 1985).

There is some evidence that learned helplessness is more prevalent in girls and self-worth concern in boys, but as yet no clear indication of why this should be so. It seems likely that a number of interacting factors are at work which come to be analysed by children's developing powers of 'meta-perception'. The implication here for teachers is that their learners' interpretations of how their parents, peers and teachers perceive them exerts a critical influence on their motivational style and thus their motivation to learn a language.

6.12 Setting and achieving goals

We have stressed that cognitive approaches to motivation view decisions to act as central components of such theories. In making decisions to engage in an activity, setting appropriate goals becomes an important part of motivated behaviour so that the decision can be carried out and the required effort sustained.

However, the concept of a 'goal' is itself more complex than might at first appear. Cognitive psychologists have come to make a distinction between the two types of goal orientation, which have been variously described as *performance* vs *mastery* goals (Ames 1992), *performance* vs *learning* goals (Dweck and Leggett 1988), and *ego involvement* vs *task involvement* (Nicholls 1979). Although there are differences in each of these approaches, they are essentially similar in distinguishing between *performance*, where the prime concern is to look good, or, at least, not to look stupid, and *learning*, where the goal is to increase knowledge, skill or understanding. 'Put simply, with performance goals, an individual aims to look smart, whereas with learning goals the individual aims at becoming smarter' (Dweck 1985: 291).

Dweck goes on to suggest that people's choices of goals reflect both their beliefs about intelligence and ability, and their typical behaviour patterns in achievement situations. Those who tend to choose performance goals are considered to tend to view intelligence as something fixed and unchangeable. If their confidence in their own ability is low, they will tend to act as if there is nothing they can do to improve their performance. If their confidence in their ability is high, on the other hand, they will account for success in terms of fixed intelligence. Situations where there is a strong possibility of failure will be avoided if at all possible because of conveying negative messages about one's ability. In contrast to this, those who pursue learning goals tend to have an underlying belief that intelligence or ability is malleable and that effort is, therefore, worthwhile. This kind of goal orientation also leads to the assumption that failure can be helpful in providing information for future action.

When the radical educator John Holt writes about children trying to read the teacher's mind, he is providing us with a graphic example of performance goal orientation. In this instance, the learners are not concerned with learning for themselves but in trying to guess the teacher's required answer and performing accordingly. Holt's writings are full of examples of a performance oriented educational curriculum which, he argues, runs directly counter to the true purpose of education and actually undermines learners' motivation to learn (Holt 1964, 1968, 1969, 1971).

However, whatever the learner's concept of goal, the important question is whose goals an individual is expected to achieve. If the goals are set by somebody else, then, as we have seen in Chapter 4 when discussing mediation, teachers will need to ensure that learners are ready, willing and able to achieve these goals in a focussed and self-directed way. In the absence of those conditions, the internal goals set by learners may be in direct opposition to those of their parents or teachers. Rollett (1987) coined the term 'effort-avoidance motivation' to describe the behaviour of people who were motivated *not* to work to achieve goals that were set for them by others. This type of motivation appears in many ways to run counter to achievement motivation. However, it cannot be accounted for by laziness or fear of failure. It appears rather that the causes of effort-avoidance are more likely to be frustrating experiences during the first contacts of the learner with the particular activity or type of tasks involved. If parents or teachers respond negatively to this kind of effort-avoidance, it seems that the tendency is likely to be increased (Rollett 1987).

Typical strategies used by learners high in effort-avoidance are either to work extremely slowly even when they are capable of working much faster, or to work very quickly but in a slipshod manner. They may even show an untypical response to praise by *decreasing* their work rate when this is given; they are adept at finding a variety of elaborate excuses for not working, and in doing so tend to produce feelings of resignation in teachers and others. It is important, therefore, when faced with such learners to focus on redirecting the energy put into effort-avoidance in creative rather than controlling ways.

An interesting approach which has taken up this point and used it constructively to motivate young children who are underachieving and have become 'switched off' from their schoolwork has been developed in the Netherlands (van Werkhoven 1990). Known as *attunement strategy*, this involves the teacher negotiating with the learner all aspects of the work to be completed, including the definition of the task, how it might be tackled, setting goals and evaluating outcomes. In addition, the learners are prompted to consider how hard the task is likely to be, how hard they will need to work and whether they will enjoy it. On completing the task, they are then required to review those predictions. The learners are also encouraged to give reasons for their successful outcomes in terms of effort and/or increasing ability. We can see in this approach the significance of the mediating role of the teacher. The attunement strategy has been successfully implemented in primary schools in the Netherlands and England. Substantial gains were found in the amount of time that previously unmotivated learners spent on their work, and they became deeply involved in it following this type of intervention (Hastings 1992).

The importance of involving learners in setting their own language learning goals has already been highlighted in Chapter 4. Here we would stress that this is a crucial component of motivation of learners to learn a language, and that this is an important step towards learner control and autonomy in this venture.

6.13   The involvement of significant others

The various theoretical perspectives on motivation that we have discussed so far have been mainly concerned with what learners bring to the learning situation, and how different tasks affect a learner's motivation. However, the reality of language learning in schools and other institutions is that learning tasks are generally introduced by another person, most often the teacher. Two main factors can be seen as contributing to the learners' motivation to participate in these activities. The first is the personality or nature of the person introducing the activity. All learners are likely to be influenced by their personal feelings about their teachers, and therefore, their perceptions of their teachers and of the interactions that occur between them and their teachers will undoubtedly affect their motivation to learn. The second is the way in which the person presents the activity and works with the learner during the completion of that activity. Thus, the role of the teacher is important at all stages of the motivational process.

In trying to identify exactly how teachers should act to motivate their learners best we have already stressed that this must involve more than notions of arousing interest. We suggest that Feuerstein's three central aspects of mediation introduced in Chapter 4 provide a useful starting point. If teachers make their intentions clear and make sure that these are understood, if they invest tasks and activities with personal significance, and if they explain clearly how performing such activities will be helpful elsewhere, then powerful motivating conditions are likely to be set. If in addition they help the learners take control of their own learning and set their own learning goals, then there is a greater chance that the learners will be motivated to learn. As well as this, they need to be aware of the importance of helping learners to develop an internal sense of control as well as feelings of effectiveness in their ability to carry out tasks.

6.13.1 Feedback

This brings us to a further aspect of the teacher's role in motivation, that is, as the provider of *feedback*. Behavioural psychologists were the first to recognise the power of feedback as a motivating influence. However, what is not always recognised is that any action (or lack of action) by another significant person, following an action on our part, may be interpreted as a form of feedback. Thus, feedback can be given (or interpreted as being given) by means of praise, by any relevant comment or action, or by silence. It can be seen that this again is a complex area involving a number of variables such as the intention of the person giving the feedback, the way in which it is given and the way in which it is construed by the person receiving it.

It is in the broader area of *reinforcement*, however, that most research has been carried out. We should begin by re-emphasising that in behavioural terms anything can act as a reinforcer if it contributes to the recurrence of behaviour. Thus, negative attention, because it is attention of any kind, can sometimes be more reinforcing than what appears superficially to be a more positive reward. However, it is the application of rewards and punishments, and, more specifically, positive (praise) and negative comments to which we shall now turn.

External reinforcers in the form of rewards, merit marks or simple praise, are often considered to be excellent ways of motivating underachieving or reluctant learners (Wheldall and Merrett 1984). Schools and classrooms are often organised according to such principles. Systems of rewards (or awards) and punishment (or sanctions) are set up as classroom management schemes or even whole-school discipline policies, with the result that gold stars, house points, tokens and even sweets are granted as rewards for, and, implicitly, motivators towards 'good' behaviour and learning progress. Extra homework, detention, reprimands and even physical punishment are administered as sanctions for bad behaviour or poor progress in learning and, equally implicitly, as intended motivators towards positive change.

There can be no doubt that in some circumstances, for some individuals, external rewards do work, at least in the short term and with regard to the specific situation in which they are applied. However, the evidence for any generalisation effect is considerably more limited. Moreover, the evidence on punishments or sanctions tends to reveal that not only are they ineffective in bringing about positive change, but they can often have the opposite effect.

Wheldall and Merrett (1987) cite a large number of studies which show that rewards, such as praise, are far more effective than punishment. They have even built an approach to teaching based on this principle which they term 'Positive Teaching' and which they claim to be highly effective (Wheldall and Merrett 1984).

Caffyn (1984) carried out an investigation into the attitudes towards rewards and punishments of more than five hundred learners and a hundred teachers in four English secondary schools. She found a highly complex set of perceptions in operation which made it impossible to make definite statements about the effectiveness of rewards, although there was virtual unanimity amongst the learners in their rejection of most traditional punishments as motivating forces. It was felt that formalised reward systems could be successful in the eyes of both learners and teachers if well-organised and operated consistently. However, public praise or the presentation of certificates was not valued nearly so highly as this being carried out in private. Moreover, too much praise was seen as detrimental by the learners, who preferred teacher interest in their work. For any sort of comment to be effective, reasons for the teacher's approval or disapproval needed to be stated. One further factor which emerged clearly was that teachers' opinions about what would or would not prove to be effective motivators often differed markedly from those of the learners.

The whole issue of the place of rewards in motivating people was taken up in several interesting studies of children by a number of researchers in the United States. Lepper, Greene and Nisbet (1973) offered prizes for drawing to a group of pre-school children who had originally chosen that activity of their own free will. Later, when offered a range of activities to choose from, the children who were rewarded for drawing were significantly less likely to choose that activity again than those children who had not been rewarded. Lepper and his colleagues confirmed and refined these findings in a number of studies which were subsequently summarised in a book entitled *The Hidden Costs of Reward* (Lepper and Greene 1978). At the same time, another group of researchers under the leadership of Edward Deci (Deci 1975, 1980; Deci and Ryan 1985) found that if people were given money for doing things they enjoyed, they lost interest in those things faster than when they were not rewarded.

From the various findings that are emerging on this topic, we can suggest some guidelines for the application of positive and negative feedback. It has been demonstrated clearly that feedback to learners which is interpreted by them as *informational* rather than controlling is likely to increase their motivation towards certain tasks as it provides them with information that helps them perform the current and subsequent tasks with a greater degree of independence (Lepper and Hoddell 1989). If feedback actually provides information to learners that enables them to identify specific aspects of their performance that are acceptable and capable of improvement by some specified means, it should prove both motivating and helpful to them to move into the zone of next development. If, on the other hand, the feedback fails to provide this kind of information, it could have entirely the opposite effect. The comment 'Well done' may make learners feel good momentarily, but it may be accepting standards below that at which they are capable of working and it does not give any indication of how they might subsequently improve their work. Similarly, indiscriminate praise or praise which is given only to those who perform well according to some general 'norm' may lower the feelings of self-competence and self-efficacy of other learners in the class.

Lepper and Hoddell (1989) offer a constructivist explanation for this phenomenon in terms of the meaning that rewards (and sanctions) convey to learners. First, praise or rewards will convey messages about the kinds of behaviour that are likely to gain the approval of teachers or parents and lead to expectations about similar rewards in the future. The future behaviour of the learners will, therefore, depend more upon how they perceive the outcomes to be valued by significant others than upon the activity itself. Second, praise may be construed as providing information about one's personal competence, which in turn will be influenced by one's view of oneself. Third, praise or reward may lead learners to feel that their involvement in any activity is in the hands of others and beyond their control, thereby decreasing their intrinsic motivation.

It should be emphasised here that the potentially negative effects of rewards and praise are more likely to occur when initial interest in an activity is high and when extrinsic motivators are superfluous and unnecessary. They are less likely to occur when rewards are seen as 'bonuses' rather than 'bribes', when they convey clear and accurate messages about high competence at an activity and where there is a natural relationship between performance on a task and positive, rewarding outcomes.

6.14 Summary

We have emphasised that making decisions to act is a central component of motivation. These decisions will be influenced by a number of different causes. Motivation can be intrinsic, that is, we do something because the act of doing it is enjoyable in itself. Alternatively, it can be extrinsic, that is, we engage in an activity to achieve other ends. If people attach a high value to the outcome of an activity, they will be more likely to be motivated to perform it. People also need to be aroused, often by curiosity or interest, and to sustain their arousal. A state of sustained arousal is known as 'flow'.

People's motivation is greatly affected by their perceptions of themselves, and by whether they see themselves as in control of their actions. They also need to believe that they are capable of carrying out an action; this is known as effectiveness motivation. Individuals have different motivational styles. Those who are mastery oriented seek to master an activity by trying to improve their performance, while those who feel a sense of learned helplessness see their failures as due to lack of ability and give up altogether.

Setting and achieving goals are important elements in sustaining motivation. Performance goals are concerned with looking good whereas mastery goals are concerned with increasing understanding.

Finally, teachers and others play a significant part in an individual's motivation. Of particular importance is the nature of feedback provided to learners. There are great dangers in relying on rewards and praise as motivators; these can have a potentially negative effect, particularly if learners are already intrinsically motivated.

6.15 Drawing it all together

In this chapter we have attempted to provide an overview of much of the recent research and different theoretical perspectives on motivation. We have also presented a model within which these different perspectives can be considered. Our approach is cognitive and constructivist, socially contextualised and dynamically interactive. Its fundamental premise is that motivation essentially involves choice about actions or behaviours: decisions as to whether to do something, how much effort to expend on it, the degree of perseverance, and so on. The decisions people make will be based on their own construction of the world. They will also depend on the internal attributes that individuals bring to the situation; their personality, confidence, and other factors. These choices will also be subject to mediating influences; the impact of mediators and significant others in the person's life. Both the learner's internal attributes and mediating influences are affected by the beliefs, the society and the culture of the world surrounding them. Hence we place decision to act at the centre of our model.

An individual's decision to act will be influenced by *internal factors*. The extent to which such factors interact with each other and the relative importance that individuals attribute to them will affect the level and extent of learners' motivation to complete a task or maintain an activity. The most significant factors identified in the research literature are listed below, but no order or priority is intended. These factors will be interacting in a dynamic manner right from the start of involvement in any activity and will certainly not be operating in a simple linear sequence.

6 *What makes a person want to learn? Motivation in language learning*

1. **Intrinsic interest of activity**
    - arousal of curiosity
    - optimal degree of challenge (zone of next potential)

2. **Perceived value of activity**
    - personal relevance
    - anticipated value of outcomes
    - intrinsic value attributed to the activity

3. **Sense of agency**
    - locus of causality (origin versus pawn)
    - locus of control re process and outcomes
    - ability to set appropriate goals

4. **Mastery**
    - feelings of competence
    - awareness of developing skill and mastery in a chosen area
    - self-efficacy

5. **Self-concept**
    - realistic awareness of personal strengths and weaknesses in skills required
    - personal definitions and judgements of success and failure
    - self-worth concern
    - learned helplessness

6. **Attitudes**
    - to language learning in general
    - to the target language
    - to the target language community and culture

7. **Other affective states**
    - confidence
    - anxiety, fear

8. **Developmental age and stage**

9. **Gender**

In relating these factors to language learning we can see that teachers need to arouse their learners' natural curiosity and interest, seek to make tasks and activities personally relevant to the learners both in the here and now and with regard to future utility whilst building up a sense of mastery and agency. Tasks should be made optimally challenging by taking into account each individual's zone of next potential. Learners should be helped to set their own goals and assess their own outcomes under conditions of minimal anxiety which promote realistic self-confidence. At the same time, positive attitudes towards the country and culture within which the target language is set should be actively encouraged.

In addition to affecting each other, these factors are subject to the influences of *external factors*, and interact with them in a dynamic way. As well as this, the external influences interact with each other. The particular culture of a country or region will influence what happens within that country's education system, and this in turn will have an effect on schools, teachers, parents and others. Since learning never occurs in a vacuum, it is essential to take into account those contextual variables which will be interpreted differently by each individual learner, but which will nevertheless have a profound impact on a person's initial level of motivational arousal and also their continuing persistence in seeking to achieve selected goals.

Some important external factors are:

1   **Significant others**

- parents

- teachers

- peers

2   **The nature of interaction with significant others**

- mediated learning experiences

- the nature and amount of feedback

- rewards

- the nature and amount of appropriate praise

- punishments, sanctions

3   **The learning environment**

- comfort

- resources

- time of day, week, year

- size of class and school
- class and school ethos

4   **The broader context**
- wider family networks
- the local education system
- conflicting interests
- cultural norms
- societal expectations and attitudes

Some of these factors will be discussed in greater detail in Chapter 9 when we consider the learning context.

Thus, another way in which motivation can be conceptualised is shown in Figure 21 below. This model is discussed further in Williams (1994).

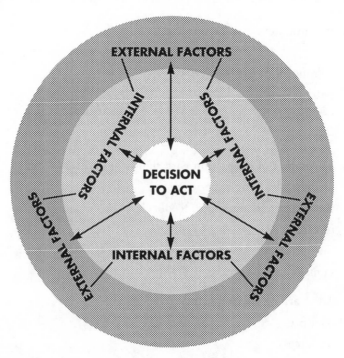

Figure 21   *Motivation: a cognitive model*

6.16   Conclusion

In this chapter we have attempted to draw together key aspects of the ever-growing literature on motivation. We began by presenting an overview of early psychological approaches to the topic which we saw were heavily influenced by behaviourism and mainly concerned with drive reduction theories. We also provided a brief summary of approaches that have been taken to this topic in foreign language teaching.

We then discussed what is meant by a cognitive approach to motivation. However, we are also acutely aware of the dangers involved in taking an entirely cognitive perspective, since this would be at odds with our emphasis upon the whole person, the importance of social interaction and the influence of the context. We have, therefore, presented the most significant messages to be drawn from the literature on motivation within a social constructivist framework. We shall conclude by offering some tentative suggestions as to ways in which language teachers might draw upon this model and the findings summarised in this chapter to direct their own practice in motivating their learners.

1   **Recognise the complexity of motivation**
    Motivation is such a complex area involving so many interrelated factors that it would be a mistake to take one simplistic view. If one approach does not appear to be successful then another might produce different results. In addition, it is important to recognise that motivation is far more complex than simply providing interesting language learning activities or making learning fun.

2   **Be aware of both initiating and sustaining motivation**
    The literature has tended not to differentiate clearly between what initiates motivation, i.e. 'turns someone on' to an activity, and what sustains the involvement in the activity, i.e. keeps them interested in pursuing a particular goal. There are a multitude of reasons why learners may well be highly motivated to begin learning a foreign language, but it is quite another matter to sustain that motivation.

3   **Discuss with learners why they are carrying out activities**
    This would include discussing why they are learning the language and how each task helps them towards this goal.

4   **Involve learners in making decisions related to learning the language**
    This could include decisions about what activities to perform, how to go about them and how much effort to expend.

5 **Involve learners in setting language learning goals**
This is a crucial element in motivation to help individuals to develop internal feelings of control and to move towards autonomy.

6 **Recognise people as individuals**
Individuals need to be allowed to learn in ways that are personal and significant to them.

7 **Build up individuals' beliefs in themselves**
An important element in motivating learners is enhancing their self-image as language learners, and their beliefs in their own effectiveness at learning a language.

8 **Develop internal beliefs**
These are feelings that one is the cause of one's own actions as well as in control of the outcomes of one's actions.

9 **Help to move towards a mastery oriented style**
People who are mastery oriented feel in control of their actions, and aim to find ways to improve their performance and to succeed in an activity.

10 **Enhance intrinsic motivation**
It is important to help learners see value in carrying out activities for their own sake rather than only doing things for external reasons.

11 **Build up a supportive learning environment**
A context which is supportive and fosters the will to learn, and where individuals are encouraged to express themselves and develop their full potential and individuality creates powerful motivating conditions.

12 **Give feedback that is informational**
In this way learners know why they did or did not do well, and what they can do to improve. Teachers need to be aware of the dangers of an over-reliance on praise, and of the negative effects of punishments and reprimands.

7 How does the learner deal with the process of learning?

7.1 Introduction

In the previous two chapters we considered various attributes that learners bring to the learning process. We discussed how learners' motivation affects their learning in important ways. We have seen too that learners bring their own individual characteristics, personalities, attributions and perceptions of themselves to the learning situation. In this chapter we shall consider ways in which learners draw upon their existing skills and knowledge, and use their personal attributes in the process of learning. What we are concerned with here is *how* learners go about learning something; that is, the skills and strategies that they use and the processes that they go through in order to make sense of their learning. We first provide an overview of what is meant by skills and strategies, together with the notion of 'learning to learn'. We then focus on language learning strategies, before considering strategy training.

Until recently the notion of learning strategies has been relatively neglected. In recent years, however, there has been a growing interest amongst psychologists in the cognitive strategies people use to think, to learn and to solve problems. The impetus for this arose mainly from information-processing models of learning (see Chapter 1), and has given rise to a proliferation of research and writing on these topics. Research into different aspects of thinking is being carried out in various countries in both Western and Eastern Europe, Russia, the USA and Australia. This has led to the production of a number of so-called 'thinking skills' programmes, and courses on thinking are now offered in several universities in the USA. The Somerset Thinking Skills programme (Blagg *et al.* 1988), The Oxfordshire Skills programme (Hanson 1991), and Matthew Lipman's Philosophy for Children (Lipman 1988; Whalley 1991) are examples of commercial 'packages' which claim to teach thinking skills to both children and adults.

There are a number of recent books describing work in this field. Clear and readable accounts are provided by Nisbet and Shucksmith (1991) in their book *Learning Strategies*, and by Coles and Robinson (1991) in their edited collection of papers entitled *Teaching Thinking*.

7.2   Learning strategies

One outcome of such work has been an interest in the broader notion of learning strategies. What is clear from cognitive psychology (see the overview in Chapter 1) is that learners are far from passive in their learning; rather, they are actively involved in making sense of the tasks or problems with which they are faced in order to learn. When confronted with a learning task, learners have various resources at their disposal and make use of them in different ways. Cognitive strategies are only one of the resources people have available to them. As we shall see, we also make use of a variety of other processes to help us to learn something. We use our minds, but also our feelings and our social and communicative skills in active ways.

Over the last twenty years there has been a growing amount of research into language learning strategies. This work, which has been mainly descriptive in nature, is concerned with investigating how individuals go about the task of learning something, and attempting to discover which of the strategies that learners use are the most effective for the particular type of learning involved.

Before we embark on a survey of the field, it is important to clarify what we mean by a learning strategy. Most of us have probably used some or all of the following in learning a foreign or second language:

- repeating words over and over again;
- listening attentively to try to distinguish words;
- trying to work out the rules of the language by forming hypotheses about how it works;
- trying out these hypotheses to see if they work;
- testing yourself to see if you remember words;
- guessing the meanings of unknown words;
- using your knowledge of language rules to try to make new sentences;
- rehearsing in your head what you are about to say;
- practising the sounds of the language to yourself;
- asking a speaker to repeat something;
- pretending that you understand in order to keep the communication going.

These are some of the many strategies that people use to try to succeed in the complex task of learning a language. There are a number of differences between them. Some of them are used *consciously*, that is, we made a conscious and deliberate decision to do this in order to help us to learn, but we can also use strategies *unconsciously*. Sometimes a strategy can be observed, such as when we repeat words aloud, and sometimes they are not observable, such as when we try to work out rules in our heads. In fact, learning strategies are notoriously difficult to observe, which is one reason why research in this area is so problematic. From the above list it can also be seen that some of these strategies are *cognitive*, that is, they involve processing language in our own minds, while others, such as the last two, are rather more *social* in nature.

7.3 Skills and strategies

It has also proved difficult to define and to classify learning strategies, partly because terms such as skills, strategies, executive processes, micro-strategies and macro-strategies are used differently by different people.

First, a distinction is sometimes made between a skill and a strategy. In this distinction, learning strategies are conceived of as operating at a level above skills; they can be seen as the executive processes which manage and co-ordinate the skills. Nisbet and Shucksmith (1991:24–5) explain the distinction by using an analogy of a football team. A player possesses a range of skills, such as how to pass the ball to another player. However, to succeed in a football match he has to know when to use these skills and how to put them together. Thus, he uses tactics to co-ordinate them. In order to employ a good tactic, he has to be aware of other things that are going on around him, to choose the appropriate strategy for the particular moment, and to monitor whether it is successful.

A learning strategy is like a tactic used by a player. It is a series of skills used with a particular learning purpose in mind. Thus, learning strategies involve an ability to monitor the learning situation and respond accordingly. This means being able to assess the situation, to plan, to select appropriate skills, to sequence them, to co-ordinate them, to monitor or assess their effectiveness and to revise the plan when necessary. So, for example, guessing the meaning of a word or skimming a text are skills, but the learner has to be able to use them in a purposeful way when appropriate. In other words, strategies are *purposeful* and *goal-oriented*.

Other authors have made similar distinctions between more general and more specific strategies. Sternberg (1983), for example, distinguishes *executive skills* from *non-executive skills*, while Kirby (1984) sees them as *macro-strategies* and *micro-strategies*. While these distinctions are useful, the main problem with them is that they are not always that clear-cut in practice, and it may be more realistic to conceive of strategies as more or less global or task specific; in other words as higher order or lower order. We shall, therefore, often use the term 'strategies' in this chapter to refer to a range of such processes rather than making a distinction between skills and strategies.

Nisbet and Shucksmith (1991:28) provide a useful table of what they term 'super-skills or strategies' which might be commonly needed to carry out a learning task well. (See Figure 22.) It is easy to see their application to language learning.

An important question to ask at this point is why we should be interested in learning strategies. We can go some way towards answering this by looking at what makes learners successful at learning something. Why are some people more effective at learning than others? Effective learning is not merely a matter of an individual having a high IQ. (In Chapter 1 we discussed the limitations of viewing IQ as something fixed.) What appears to be important is the learners' ability to respond to the particular learning situation and to manage their learning in an appropriate way. Studies of successful and unsuccessful learners show that people who succeed in learning have developed a range of strategies from which they are able to select those that are most appropriate for a particular problem, to adapt them flexibly for the needs of the specific situation, and to monitor their level of success (Nisbet and Shucksmith 1991:6). Nisbet and Shucksmith (ibid.:5) make the disturbing observations that most adults will avoid the need to learn if they can by sticking to familiar routines, and, when faced with an unfamiliar task, most people will not know how to set about solving it.

a	Asking questions:	defining hypotheses, establishing aims and parameters of task, discovering audience, relating task to previous work, etc.
b	Planning:	deciding on tactics and timetables, reduction of task or problem into components: what physical mental skills are necessary?
c	Monitoring:	continuous attempt to match efforts, answers and discoveries to initial questions or purposes
d	Checking:	preliminary assessment of performance and results
e	Revising:	maybe simple re-drafting or re-calculation or maybe involving setting of revised goals
f	Self-testing:	final self-assessment both of results and performance on task

Figure 22 *A list of commonly mentioned strategies (Nisbet and Shucksmith 1991:28)*

7.4   Learning to learn

This brings us back to one of the major themes of this book, that education is a lifelong process, one purpose of which is to equip learners to cope in a changing world. As Knowles (1976:23) similarly reminds us, one of our main aims in education is 'helping individuals to develop the attitudes that learning is a lifelong process and to acquire the skills of self-directed learning'. Two questions follow naturally from this. Can individuals learn to become more successful at learning, and, can we as teachers help people to learn more effectively? There is increasing evidence that we can answer both of these questions in the affirmative. As Wenden and Rubin claim (1987:8), '[o]ne of the leading educational goals of the research on learner strategies is an autonomous language learner', one who is equipped with the appropriate skills and strategies to learn a language in a self-directed way. This has initiated interest in what is now termed *learner training* in second and foreign language teaching, which is concerned with ways of teaching learners explicitly the techniques of learning a language, and an awareness of how and when to use strategies to enable them to become self-directed. This we would see as one of the most important functions of teachers as educators. An important question though is, how do we do it?

Traditionally, curricula have tended to concentrate on imparting knowledge and skills, and have neglected the teaching of how to learn. In language teaching, for example, we have often tended to focus on teaching the form of the target language by presenting pieces of the language in carefully graded steps, at the cost of teaching people *how* to learn the language.

It might be argued that in school, children will pick up a knowledge of how to learn from their experience of being involved in learning. Sadly, although learners do pick up some knowledge of how to learn, it is not always the most appropriate type. Instead, many learners develop strategies which are merely concerned with coping with the demands of the school curriculum, of finding ways to meet the requirements imposed by teachers, strategies which will pay off in the classroom situation but serve no useful purpose in later life. The radical educator, John Holt, makes this point in many of his books (Holt 1964, 1968, 1969).

Nisbet and Shucksmith's description of a typical child called Bill is salutary:

> Bill is one of life's plodders, conscientiously looking for and sticking to the one 'right' method of working. It is a strategy which, unfortunately, pays off in many school situations, and he will probably end up with a reasonably good set of grades and a school report which describes him as a 'good student'. His inability to adapt to changing requirements and his lack of self-knowledge may start to be a problem when he is expected to

147

study on his own. But for the present, his teachers do not see him as a problem and are quite glad to have a few like Bill in their classes.

(1991:3)

There are many 'Bills' in our language classes. In a similar vein, Coles and Robinson (1991:91) argue persuasively that 'schools should be less concerned with imparting information and more concerned with encouraging the kind of teaching which pays attention to the way children learn'. We shall return to this notion later. However, we shall turn now to one of the central skills needed in order to learn how to learn effectively, metacognition.

7.5 Metacognitive strategies

A useful distinction is made in the literature on learning strategies between cognitive and metacognitive strategies. Cognitive strategies are seen as mental processes directly concerned with the processing of information in order to learn, that is for obtaining, storage, retrieval or use of information.

However, there is another set of strategies operating at a different level to these, which involve learners stepping outside their learning, as it were, and looking at it from outside. Such strategies include an awareness of what one is doing and the strategies one is employing, as well as a knowledge about the actual process of learning. They also include an ability to manage and regulate consciously the use of appropriate learning strategies for different situations. They involve an awareness of one's own mental processes and an ability to reflect on how one learns, in other words, knowing about one's knowing. This different level is called *metacognition*, a term first introduced by John Flavell (1970, 1976, 1981). The main point to make at this stage is that metacognitive awareness is important for effective learning. It is a concept we shall develop in more detail later.

7.6 Summary

We are now in a position to summarise some points about the skills and strategies used in learning, following Wenden (1987a:7–8). They are the various operations that learners use in order to make sense of their learning. They can be of a higher or lower order. They refer to specific actions that a learner uses in response to a particular problem, rather than describing a learner's general approach to learning. They may be concerned with any stage in the learning process, that is, they may be concerned with obtaining information, storage, retrieval or use of the information. Some strategies are observable and some are not. They may be used consciously or unconsciously, and they are amenable to change, in other words, they can be learned. Strategies can be cognitive, that is, they can involve mental processing, or they can be more social in nature, and their effective use is enhanced by metacognitive awareness.

7.7   Language learning strategies

Research into language learning strategies began in the 1960s, since when a considerable amount of descriptive work has been carried out in this area. Much of this has clearly been influenced by developments in cognitive psychology. Good surveys of this field are provided by Wenden and Rubin (1987), O'Malley and Chamot (1990), Ellis (1994) and Oxford (1990). For a practical application at classroom level and a selection of activities for teaching strategies to pupils, the reader is referred to Ellis and Sinclair's book, *Learning to Learn English* (1989).

It has already been suggested in Chapter 6 that learning a language is different in many ways from learning most other subjects because of its social and communicative nature. Learning a language involves communicating with other people and therefore requires not only suitable cognitive skills but also certain social and communicative skills. It is not surprising, therefore, to find in the literature on language learning strategies that further categories are identified. Joan Rubin, who pioneered much of the work in this field, makes the useful distinction between strategies that *contribute directly to learning,* and those that *contribute indirectly to learning.* Thus, operations concerned with memorising, inducing rules, guessing meaning and rehearsal contribute directly to the learning of the language at a cognitive level; they are the mental processes by which learners acquire a knowledge of the language system. However, there is another group of processes that we employ to help us to learn a foreign language more efficiently in an indirect way by bringing us into closer contact with the target language. This serves to give us more input of the language, or an increased opportunity to try out the language with other people. Seeking opportunities to speak to tourists, listening to the radio or writing to a penfriend would be examples of indirect strategies.

Rubin (1981, 1987) suggests that there are three major types of strategies used by learners which can contribute directly or indirectly to language learning. The first group she calls *learning strategies.* These contribute directly to the development of the language system which the learner constructs. They include both cognitive and metacognitive strategies. She identifies six main cognitive strategies contributing directly to language learning.

1 *Clarification/verification* refers to strategies used by learners to check whether their understanding of a rule or language item is correct.

2 *Guessing/inductive inferencing* refers to various strategies concerned with making hypotheses about how the language works. In order to make suitable hypotheses, learners need to be able to select appropriate information, attend to what is important, hold a number of pieces of information in the head, and use information from the context and their world knowledge as well as samples of the language.

3 *Deductive reasoning* is a strategy where the learner uses a knowledge of general rules to produce or understand language.

4 *Practice* is concerned with storage and retrieval of language. This includes such strategies as repetition and rehearsal.

5 *Memorisation* is also concerned with storage and retrieval of information, and ways of organising the information for storage. This category includes mnemonic strategies and using lexical groupings.

6 *Monitoring* refers to learners' checking of their own performance, including noticing errors and observing how a message is received.

(Rubin 1987: 22–7)

Metacognitive strategies, in Rubin's categorisation are used to oversee, regulate or self-direct language learning, as discussed above. Various classifications of metacognitive strategies can be found, e.g. in O'Malley and Chamot (1990). They involve such processes as planning, prioritising, setting goals and self-management.

Secondly, *communication strategies* are those used by a learner to promote communication with others. They are strategies used by speakers when they come across a difficulty in their communication because of a lack of adequate knowledge of the language. These processes are particularly important to language learners as, by finding ways to continue the communication rather than abandon it, the speaker indirectly obtains more exposure to the language and an increased opportunity to practise it. In this way they can increase their input of the language to be processed by their cognitive strategies.

Some examples of communication strategies used between Japanese adult learners of English are shown below.

1 Speaker A: Aah, some green, some green . . .
Speaker B: What's that?

Speaker A: A little pot, in that, trees.
Speaker B: Ah, plants.

(Ishida: 1993)

Here, speaker A does not know the word 'plant' and attempts to describe it instead. Speaker B understands the explanation and supplies the correct word, allowing the conversation to continue.

In the next example, student C uses the strategy of 'indirect appeal', where she was unable to complete her utterance, and appealed to the teacher to finish it for her, thus continuing the discourse.

2   Student C: I thought, um, British people are similar to American people, but . . . but . . .
                (*She uses eye contact to ask for the teacher's assistance.*)
    Teacher: You thought, because we speak the same language, they must or could be the same.

(Ishida: 1993)

Building on work by Tarone (1977), the third of Rubin's categories is *social strategies*. These refer to the activities that learners use in an attempt to increase their exposure to the language. Like communication strategies, they contribute indirectly to learning. Strategies in this category include initiating conversations in the foreign language, watching films and reading books.

The definition and categorisation of language learning strategies was further developed by Rebecca Oxford (1990) in her book *Language Learning Strategies: What Every Teacher Should Know*. Oxford sees the aim of language learning strategies as being oriented towards the development of communicative competence, and that they must, therefore, involve interaction among learners. Learning strategies, she argues, must both help learners to participate in communication and to build up their language system. Oxford (1990:9) provides a list of twelve features of language learning strategies, which usefully serve to pull together the discussion so far.

1   **They contribute to the main goal, communicative competence.**
They can foster particular aspects of that competence:
grammatical competence, sociolinguistic competence, discourse competence, and strategic competence.

2   **They allow learners to become more self-directed.**
As we have already described, the aim of teaching learning strategies is to help learners to take control of their own learning.

3   **They expand the role of teachers.**
We shall discuss this point further below.

151

4 **They are problem oriented.**
In other words, they are used in response to a particular problem.

5 **They are specific actions taken by the learner.**
That is, they are specific behaviours in response to a problem, such as guessing the meaning of a word, rather than more general aspects such as learning style, personality or motivation.

6 **They involve many aspects of the learner, not just the cognitive.**
They involve affective and social aspects as well.

7 **They support learning both directly and indirectly.**

8 **They are not always observable.**

9 **They are often conscious.**
Strategy training helps learners to become more aware of the strategies they use, and to distinguish between appropriate and inappropriate ones. However, the aim must be to enable learners to use appropriate strategies automatically and unconsciously.

10 **They can be taught.**
People can improve their learning through strategy training.

11 **They are flexible.**
Learners exert choice over the way they use, combine and sequence strategies.

12 **They are influenced by a variety of factors.**
For example, stage of learning, task requirements, age, sex, nationality, general learning style, personality, motivation and purpose for learning the language.

Oxford has developed also a somewhat different system of categorisation which, while containing most of the features of previous classifications, is more detailed. She divides strategies into two main classes, *direct* and *indirect*, which are further subdivided into six groups (see Figure 23). Rather than being seen as isolated entities, each type can support and connect with another.

In Oxford's system, *metacognitive strategies* help learners to regulate their learning. *Affective strategies* are concerned with the learner's emotional requirements such as confidence, while *social strategies* lead to increased interaction with the target language. *Cognitive strategies* are the mental strategies learners use to make sense of their learning, *memory strategies* are those used for storage of information, and *compensation strategies* help learners to overcome knowledge gaps to continue the communication. Oxford's book provides us with a detailed taxonomy of sub-strategies under each of these headings.

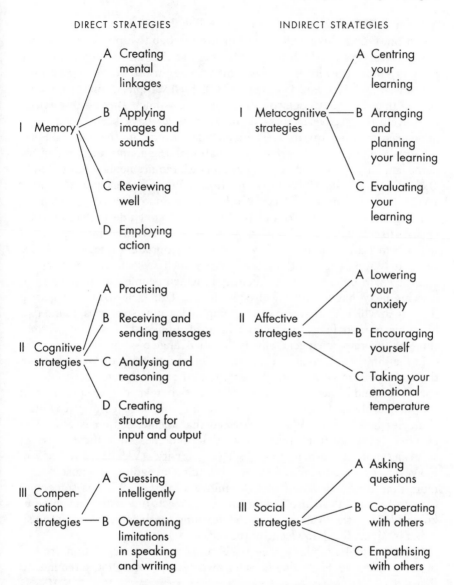

DIRECT STRATEGIES   INDIRECT STRATEGIES

I Memory
- A Creating mental linkages
- B Applying images and sounds
- C Reviewing well
- D Employing action

I Metacognitive strategies
- A Centring your learning
- B Arranging and planning your learning
- C Evaluating your learning

II Cognitive strategies
- A Practising
- B Receiving and sending messages
- C Analysing and reasoning
- D Creating structure for input and output

II Affective strategies
- A Lowering your anxiety
- B Encouraging yourself
- C Taking your emotional temperature

III Compensation strategies
- A Guessing intelligently
- B Overcoming limitations in speaking and writing

III Social strategies
- A Asking questions
- B Co-operating with others
- C Empathising with others

Figure 23 *Diagram of the strategy system showing two classes, six groups and 19 sets (Oxford 1990:17)*

It can be seen that much of the recent work in this area has been underpinned by a broader concept of language learning strategies that goes beyond cognitive processes to include social and communicative strategies.

A point worth emphasising here is the link between the emotions and cognition. Our feelings will affect our use of cognitive processes and vice versa. Gardner and MacIntyre (1992) suggest that affective variables are probably more powerful in influencing strategy use than intelligence and aptitude. MacIntyre and Gardner (1989), for example, come to the conclusion that the use of cognitive strategies is very much affected by anxiety.

As well as affective factors, learning strategies have been found to be influenced by other variables. These include attitude, motivation, age, personality, gender, general learning style, national origin, aptitude, proficiency in the language, perceived proficiency and task requirements (Oxford 1989; Oxford and Nyikos 1989; Rost and Ross 1991; Gardner and MacIntyre 1992). In reviewing the effects of different factors on the deployment of learning strategies, Oxford and Nyikos (1989) conclude that motivation appears to correlate best with strategy use, and that increased motivation and self-esteem lead to more effective use of appropriate strategies and vice versa. It is apparent also that social factors such as socio-economic group and the environment influence the way in which people use strategies, and it seems likely that culture will also play a part. Tran (1988), in investigating the way in which Vietnamese women employ learning strategies, found that his subjects used fewer strategies than men, unlike studies with Western subjects, where women generally use a wider range of strategies.

In the same way, we also feel that it is helpful to take a broader view of the notion of metacognition. We emphasised above that metacognition is conscious, and generally involves at least two related concepts; first, a knowledge about learning, and second, an ability to employ cognitive strategies intelligently. We also stressed that metacognition is central to effective learning. It is 'the process that underlies the efficient use of strategies and the essence of intelligent activity' (Wenden 1987b:573). However, if we are to take a broader view of metacognition, it must involve more than a knowledge of one's cognitive strategies. What is sometimes forgotten is that it can also include affective aspects of learning; a conscious knowledge of the feelings that the learning problem evokes. It must, therefore, include a knowledge of the self.

Quicke (1994) similarly views the concept of metacognition from a broad perspective. Following Flavell's own perceptions, Quicke reminds us that:

> A metacognitive approach to teaching and learning is in fact a step away
> from a narrow cognitivist view of education to a more holistic view
> which encompasses 'total development' and 'development of the self' as
> agent.
>
> (Quicke 1994:249)

He argues that by taking such a view, the distinctions between emotion and cognition break down. He sees education as involving the development of 'whole' persons as self-directed agents and autonomous learners, with metacognitive awareness being crucial in this process.

Metacognition in our view, therefore, includes not only a knowledge of mental processes, as these are necessarily linked to and affected by emotions and feelings. It must also encompass a knowledge of factors relating to the self, and the way in which these affect the use of cognitive processes. Thus, an awareness of one's personality, feelings, motivation, attitudes and learning style at any particular moment would be included within such a concept of metacognitive awareness.

To set this argument within the social constructivist model of learning adopted in this book, it is also important to realise that there are a number of factors that will affect the way learners will actually construct their metacognitive knowledge. So, there will be various influences from within the context in which the learning occurs that affect the learners' beliefs about themselves, their feelings and their motivation. These in turn will influence their employment of cognitive strategies, and the way in which they consciously develop and build up an awareness of their use.

Another point that is worth emphasising here is that metacognitive awareness is a necessary step in learning to regulate learning. However, the final aim is not to be constantly thinking about our learning, but to move towards a situation where the use of appropriate strategies becomes unconscious, where the skills of learning become intuitive. Effective learners need to be able to employ strategies unconsciously, and then to be able to call their metacognitive awareness into play as and when necessary when faced with a difficulty.

There have been several attempts at categorising metacognitive strategies. Wenden (1987b:574) builds on several of Flavell's original writings to make the distinction between three types of metacognitive knowledge: knowledge about *person*, knowledge about *task* and knowledge about *strategy*. Knowledge about person involves everything that one believes about oneself and others as learners. This includes beliefs about one's personal attributes and preferred style of learning, knowledge about what one knows and does not know and what one can and cannot do, and an awareness of one's progress. Flavell's person variables, however, only refer to cognitive knowledge, and this concept was extended by Wenden to include affective factors such as 'I became angry when . . . ' or, 'I felt depressed when . . . ' (ibid.:576).

Knowledge about task refers to an awareness of the purpose and demands of the task, as well as an ability to assess the information provided, and to select what is relevant from what is irrelevant. Knowledge of strategy involves an understanding of which strategies should be used for different types of tasks as well as a general knowledge about learning languages, for example, 'The best way to learn languages is . . . '.

In addition to these different types of knowledge, 'regulatory skills' are also included as a part of metacognition. Wenden divides these into pre-planning and planning-in-action. Pre-planning involves determining objectives, selecting materials and methods, assessing proficiency level and predicting difficulties. Planning-in-action includes such strategies as monitoring, evaluating outcomes and revising plans. It is worth pointing out that these two aspects of metacognition, knowledge about learning and the regulation of learning, exist in a reciprocal relationship. The insights gained from one feed into the other.

We shall consider strategy training next in this chapter. However, it should be noted at this point that training in metacognitive awareness must include awareness of what learning a language involves as well as training in the selection of appropriate strategies for different situations. By 'appropriate' we would include the notion of appropriateness for the individual. In addition to this, metacognitive training should include heightening awareness of the feelings involved in different aspects of language learning, and of individuals' own personalities and strengths and how these could best be employed in language learning.

In the next chapter, we shall move from this broad view of learning strategies and focus on the cognitive processes that are involved in learning something. However, the questions to which we now turn are: what can teachers do to help their learners employ appropriate learning strategies, and what evidence is there that such approaches actually influence learners' ability to learn how to learn?

7.8   Strategy training

We shall first provide a brief review of some of the attempts to teach thinking and learning skills, before we discuss the teaching of language learning strategies. Despite our accumulation of knowledge about the kinds of skills and strategies involved in effective learning, it has not proved an easy task to incorporate this information into the teaching process. One of the debates in this area centres upon the issue of whether thinking strategies are best taught independently as lessons in their own right, or whether, by a process of 'infusion', they are better taught as part of a specific subject.

Proponents of the former school believe that the language, concepts, skills and strategies of effective thinking and problem-solving can and should be taught directly by means of a specifically designed programme. Probably the most universally employed programme of this nature is Feuerstein's *Instrumental Enrichment* (IE), which has been introduced into the education systems of more than 40 countries across the world (Sharron 1987). Instrumental Enrichment is a highly structured series of tasks directly related to identified aspects of thinking such as making comparisons, categorising, organising one's thoughts and drawing inferences. The programme has been the subject of numerous evaluation studies (Savell *et al.* 1986; Weller and Craft 1983). Although not all studies have produced unequivocally positive results, there is now sufficient evidence to indicate that under appropriate conditions, with properly trained teachers, this programme can and does have a positive effect on the cognitive abilities, educational attainments, feelings of self-worth and general levels of motivation of many learners who were previously failing in school (Burden 1987). Moreover, an even more striking positive effect has been found on the attitudes of teachers who have become involved in teaching this programme (Blagg 1991). This programme will be described further in the next chapter.

Other programmes designed to teach thinking skills include the *Somerset Thinking Skills Programme* (Blagg *et al.* 1988), de Bono's emphasis on lateral thinking exemplified in his *CORT* programme (1977, 1979, 1993), and Lipman's *Philosophy for Children* (Lipman 1988; Whalley 1991). However, none of these have been subject to anything like the same degree of rigorous evaluation as Feuerstein's programme.

The alternative 'domain-specific' approach has been advocated most persuasively by the metacognitive theorist and researcher Anne Brown and her colleagues, who argue that skills and strategies are best taught in relation to specific curriculum subject areas (Brown *et al.* 1983; Brown and Campione 1986). This has been followed up with regard to such subject areas as mathematics (Halpern 1992; Lawson and Rice 1987) and, most notably, reading comprehension (Palincsar and Brown 1984). Brown and her co-workers have admitted to being heavily influenced by Vygotsky's ideas and have sought in their work on the assessment and teaching of children with learning difficulties to find ways of gradually transferring, by drawing upon the idea of Vygotsky's zone of next potential, the control of cognitive skills from teachers to learners. Particularly successful has been the improvement of reading comprehension in seventh grade retarded readers by means of a technique described as *reciprocal teaching* (Palincsar and Brown 1984). The teacher and learners begin by working together, with the teacher initially doing most of the work, but gradually passing on more and more responsibility to the learners as their skills increase so that they are eventually able to work independently.

By analysing the strategies used by good readers in text comprehension, Palincsar and Brown identified four main features: (a) they periodically stop and *summarise* what they have just read, (b) they formulate *questions* to ensure that they have grasped the main points, (c) they check back and clarify any points about which they feel uncertain, (d) they try to *predict* what will come next. Poor readers tend to use few, if any of these strategies.

In order to improve the skills of retarded readers by strategy training, Palincsar and Brown instructed teachers first in how to carry out an ongoing assessment of each learner's current level of skill. (It is only possible to carry out this work with small groups.) By modelling the processes of summarising, asking appropriate questions, clarifying ambiguity and predicting, the teacher gradually begins to hand over the responsibility for these tasks to each of the learners in turn. At the same time their performance is monitored by the teacher, who provides feedback and further modelling where necessary.

In this way it was possible to demonstrate not only impressive gains by most learners on reading comprehension tests but also transfer to other similar activities and spontaneous use of strategies where none had previously been in evidence.

7.8.1 The Strategic Teaching Model

Not unexpectedly, most of the published work on learning strategies focusses almost entirely on what the learner does or should do. The often neglected part that the teacher plays has been emphasised by the *Strategic Teaching Model* of Jones *et al.* (1987). Six assumptions drawn from cognitive learning theory are used to guide teachers in their preparation and presentation of lessons. These assumptions are an amalgam of much that has previously been covered in this chapter, namely that effective learning is goal oriented, draws upon prior knowledge, requires knowledge organisation, involves the use of strategies, occurs in recursive phases and follows a developmental pattern. The guidelines for employing this model are reproduced in Figure 24, but the interested reader is referred to O'Malley and Chamot (1990:187–90) for a fuller description of what these assumptions entail.

The important point here, to which we shall return later, is that teachers are expected to become actively involved in assessing, planning and decision-making about what their learners already know, what they need to know and exactly how they can be helped to become independent learners. Essentially, the teacher is required to assess the type and level of current strategy use, to select and describe an alternative strategy, if this is felt likely to be more helpful, to model the new strategy, and finally to support the learner's use of that strategy by a process of *scaffolding*. Claims have been made for the successful application of this kind of instruction with regard to the acquisition of declarative knowledge (information) and the development of procedural knowledge (skills) in different curriculum content areas.

The sequence of steps used in the Strategic Teaching Model is shown in Figure 24.

1 Assess strategy use with:
   - think-aloud
   - interviews
   - questionnaire

2 Explain strategy by:
   - naming it
   - telling how to use it, step by step

3 Model strategy by:
   - demonstrating it
   - verbalising own thought processes while doing task

4 Scaffold instruction by:
   - providing support while students practice
   - adjusting support to student needs
   - phasing out support to encourage autonomous strategy use

5 Develop motivation by:
   - providing successful experiences
   - relating strategy use to improved performance

Figure 24 *Strategic Teaching Model (Jones* et al. *(1987) in O'Malley and Chamot 1990:158)*

7.8.2 Process-based instruction

A particularly promising variation on this work that has been employed successfully with children demonstrating learning difficulties is the *process-based instruction* model of Ashman and Conway (1989, 1993). This approach has its origins in the work of the Russian cognitive psychologist Luria, later taken up by Das *et al.* (1979) and incorporated into their 'Information-integration' model of cognitive functioning. As its title implies, this model takes an information-processing approach to learning and views cognition as an interaction between input, storage and retrieval activities (called coding) and planning.

At this level, process-based instruction is essentially similar to several other information-processing models for teaching learning strategies. However, their review of the problem-solving literature led Ashman and Conway to conclude that such information-processing models could only be of practical relevance if employed within an interactionist framework. They noted the importance of taking into account teacher, learner and procedural variables and translated these into what they termed *teacher-learner obligations.* Placing a heavy emphasis on co-operative learning and teaching they developed a 'classroom integrated' model which stressed the importance of teaching learning strategies according to a systematically prepared plan which focussed upon specific curriculum topics and the development of learners' knowledge bases.

The final process-based instruction model involves five phases – *assessment, orientation, strategy development, intra-task transfer, consolidation* and *generalisation*. Lack of space precludes a detailed account here of exactly how the teacher should deal with each of these phases. However, it is worth noting that the teacher's responsibility for helping learners develop and employ appropriate learning strategies involves far more than just a knowledge about strategies. Such strategies have, in fact, proved far more difficult to teach than to identify. Ashman and Conway claim that only a thorough, step-by-step, integrated approach will bring this about.

7.9   Learner training in foreign language teaching

In recent years the notion of learner training, i.e. the explicit teaching of strategies, has received a considerable amount of attention in ELT. The premise underpinning much of this work is that we can identify the strategies used by good language learners and then teach these to learners, thus increasing their ability to learn. However, a number of important questions remain:

- How can teachers best foster learners' strategies?
- How can teachers ensure that these strategies are transferred to other situations?
- Are the strategies used by good language learners the right ones to teach all learners?
- How do we cater for individual differences?

Several published collections of learner training materials are now available, e.g. Ellis and Sinclair (1989). In addition, many recent coursebooks claim to include elements of strategy training. A good survey of the provision made in EFL coursebooks for learner training is provided by Sinclair and Ellis (1992).

The research literature contains numerous descriptions of attempts to teach language learning strategies. Some interesting accounts of these can be found in O'Malley and Chamot (1990) and Wenden and Rubin (1987), and they will, therefore, not be repeated here. Strategy training has included such aspects as teaching ways of learning vocabulary (e.g. using mnemonics, keywords and word chains), teaching techniques for listening (e.g. guessing, self-correction or directed attention), teaching strategies for reading such as semantic mapping, and teaching a variety of metacognitive strategies and self-awareness. Rather less attention has been devoted to strategies concerned with the productive skills of speaking and writing. An excellent review of the findings from some of these projects is provided by Oxford and Crookall (1989).

What the results of most of these studies indicate is that treatment groups, i.e. those who were explicitly taught strategies, particularly those who were taught metacognitive strategies, performed better on a range of language tasks than did the control groups who received no strategy training. Such findings, however, are limited in their generalisability. They can do little more than tell us that after treatment the learners performed better on certain language tasks, while they give us limited information about the long-term effects of such training, or its transferability to other situations. What we also need to know is how different learners react to training, how they acquire strategies, and how the teachers' actions and attitudes affect the process.

However, several findings emerged from these studies that are worth noting. First, different cultural groups responded differently to strategy training. For example, Hispanic learners were found to benefit more than Asian learners, who preferred to use the strategies to which they were accustomed (op. cit.:412–13). It appeared that if the new strategies ran counter to those preferred by the cultural group, the learners understandably resisted using them. Rees-Miller (1993) postulates that a reason behind this may be that 'the behaviours defined as exemplary of successful learning strategies practised by good language learners may be based on cultural models that are not universal' (1993:684), i.e. they are based on highly ethnocentric assumptions (Politzer and McGroarty 1985:14). Oxford and Crookall (1989) describe how Sutter, in his work with refugees in Denmark, attempted to overcome this by 'camouflaging' new strategies under the guise of familiar ones, a solution we would not support.

There is also evidence of gender differences in the choice of strategies, as well as personal differences based on different personalities and learning style preferences.

As Rees-Miller (1993) concludes 'attempts to translate the theory behind learner-training into practice have produced only qualified success' (1993:279). The issue of strategy training is far more complex owing to the different factors that interact to influence the teaching and learning of strategies: culture, situation, age, gender, personal learning style and teachers' attitudes and beliefs.

It also appears that attempts to characterise good and poor language learners according to the strategies they use are oversimplistic. A number of studies indicate that unsuccessful learners actually employ the same strategies as those used by successful learners. In this case, the reasons for their lack of success may be far more complex, and the teaching of more learning strategies may not be the answer.

7.10 Procedures for strategy training in foreign and second language teaching

Various models for the teaching of language learning strategies have been proposed. Some are concerned with teaching strategies separately, and others with integrating the strategy instruction with language tasks. Generally, direct or explicit teaching, where the learners' attention is directed to the strategy being taught, is preferred to indirect teaching where learners are not told the purpose of the tasks. O'Malley and Chamot (1990:157–60) summarise some of the different procedures for teaching strategies. These generally involve a sequence of first helping students to *identify* or become aware of strategies that they are already using, then *presenting* and explaining a new strategy, with a rationale for using it. At this stage the teacher might *model* the strategy. This is followed by *practising* it, at first with substantial support or 'scaffolding', but gradually reducing this to encourage autonomous use. Finally, students are helped to *evaluate* their success.

O'Malley and Chamot (1990:158, 190–204) devised their own strategy training procedure for their ESL programme, the *Cognitive Academic Language Learning Approach* (CALLA), which is presented in Figure 25.

7.11 Conclusion

In this chapter we first discussed what is meant by skills and strategies, and the difference between cognitive and metacognitive processes. We then outlined some different categorisations of language learning strategies, showing how such classifications have included not only cognitive processes, but also social and affective factors. Following this, we presented some different approaches taken by cognitive psychologists in the teaching of thinking and of learning strategies. Finally, we provided a brief overview of work on learner training in foreign language teaching.

In this section we aim to pull together the issues discussed so far, to consider implications, future directions and further questions, and to attempt to shed some light on the field by linking the discussion to the view of learning presented in this book.

Underpinning much of the work on strategy training are a number of assumptions, some of which we would question:

- that we can identify the strategies used by good language learners;
- that we can teach these processes to our learners;
- that there will be a resulting increase in the learners' effectiveness in learning;
- that these are the right strategies to teach to all learners.

We have also indicated that evidence for the long-term effects of strategy training is as yet limited, as also is our knowledge about the transferability of strategies learned to new and different situations. Moreover, we have seen that strategy use is affected by context, culture and differences between individuals. The issue is, therefore, far from simple.

In order to link the discussion to the social constructivist approach taken in this book, we shall consider the implications under the headings *learners, teachers, tasks* and *context* (see Figure 5 on page 43), though in reality the four headings inevitably overlap and the factors interact with and affect one another.

1 Preparation: develop student awareness of different strategies through:
   - small group retrospective interviews about school tasks
   - modelling think-aloud, then having students think aloud in small groups
   - discussion of interviews and think-alouds
2 Presentation: develop student knowledge about strategies by:
   - providing rationale for strategy use
   - describing and naming strategy
   - modelling strategy
3 Practice: develop student skills in using strategies for academic learning through:
   - co-operative learning tasks
   - think-alouds while problem solving
   - peer tutoring in academic tasks
   - group discussions
4 Evaluation: develop student ability to evaluate own strategy use through:
   - writing strategies used immediately after task
   - discussing strategy use in class
   - keeping dialogue journals (with teacher) on strategy use
5 Expansion: develop transfer of strategies to new tasks by:
   - discussions on metacognitive and motivational aspects of strategy use
   - additional practice on similar academic tasks
   - assignments to use learning strategies on tasks related to cultural backgrounds of students

Figure 25 *Strategy training sequence used in CALLA (O'Malley and Chamot 1990:158)*

Learners

We have already emphasised that learners bring to the task of learning different characteristics such as age, gender, personality, motivation, self-concept, life experience and cultural background, all of which influence the way in which they go about the task of learning. It is, therefore, over-simplistic to assume that all learners will use or should be taught the same strategies in the same way. What is apparent from a constructivist view of learning is that individuals construct their own meaning from their learning; they make their own personal sense of the skills and strategies they are taught, and the way in which they do this will depend on the other influences that surround them. It may, therefore, be more fruitful to consider the ways in which individuals perceive the importance of the strategies which are introduced to them, and their attitudes towards learning these strategies. It may also be more productive to consider the way in which learners construct their own metacognitive awareness and their self-knowledge.

We propose, therefore, that a crucial aspect of strategy training is that learners develop a sense of *personal relevance* or *personal authenticity*. Rather than asking them to use particular strategies simply because the teacher tells them to, we feel it is more beneficial to help individuals to discover and develop those that are most significant and personally relevant to them. Within this process, the learner's metacognitive knowledge, in its broader context of knowledge of the self, feelings and emotions, personal aims and motivation, will be significant in discovering personal authenticity in how to learn.

Linked to this is the sense of purpose that we discussed in Chapter 4 on mediation, and the notion of choice we considered when discussing motiv-ation in Chapter 6. Individuals will choose to use certain strategies if they have a clear purpose for using them and they feel that accomplishing a particular task has value to them personally. In other words, they will employ particular strategies if they have a sense of ownership or choice in the strategies used, they are clear why they are using them, and they want to complete a task to achieve a goal that they have identified as worthwhile. The teaching of learning strategies, therefore, should reflect the first three aspects of mediation, whilst autonomy is gradually transferred to the learners, so that they develop the ability to select strategies intelligently and to use them in a focussed and self-directed way.

Teachers

We suggest that it may be of limited value merely to add strategy training as another element of the syllabus without considering the implications for teachers. Simply adding learner training tasks to the language syllabus may result in little more than yet another curricular activity that learners perform because the teacher tells them to, resulting in doubtful long-term gains and not necessarily leading to autonomy.

What is needed is a reorientation of teachers' roles. First, teachers need to become effective mediators. Second, they need to be able to take on such roles as advisors, facilitators, consultants, co-communicators, partners and joint problem-solvers. Third, teachers' attitudes towards the value of learning strategies is crucial, as this will inform everything that the teacher does and therefore pervade the delivery of the whole curriculum.

We propose, therefore, an alternative perspective on the issue of strategy training. The successful teacher may not be one who merely provides specific learner training tasks, but rather, one who is aware of the strategy implications of every language learning task that they give. Teachers would then habitually draw the attention of their learners to the processes they are going through in language learning, help them to develop an awareness of how they go about their learning, and seek, through the process of mediation, to gradually give control to their learners.

This of course raises the question of how teachers can be taught to provide strategy training. Equipping teachers with procedures to follow is not likely to be sufficient. It may be more important to help teachers to develop their own metacognitive awareness and to consider the implications of this for their day-to-day teaching. Such a heightened awareness should better inform teachers of the ways in which their learners can be helped to develop a knowledge of their learning processes.

Tasks

There are a number of implications for the design of tasks, which we consider in more detail in the next chapter. First, there is a need to start with simpler tasks with more control over how they are solved, moving towards more complex activities requiring learners to select their own strategies to achieve these goals, and to evaluate their own level of success. In doing this, it is important to teach learners to ask themselves the fundamental questions involved in mediation: What do I want to achieve? Do I know exactly what I am doing? Why am I doing it? How will it be of value to me? Which strategies shall I use to achieve my aim best? How do I tell when I have succeeded?

There is also a need to allow periodically for megacognitive reflection on the processes used in carrying out tasks, as well as reflection on the feelings and emotions involved.

Context

The use of strategies will be affected by the whole context of the learning situation, including the classroom culture and ethos. A classroom where a competitive culture prevails will encourage the use of different strategies to one with a co-operative environment. For example, in the former, learners might develop strategies to assist speed, independence, and measuring themselves against others, while the latter might encourage social strategies, requesting help, and measuring themselves against their own goals. In addition, learners will be influenced by their home culture and that of the community surrounding them.

We must re-emphasise in conclusion that the issue of strategy use is complex, and there are no simple solutions to the questions of how to promote efficient employment of strategies. What is more significant is teachers' sensitivity to the ways in which their learners learn, their attitudes towards teaching their learners to think and to learn, and an awareness of the part the learners must play in taking control of their learning.

8 The place of tasks in the language classroom

8.1 Introduction

In this section of the book we shall consider the third aspect of our model, the place of the *task* in the teaching-learning process. We shall first set the scene by providing a brief overview of the use of tasks in foreign language teaching. We shall then look at tasks from a cognitive viewpoint and consider the cognitive processes involved in carrying them out. Following this, we focus on the notion of purposefulness of learning activities. To illustrate this, we shall use Feuerstein's thinking skills programme known as 'Instrumental Enrichment' and present a selection of tasks that teach both language and thinking skills. Finally we consider tasks from an educational perspective, taking a constructivist approach. Our focus will be upon an educational rationale for the selection and presentation of tasks, upon the ways in which teachers exemplify their theories of learning by the kinds of tasks they present to their classes, and the sense that learners make of their learning experiences.

8.2 Tasks in foreign language teaching

In this first section we shall explore briefly some issues involved in the use of tasks for language learning. This is well covered elsewhere in the literature, so we shall make brief mention only of aspects of tasks that relate to our subsequent discussion in this chapter of psychological and educational perspectives on learning tasks.

What is involved in a language learning task has been interpreted differently by language teachers as approaches to foreign language teaching have changed. In a grammar-translation approach, for example, a reasonable task might be to complete sentences with the correct form of the verbs supplied. In a topic-centred approach, an appropriate task might be to observe plants growing and describe the ways in which they change. Basically, a task is anything that learners are given to do (or choose to do) in the language classroom to further the process of language learning. The important point is that the specific interpretations taken will be determined by the different views that teachers have of the teaching-learning process, how they believe second language acquisition is best facilitated, and the approach to language teaching that they subscribe to either implicitly or explicitly.

The language teaching literature provides a multiplicity of definitions and interpretations of the term 'task', which are well surveyed by Kumaravadivelu (1993:70–2). However, we shall take a broad definition, as explained above, that a task is any activity that learners engage in to further the process of learning a language.

In recent years, however, the term 'task' has taken on a particular meaning, as increasing attention has been focussed on what has become known as a 'task-based' approach to foreign and second language teaching. There is now a considerable volume of literature on this (Nunan 1989; Candlin and Murphy 1987; Crookes and Gass 1993a; Legutke and Thomas 1991), as well as on task-based syllabi (Prabhu 1987; White 1988; Long and Crookes 1993; Nunan 1993). In addition, tasks have increasingly been used as units for research into second language acquisition (e.g. Crookes and Gass 1993b). Thus, the task has recently become a central pedagogical tool for the language teacher as well as a basic unit for language syllabus design and research.

One of the driving forces behind the current surge of interest in tasks within the foreign language classroom has been psycholinguistic. Studies of second language acquisition and theories about the way in which individuals acquire a foreign language suggest that a learner's language system develops through communicating meaningfully in the target language. In other words, individuals acquire a foreign language through the process of interacting, negotiating and conveying meanings in the language in purposeful situations. Thus a task, in this sense, is seen as a forum within which such meaningful interaction between two or more participants can take place. It is through the ensuing exchange and negotiation of meanings that learners' knowledge of the language system develops.

Arising from the notion of task-based methodology is an approach to syllabus design which takes the task as its basic unit. A task-based syllabus is one that is based on the *process* of learning, that is, on how individuals learn a language rather than on a pre-selection of language items to be taught. This type of syllabus consists of a series of tasks, and it is in carrying out these tasks that learners are engaged in meaningful communication in the target language, thereby acquiring the language.

Different versions of a task-based syllabus have been proposed. One is the *procedural syllabus* which arose from the work of Prabhu and his co-workers in Bangalore, in India (Prabhu 1987). Prabhu's concept of task involved cognitive processes, and was defined as:

An activity which required learners to arrive at an outcome through some process of thought, and which allowed teachers to control and regulate that process.

(1987:24)

A procedural syllabus consisted of a series of tasks that were intellectually challenging, and which the learners carried out in the target language, thereby focussing on meaning rather than form. The main difference between this and other task-based approaches lay not so much in the tasks themselves but in the absence of any focus on the formal properties of the language. Other approaches to task-based syllabus design generally include a conscious focus on the form of the language, while still conceiving of the task as a forum for meaningful interactions to take place.

8.2.1 Task components

Many attempts have been made by those involved in language teaching to identify the elements that make up a task. One such analysis is that of Nunan (1989, 1993), who sees tasks as consisting of six elements. The first of these is the *input data*, which is the material that the learners work on, for example a newspaper article or a radio broadcast. Tasks also involve one or more *activities* or *procedures*, which is what the learners actually do with the input. In addition they include *goals, roles of teachers, roles of learners* and a *setting*.

In our discussion of tasks we shall mainly be concerned with the first two elements; input and activities, both of which relate more specifically to the task itself, having already considered what learners bring to the learning situation and the mediating role that teachers can play. The influence of the setting will be described in the next chapter. However, it is important to stress at the same time that it is impossible to consider these factors without some reference to the others. Nunan's model is helpful as it serves to underline a point we have already emphasised, that these elements necessarily affect one another in a dynamic and interactive way.

A different perspective on the elements that constitute a task is provided by Legutke and Thomas (1991), who see tasks primarily as a part of an interactive process whose rationale lies within a social and an educational framework rather than a purely psycholinguistic one. They identify three major elements of such an interactive process; the individual, the group and the theme, which they call *I, We* and *Theme* dimensions of tasks. These maintain a 'dynamic balance' in what they term *theme-centred interaction*. Their model is shown in Figure 26. These three dimensions are in addition subject to the influences of a 'global dimension' consisting of institutional and societal pressures.

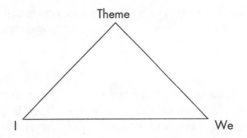

Figure 26   *Theme-centred interaction (Legutke and Thomas 1991)*

Legutke and Thomas's model deserves particular mention because of its emphasis on the interactive nature of tasks as well as the dynamic nature of the contributions made by the different dimensions. Under the *I* dimension is included all that the individual learners and the teacher bring to the learning situation. Both are significant as it is teachers who set up learning events in the classroom, but also learners who contribute to setting up these points of encounter and who interpret them in their own ways. For the learner, the *I* dimension encompasses both *implicit* contributions that learners bring, such as experience, feelings, attitudes and skills, and also what they contribute *explicitly* through language such as information or perceptions. This same distinction applies to teachers as well. Their implicit attitudes, empathy, self-knowledge, etc. affect their explicit contributions to the learning situation, such as the choice of whether they act as informant and transmitter or co-ordinator and facilitator.

The *We* dimension is a particularly interesting addition to the debate. Legutke and Thomas argue that learning takes place within the framework of the group, and any interaction generated by tasks is affected by group processes such as group anxieties, taboos, rejections, power, goals and agendas, and rivalries.

Their third dimension, the *Theme*, represents more than a topic or subject. It is seen as 'a dynamic element taking shape in an interactional process which mediates learners' interests . . . with the interests and preferences of the teacher' (1991:24). It is thus jointly constructed and is related to and determined by such aspects as the learners' world knowledge and culture. We would add that the way in which any lesson unfolds is a joint construction between all the participants, including learners and the teacher. Thus, tasks will be jointly interpreted in this way by the participants involved.

The models of Nunan and Legutke and Thomas have some similarities. Both highlight the interactive nature of tasks and point to the futility of taking an oversimplistic view of tasks in isolation without considering the role of the other elements. In any discussion of tasks it is important to consider how all of these elements interact with each other. A task may have a sound psycholinguistic underpinning, as we described above, that is, it may fit neatly within a task-based approach and be designed to generate meaningful interaction between the participants. However, it is ultimately the way in which learners and teachers interact with tasks in a specific context that will determine how they are actually used in practice. So, for example, a task that is designed to promote interaction will not in itself guarantee that it is used to achieve that purpose. It could equally well be used by some teachers in a very mechanical way. Another point worth mentioning here is that while both models include the teachers' contributions, neither gives us any detail as to how teachers carry out their different roles or how they act as mediators in designing or presenting tasks to learners. We have covered this aspect in Chapter 4, but it is worth re-emphasising here that any consideration of presenting tasks to learners must include the mediating role of the teacher as well as the actual design of the task itself.

Other important issues that have been addressed by those working in this field are the categorisation of tasks, task authenticity, interactional features of tasks, how to select or design tasks, and how to grade and sequence them. Since these concerns have been well surveyed by Nunan (1989) and others, we shall confine ourselves next to a brief mention of the grading of tasks in foreign language teaching to provide a background to our subsequent discussion of the cognitive processes involved in carrying out tasks.

8.2.2 Grading tasks and task difficulty

The grading of tasks is a particularly complex issue because of the many different elements that contribute to task difficulty, all of which overlap and influence each other. It is also notoriously difficult to determine what is easier or more difficult as this will vary from person to person and from one situation to another.

Nunan (1989:97–116) provides a useful analysis of some of these factors. First, task difficulty can be affected by the *input* provided. This includes:

- the grammatical complexity of the text;
- the length of the text;
- the propositional density (i.e. how much information is contained in the input);
- the vocabulary used;
- the speed of listening texts and the number of speakers involved;

171

- the explicitness of the information;
- the genre, discourse structure and sequencing of items in the text (see also Brown and Yule 1983);
- the amount of support in the form of pictures, etc. (see also Bransford and Johnson 1972).

A second way in which the difficulty of tasks can be affected is by changing the *activity* that the learners are required to carry out. A particular piece of text can be used in a variety of different ways. For example, learners can be asked to sequence pieces of the text, or to transfer the information provided to a different form such as a chart, to say whether they agree or disagree with the text, or to use it as a basis for discussion. Thirdly, Nunan discusses the effect of *learner factors*, which include all that the learner brings to the task, such as confidence, motivation, prior experience, learner capability and knowledge, and cultural awareness, issues we have considered in previous chapters. It is worth noting here that Nunan does not include a discussion of the cognitive operations required to carry out tasks. This is a factor we shall elaborate on in the next section of this chapter.

A different perspective on the question of task difficulty is provided by Prabhu (1987:87–8), who identifies five contributing factors:

1 the amount and type of information provided;
2 the amount of reasoning or cognitive operation needed;
3 the precision needed;
4 the learners' knowledge of the world and familiarity with the purposes and constraints of the task;
5 the degree of abstractness of the concepts dealt with in the task.

Prabhu's second factor is in fact concerned with cognitive processes. However, he does not provide us with a categorisation of these processes.

Nunan (1989:109–12) reviews three other categorisations of factors relating to task difficulty, which we shall now summarise. In the first of these, Candlin (1987) offers a taxonomy which focusses solely on the nature of the task. The factors that he identifies are:

- cognitive complexity;
- communicative difficulty;
- whether the task follows a general sequence of operations or whether this is unclear;
- linguistic complexity;
- continuity between tasks.

Candlin and Nunan (1987), on the other hand, offer a list which is based upon the cognitive operations required of the learner:

- attending to or noticing or recognising the input;
- making sense of the input, e.g. how the language is organised and structured;
- processing information (e.g. hypothesising, inferring);
- transferring and generalising what is learned.

This list shows some similarity to aspects of Feuerstein's cognitive map, which will be discussed below, particularly with regard to the notion of *phase*.

A third set of categorisations is offered by Brindley (1987) who suggests that difficulty is determined by the following factors:

- relevance to the learner;
- complexity (number of steps involved, complexity of instructions, cognitive demands, quantity of information);
- amount of context provided and knowledge of the world required;
- language demands;
- assistance given;
- accuracy required;
- time available.

Brindley has widened the range of significant variables to contain some related to the activity itself, some to the learner and some to the teacher.

Thus, it can be seen that different people have approached the question of task difficulty in a variety of ways. There is, however, one further important influence on task difficulty that has received considerable attention, that is, the different kinds of interaction generated by different types of tasks.

8.2.3   Interactional features of tasks

Much of the recent research into tasks has been concerned with different interactional features that tasks generate: how different tasks produce different types of interaction and outputs, the way in which different factors affect the quality and quantity of the communication generated, and the amount and type of negotiation. An excellent summary of the available research is provided by Nunan (1993: 60–2).

For example, alterations in the *texts*, such as the genre, will produce

173

variations in the ensuing interaction. Altering the *activity* in terms of the amount and type of collaboration required, whether the information exchanged is optional or required, whether problems are divergent or convergent, or the size of groups will also change the nature of the interaction. In addition, a number of factors concerned with *participants* such as their familiarity with each other or the task, their gender or proficiency level, their language backgrounds and individual learning preferences can affect the interaction generated by tasks.

8.2.4 Summary

In this section we looked briefly at the concept of task as it is used in foreign language teaching. To summarise, tasks involve *input* in the form of a piece of text or language, either written or spoken; they involve *activities*, which are what the learner is required to do; and they involve *cognitive operations*, which are the cognitive processes needed in order to carry out the activity. However, it is difficult, if not impossible, to consider tasks in isolation from other key variables within the teaching-learning process. Tasks are normally designed or selected by teachers to achieve some purpose which reflects their implicit views about learning and education. These tasks or activities can vary in different ways which will reflect those educational views, for example about the importance of experiential learning, or about the importance of encouraging co-operation. The selected tasks will then be carried out by learners who will employ a range of cognitive and social processes to make sense of and attempt to complete them. The tasks will also arouse a range of feelings and emotions on the part of the learners, which will affect the ways in which they make sense of and carry out the activities.

Having looked at tasks from a language teaching perspective, we shall now take a psychological approach and turn our attention to the question of the mental operations involved in carrying out tasks. This should help language teachers to examine the tasks they give their learners from a cognitive point of view. We shall then discuss the light such a perspective can throw on what is involved in carrying out language learning activities.

8.3   A cognitive processing approach

In order to explore more deeply what might be involved in any cognitive act, cognitive psychologists have suggested a number of models to describe the thinking process. These can help us to understand the cognitive strategies used when carrying out a learning task, as well as providing us with insights into the mental processes involved in learning a language. However, while many of these representations help to describe what goes on when a learner is performing a mental act, few of them take us forward in terms of their practical application.

In this section, we have decided to focus on one such model, the *cognitive map* of Reuven Feuerstein, as we feel that this provides a coherent and carefully worked-through model with concrete practical outcomes for the teacher in terms of designing tasks and helping learners with their learning (Feuerstein *et al.* 1979, 1991). In Chapter 2 we introduced Feuerstein's theory of structural cognitive modifiability, and in Chapter 4 we focussed on his notion of mediated learning experiences. We shall now first present Feuerstein's cognitive map and then describe his *Instrumental Enrichment* programme, which is a carefully graded programme designed to teach thinking and problem-solving skills. We shall then demonstrate the way in which we can draw upon the tasks of Instrumental Enrichment to design activities which teach both language and thinking skills.

8.3.1 Feuerstein's cognitive map

The cognitive map is a model that represents the significant factors involved in the performance of any mental act. These include some elements that are brought to the learning situation by the learners themselves, and some that are provided by the tasks with which they are faced. The cognitive map is a part of Feuerstein's more general theory of learning, and was used to construct the Instrumental Enrichment programme.

The seven elements of the cognitive map are as follows:

1   The universe of *content* around which any mental act is centred. The learners' background experience and familiarity with different kinds of learning content will play an important part in affecting their responses to tasks.

2   The *modality* or language in which the mental act is expressed. This refers to the medium in which the task is presented. This may be written language, spoken language, pictorial, numerical, symbolic or a combination of these. Some people will feel more comfortable in dealing with one medium than another.

3   Level of *complexity*. Feuerstein defines this as the quality and quantity of units of information necessary to carry out a particular mental act. Learners will vary in their ability to deal with tasks of different levels of complexity. Those who have only been exposed to simple, straightforward tasks, or for whom expectations have been too low, will not be equipped to deal with more complex tasks.

4   Level of *abstraction*. This is seen as the distance between a mental act and the concrete object or event it relates to. A low level of abstraction might involve sorting out concrete objects. At the opposite extreme, a high level of abstraction might involve sorting and classifying hypothetical constructs. Learners differ in the degree of abstract thinking they are capable of. In this, Feuerstein agrees with Piaget regarding the developing child's need to move from concrete to abstract tasks, but he also argues that abstract thinking can be taught. If tasks are presented that involve the need to think in abstract terms and help is provided in ways of dealing with such tasks (mediation), learners will be helped to develop higer-order thinking skills.

5   Level of *efficiency* with which the mental act is performed. Efficiency will involve a combination of rapidity and precision. This entails a balance between fluency and accuracy that will lead to the most efficient performance of the task. Learners will differ in the efficiency with which they can perform different kinds of tasks.

6   The *cognitive operations* required by the mental act. This refers to the different processes involved in thinking. Examples are recognition, identification, classification, ordering, comparing, organising, analysing, recognising temporal relations, recognising spatial relations, understanding instructions, recall or formulating hypotheses.

7   The final element of the cognitive map is known as the *phase* of the cognitive functions required by the mental act. Learning phase is organised into a simple sequence of: input → elaboration → output although this is not considered to be necessarily linear.

Phase

In order to learn or to solve a problem, a person must be able to select, gather and take in appropriate information (input). The input needs to be processed and used in some way (elaboration). Finally, the person will need to express a message or their findings appropriately (output). Feuerstein adds detail as to problems that can occur at any of these stages, which he terms *cognitive deficiencies*. To be an effective learner requires optimum functioning in all three aspects of phase. Difficulties in any area can be remedied through the use of the Instrumental Enrichment programme.

The essential aspects of the different elements of learning phase are shown in Figure 27. At the *input* phase of solving a problem, learners are involved in perceiving and exploring the information available to them. This may be the information they are given to carry out a task. It may be linguistic

Input Stage
At this stage learners need to be able to:
- systematically explore a learning situation rather than act impulsively;
- develop an increasingly accurate understanding of words and concepts;
- position themselves in time and space;
- gather information from more than one source.

Elaboration Stage
At this stage learners need to be able to:
- define the nature of any problem with which they are faced;
- draw upon information stored in the brain;
- select relevant cues and ignore irrelevant information;
- make relevant comparisons;
- relate objects and events to previous and anticipated situations;
- summarise all the relevant information at their disposal;
- construct a logical plan of action.

Output Stage
At this stage learners need to be able to:
- express their thoughts and feelings in a controlled and planned way;
- employ words and concepts accurately in order to do so;
- develop an awareness of other people's reactions in order to communicate effectively.

Figure 27 *The three aspects of learning phase (after Feuerstein et al. 1980)*

information that is presented, in which case this is the stage at which they carefully explore this data. There are a number of crucial skills that are needed at this stage, as shown in Figure 27. If any of these are absent, then problems are likely to occur in learning.

At the input level, Feuerstein identifies learning difficulties occurring due to blurred and sweeping perception, to unplanned, impulsive and unsystematic exploratory behaviour, to inadequate receptive verbal tools (linguistic receptive skills), and to an underdeveloped need for precision and accuracy in data gathering. Other problems can arise at this stage from an inability to cope with more than one source of information at a time and to underdeveloped spatial and temporal concepts.

The *elaboration* phase is where the input is processed and accommodated with the existing information. This is the stage at which the learner works out how the language functions. Here, there is a need for the ability to experience and define problems when they exist, to discriminate between relevant and irrelevant information, to make spontaneous comparisons and to relate objects and events to previous and anticipated situations. There is also the need to have ready access to information stored in one's brain, to enter into problem-solving behaviour involving logical thinking, to summarise and to plan ahead. One temperamental requirement here is the ability to stay with a problem rather than drifting off into fantasy or onto a totally irrelevant task.

The *output* phase is concerned with expressing meanings arising from the processing that has occurred. Problems may occur at this stage if a person can only communicate in an egocentric way that does not recognise or take into account the needs of others. The impulsive expression of thoughts or actions will often be inappropriate, and underdeveloped expressive language tools may lead to inadequately elaborated responses. Here also there may be emotional or physiological blocking of responses.

Lidz (1987) took up Feuerstein's notion of learning phase and produced a more coherent model of the input, elaboration and output processes. She conceptualised *input* as encompassing *arousal, sensation, attention* and *perception* – basically, orientation to a task, plus simple comprehension of what is involved in order to achieve what is required. Useful strategies here would include scanning techniques and concentration management. *Elaboration* involves short- and long-term memory, processing skills and executive systems. The kinds of strategies involved here would be rehearsal, grouping, visual imaging, the development of acronyms and acrostics, linkage to stored information and the use of cues. *Output* involves the execution of some kind of response or performance which may involve verbal, written, gestural, or figural communication. Suitable strategies here would include paraphrasing, outlining and summarising.

Feuerstein's cognitive map has not yet been applied to language tasks. This map formed the basis of his Instrumental Enrichment programme which we shall now present. An interesting description of a preliminary study of the way in which a number of his Instrumental Enrichment tasks were adapted and used with child EFL learners from Japan, Italy and Kuwait is provided by Warren (1995).

8.3.2 Instrumental Enrichment

Instrumental Enrichment is essentially a series of some 400 cognitive tasks which have been constructed by Feuerstein and his co-workers by means of the cognitive map to teach the skills of thinking, problem-solving and learning-how-to-learn (Feuerstein *et al.* 1980). In the first instance, these materials were designed to improve the mental and educational functioning of 'retarded performers' who for reasons of cultural difference or deprivation (a term used in a very specific way by Feuerstein) were not able to function adequately within the normal school system. However, an enormous body of research has come to demonstrate the utility of this programme in affecting the thinking and behaviour of a wide range of specific groups including the deaf, the learning disabled, and the intellectually gifted (Burden 1987). It is important to reiterate here the emphasis that Feuerstein also places on the importance of *mediation* in the presentation and use of the Instrumental Enrichment materials. The interested reader is referred to Sharron's *Changing Children's Minds* (1987) for an informative and highly readable account of this work.

Fourteen specific aspects of cognitive functioning form the basis of the Instrumental Enrichment programme. These range from the simple organisation of our thoughts, through orientation in time and space, making comparisons, categorisation, establishing logical relationships, through to inductive and deductive reasoning.

The instruments of the Instrumental Enrichment programme are as follows:

- Organisation of Dots
- Analytic Perception
- Orientation in Space (1)
- Orientation in Space (2)
- Comparisons
- Illustrations
- Family Relations
- Instructions
- Temporal Relations
- Categorisation
- Numerical Progressions
- Representative Stencil Designs
- Syllogisms
- Transitive Relations

Each relates to a different aspect of the cognitive map, and illustrates a developmental model of the thinking process. Thus, we can take, for example, the ability to make comparisons as an essential cognitive skill and work from a simple level of visual discrimination up to the ways in which complex, abstract ideas can be classified. Each instrument contains a series of graded tasks which progress from simple to highly complex. By varying the nature of the content, the modality in which they are presented, the level of abstraction, and the kinds of cognitive operations required for their performance, learners can be helped to move efficiently into more complex modes of thinking.

Using Instrumental Enrichment tasks for language learning

We explained on page 169 that Legutke and Thomas (1991) argue for an educational underpinning to language tasks. Similarly Williams (1991) proposes that tasks for young learners should have an educational rationale. She makes the distinction between *meaningful* and *purposeful* activities. A communicative approach to language teaching has yielded a set of techniques such as information-gap exercises, which entail the use of *meaningful* language, that is, language that conveys meaning. However, such activities do not necessarily contain *purpose* to a child, such as an educational purpose, or enjoyment (such as reading a story), or achieving an end that is personally important to the child; nor do they necessarily belong within a child's world. Purpose, then, entails the concept of personal relevance. Examples of such non-linguistic purposes might be to find out about the world, to find out about people, to express opinions, to study a topic such as how plants grow, to enjoy books, to sing songs, to play a game, to act in a play, or to make a puppet. The concept of educational purpose also incorporates the notion of empowerment discussed earlier in this book. Can activities also empower learners to take control, to become autonomous and to become better language learners?

One such purpose that we shall now explore is the development of thinking skills. In the remainder of this section we shall show how some of Feuerstein's Instrumental Enrichment tasks can be used to teach both language and thinking. Learners are then engaged in using the target language for a purpose, that is, to develop their thinking ability, and it is through this that their language competence develops.

The following task is based on Feuerstein's Orientation in Space instrument. (See Figure 28.) In order to complete this task, the learner is required to take in specific pieces of information, to engage in a number of thinking processes concerned with spatial orientation, and at the same time to express this through appropriate language.

The next task is from Feuerstein's Temporal Relations instrument. (See Figure 29.) In this exercise, learners have to understand the meanings of the propositions expressed in each pair of sentences. They then need to understand the range of possible relationships between the sentences in terms of time sequence, logical consequences, and cause and effect. They also need to understand that each pair of sentences is open to more than one possible interpretation. As it stands, it is already a feasible language activity involving a deep level of comprehension as well as thinking.

There are a number of possible ways in which this task can be extended.

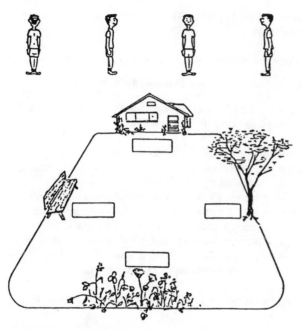

1. Write

   house   tree   bench   flowers

   next to the objects.

2. Draw or paste one of the boys in the centre of the drawing.

3. Complete the sentences using

   ┌─────────────────────┐
   │ on the right of   │
   │ on the left of   │
   │ in front of   │
   │ behind   │
   └─────────────────────┘

   The bench is _____ the boy.

   The tree is _____ the boy.

   The house is _____ the boy.

   The flowers are _____ the boy.

Figure 28   *From Feuerstein's Orientation in Space instrument*

1. In each exercise below, two things are happening. On the line provided next to each exercise, write:

   | M | if there must be a connection between the happenings.

   | C | if there can be a connection between the happenings.

   | N | if there cannot be a connection between the two events and they just happened to occur at the same time.

   ____ 1) I turned on the radio. My doorbell rang.
   ____ 2) The girl fell off the chair. The woman was very frightened.
   ____ 3) The man took an umbrella. It was pouring outside.
   ____ 4) The bus stopped. Many people were waiting at the station.
   ____ 5) A man crossed the street. A car stopped with a screech.
   ____ 6) There was no hot water. The drain was clogged.
   ____ 7) The principal was very angry. A pupil was sent out of the room.
   ____ 8) The water streamed out of the container onto the floor. After a quarter of an hour, the container was empty.

Figure 29   *From Feuerstein's Temporal Relations instrument*

One would be to ask learners to supply suitable linking words to show a connection between the sentences. An example might be

> Join the following sentences together using *and*, *when* or *because* so that there is a connection between them.

It is clear that in most instances there is more than one possibility. Learners could be asked to justify their choice of a particular linking word.

The third example is taken from Feuerstein's Comparisons instrument. (See Figure 30.) This task requires language proficiency at an advanced level. While trying to find one word that expresses what is common, or two words to express what is different, learners are forced to use words as precisely as possible. If this task is completed in groups, each group can be asked to justify their own choice of words. The interaction enables them to explore subtle differences between words and nuances of meaning, for example, the difference between a *feeling* and an *emotion*.

The final example is based on Feuerstein's Temporal Relations instrument (see Figure 31). This activity is designed to help children understand the concept of past, present and future, looking at it from different perspectives: the past, present and future as it relates to them personally and also as it relates to the world. It is important that learners understand these concepts and how such notions relate to themselves if they are to understand the use

Indicate what is common to each pair of words and the differences between them.

	COMMON	DIFFERENCES
Church Factory	_____	_____
Milk Salt	_____	_____
Love Hate	_____	_____
Ugly Wicked	_____	_____

Figure 30   *From Feuerstein's Comparisons instrument*

of tenses to express these concepts. The task can be completed individually, before learners share their ideas in groups or as a whole class. This activity can also be used successfully with adults, as a means of sharing personal histories, developing active listening, and to explore the notion of time, its relevance to them, and its significance in different cultures.

Although in this section we have been focussing narrowly on a cognitive perspective, it is important to emphasise that such an approach must be viewed within an interactionist framework. Thus, it is vital that teachers mediate these tasks in appropriate ways, that the nature of the interactions that occur are conducive to learning, and that a supportive environment exists. In order to draw some of these threads together, we shall conclude this chapter with a reconsideration of the educational value of tasks.

8.4   An educational perspective on tasks

In the first section of this chapter we discussed briefly some aspects of language learning tasks. In the second section we considered a cognitive approach to tasks and discussed how we could use some tasks from Feuerstein's Instrumental Enrichment programme to teach a foreign language.

In this concluding section, we shall look at tasks from an educational perspective. The first point we wish to emphasise is that tasks can be seen as a manifestation or embodiment of the theories of learning subscribed to by teachers and their perceptions of the whole spectrum of the teaching-learning process. Teachers will select tasks which reflect their beliefs about

PAST–PRESENT–FUTURE

Things that have already happened are _____ .

Things that will happen are _____ .

Things that are happening now are _____ .

present		future
	past	

The year 2020 belongs to the _____ .

The year 1960 belongs to the _____ .

The year _____ belongs to the present.

MY OWN PAST, PRESENT AND FUTURE

The age of 5 is _____ .

The age of 35 is _____ .

My present age is _____ .

These things belong to my past:
  birth
  being a baby

_____

_____

_____

_____

These things belong to my present:
  going to school

_____

_____

_____

_____

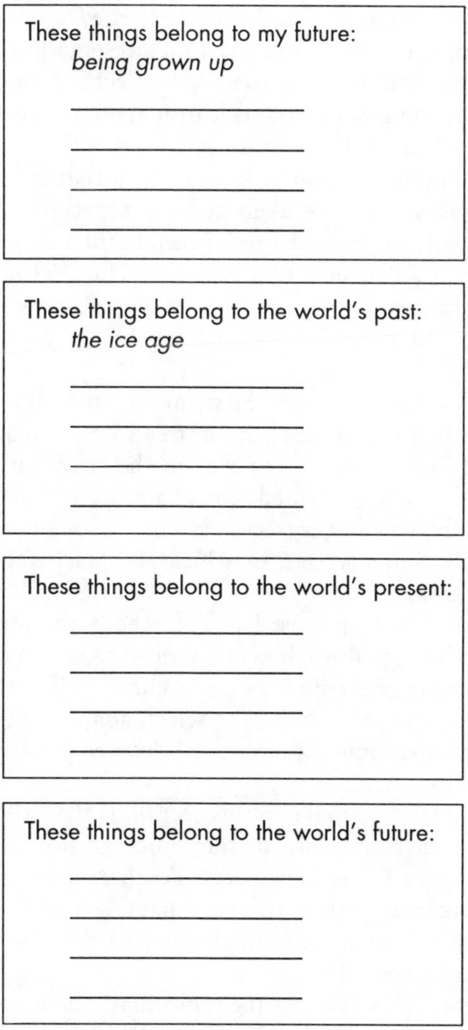

These things belong to my future:
  being grown up

_____

_____

_____

_____

These things belong to the world's past:
  the ice age

_____

_____

_____

_____

These things belong to the world's present:

_____

_____

_____

_____

These things belong to the world's future:

_____

_____

_____

_____

Figure 31   *Past, present and future (from Feuerstein's Temporal Relations instrument)*

teaching and learning, including beliefs about such aspects as co-operation or competition, learners' roles, learning style, independence, level of challenge and so on. So, if a teacher believes that language is learned through meaningful interaction in that language, then the tasks selected are likely to reflect this belief. If, on the other hand, the teacher believes, either implicitly or explicitly, that learning is best facilitated by the presentation and practice of pre-selected items, then the activities used will reflect this view. Similarly, if a teacher believes that competition assists learning, then the tasks will tend to have a competitive element; if rewards are considered to be important, then teachers may well build this into tasks; if it is felt that individual needs should be met, then tasks are more likely to be tailored to individuals; if teachers believe that learners should be self-directed, then they are likely to find tasks which contain an element of autonomy. Thus, we see tasks as a vehicle for the embodiment of the teacher's, task designer's or textbook writer's attitudes and philosophies, and as pivotal in conveying these attitudes to learners.

This gives rise to two further issues. First, many tasks are designed by coursebook writers to be used by teachers. In this case the teacher's views will not be embodied in the task design, but in the selection, the way in which the activity is actually presented (for example, whether it is done in groups or individually, whether correct answers are sought, and whether creativity is permitted), and the way in which the teacher mediates the various aspects of the task.

Second, we have already emphasised in Chapter 3 the importance of teachers making their views, philosophies and deeply ingrained beliefs about education explicit. Within the context of the current discussion, this is important in developing teachers' abilities to select, adapt and present tasks that are in keeping with their philosophies in an educated and well-informed way.

The second point we wish to make in this section is that we believe that the ways in which teachers mediate in their presentation of tasks is a crucial aspect of any debate on learning tasks. Teachers may have access to innovative activities, but present them in a way that fails to generate feelings of confidence, competence, control, individuality, or the other aspects of mediation discussed in Chapter 4.

The third point is the importance of the sense that the learners make of the activities or experiences provided for them. We have seen from our discussion of constructivism in Chapter 2 that learners will construct their own meaning from, or make their own sense of the tasks with which they are presented. Not only will the meanings they construct differ, but their emotional responses will also vary. The ways in which learners respond to the tasks with which they are presented provide teachers with vital information as to how to proceed in future learning activities. Learner response can help the teacher to identify their needs, which cognitive aspects need developing, and what forms of mediation are required.

Thus, we see tasks as pivotal in the interaction between teachers and learners. They provide one of many routes through which teachers and learners convey attitudes and messages about the learning process to each other, as well as providing a vehicle within which learning takes place. Much of the work on tasks in foreign language teaching has focussed on the design of good learning tasks, drawing on second language acquisition research and theory. However, of equal importance is a consideration of the way in which these tasks are presented, mediated, carried out and evaluated. Even the most innovative and well-designed tasks can be used in a range of different ways. A coursebook of communicative tasks, if used by a teacher who believes that language is learned best as individual grammar items, will give rise to a series of structurally based lessons. Conversely, a more structured task can be interpreted by a teacher in a communicative way. The important message for coursebook designers or those responsible for syllabus design is that whatever is specified in the book or syllabus will be interpreted in a variety of ways depending on the beliefs that both teachers and learners bring to them.

Having looked at the way in which learners and teachers interact through tasks, in the next chapter we turn to the fourth component of the model, the *context* within which these interactions take place.

9 The learning context

9.1 Why study learning environments?

Learning never takes place in a vacuum. Whether one adopts a Piagetian perspective, which conceives of the developing child individually exploring his or her environment, or the approach we have strongly advocated in this book that right from birth learning is the result of social interactions, it always occurs within a particular context. Or rather, we would argue, learning occurs within a variety of often overlapping contexts, some of which are more conducive to the process of cognitive, affective, moral and social development than others.

The importance of the appropriate environmental conditions for learning to take place cannot be underestimated. The cognitive psychologist, Robert Sternberg, has argued convincingly that we cannot judge the intellectual quality of any behavioural act outside of the context in which it occurs. What may be deemed intelligent at one time and place will by no means necessarily be the case at another (Sternberg 1984). Thus, teaching a child how to understand the demands and often subtle nuances of different social and cultural contexts can be seen as helping that child to act intelligently. At the same time, by providing learners with the kind of learning environments which enable them to learn how to learn and to develop as fully integrated individuals, we can help to foster such intelligent behaviour. This is equally true of non-intellectual influences within the environment and their effects upon emotional development (Greenhalgh 1994).

An understanding of the ways in which aspects of the environment affect learning is particularly important for language teachers and learners. At the broadest level, it is clear that national and cultural differences have a profound influence upon the development of a language and the way in which it is used. One of the primary functions of a language is to describe our environment so that we can form an image of ourselves in relation to it. The better we can come to understand the cultural context which gives rise to the language we are trying to learn, the more likely we are to come to understand the essential differences between the way in which that language is used and our own.

At another level, a country's educational system will affect the learning environment. There are clearly vast differences between the avowed aims of the educational systems of such countries as China, Japan, the UK and the USA. Even within such countries there is not necessarily a universally recognised set of educational policies about how such aims should be achieved. At the school level, the ethos that exists within a school will affect the type of learning that goes on in that school. What makes a successful school must, therefore, be judged in terms of the expressed educational aims of that school within the broader national and cultural context of the country's educational system.

At an even more basic level, the immediate physical environment of the classroom and the nature of the personal interactions which occur within it will have a profound influence upon whether, what and how any individual learns a language. As Rutter tells us, many children will spend some 15,000 hours in classrooms during their school career (Rutter *et al.* 1979). We shall focus particularly in this chapter on the personal interactions that give rise to a particular learning *ethos* or *climate*. More specifically, we shall be looking closely at the ways in which the members of any class or learning group interpret those interactions and construe them as facilitative or otherwise. First, however, we shall examine some of the theoretical perspectives that have been brought to bear on this area and some of the attempts that have been made to assess the quality of learning environments.

9.2   Ecological perspectives

One helpful way in which some psychological researchers and practitioners have made sense of the various forms of influence exerted by different aspects of the learning environment is by applying what has come to be known as an *ecological* perspective. This term emanates from the work of the social and clinical psychologist Uri Bronfenbrenner. In order to understand properly any person's development, Bronfenbrenner (1979) argues that we need to take into account their ecology, i.e. the environmental systems surrounding them. At the closest level there is the *microsystem*, which contains the developing child's more important relationships with parents, teachers, siblings and peers. Next comes the *mesosystem* within which are contained a broader range of interactions of significant people in the developing child's life, e.g. home-school relationships. At one level further removed is the *ecosystem* where the interactions of others will have an indirect rather than a direct effect on the learner. An example here might be the nature of a teacher's personal relationships outside school or the kind of ethos that exists within a school. Finally, there is the *macrosystem*, which involves the whole culture of the society in which people live. This will affect

189

learning in a number of possible ways, e.g. formally, by the imposition of a national curriculum, or informally by often subtle cultural customs and mores.

A variation on the ecological perspective which has been particularly influential in its effect on school psychology is the *systems* approach (Molnar and Lindquist 1989; Kaiser 1993). No one particular theorist dominates this approach to learning and even the term 'systems' itself is open to a variety of interpretations (see Burden 1981 for a full discussion of alternative definitions of 'systems'). However, there are some key elements which all advocates of the systems approach have in common.

Each individual is viewed as an inseparable part of a social system. Sometimes these systems have clearly defined boundaries, e.g. schools, classroom groups, families. However, these boundaries are often permeable, so systems are constantly changing but also resistant to change. To understand why people are more or less successful at learning within a particular system such as a school, it is necessary to consider how the system works as a whole and the kind of influence that systemic factors bring to bear on different individuals. The way in which schools function in Japan is likely to be very different from how they function in Namibia or in the USA. The interactions between teachers and learners are likely to vary considerably both between and within each of these countries, and thereby to give rise to wide variations in kinds of learning processes and outcomes.

It must be emphasised that the interactive process within systems is both dynamic and multifaceted. Thus, when something goes wrong within the system, it should not be seen as the fault of any individual, but a lack of balance in the system. Learning failure should, therefore, be seen in terms of a disparity between what the individual brings to the learning situation and the demands or expectations of the environment (Apter 1978).

In taking a systems approach to learning, an effort is made to synthesise information from different aspects of social situations (physical, social, psychological and cultural). An underlying assumption is that by gathering such information from a number of different sources it should be possible to facilitate a 'congruent' environment within which the learning of all those involved can be optimised.

What is of particular significance to us here is that ecological or systems approaches emphasise the importance of taking into account the total environment of the learner if we are to explain adequately how and why people learn. They also emphasise the dynamic, interactive nature of all the variables involved and argue strongly against taking a simple linear view of cause and effect.

Thus, it is argued that learning must be viewed holistically with as much emphasis being placed on relationships and interactions as on the participants and the content of what is learned. The whole learning process, therefore, becomes more than merely the sum of its parts (Plas 1986).

9.3   Environmental references

There is a growing body of evidence to show that different individuals, and probably also groups of individuals, find certain environmental conditions more conducive to learning than others. Somewhat inexplicably many of these studies are grouped under the heading of *learning styles*. This really is a misnomer because the studies have very little if anything to do with the person's style of learning and much more to do with preferred conditions for learning.

Thus, the most widely used assessment instrument in this area, Dunn *et al.*'s *Learning Style Inventory* (LSI), defines learning style in terms of four pervasive learning conditions and 22 different elements. The four learning conditions are identified as (a) *environmental* (noise, temperature, lighting, etc.), (b) *emotional* (motivation, persistence, conformity, etc.), (c) *sociological* (preference for learning alone or with others), and (d) *physiological* (time of day preference for learning, need for food intake, etc.) (Dunn, Dunn and Price 1986). It seems highly likely that individual preferences are strongly linked to cultural background (Griggs and Dunn 1989; Dunn, Baudy and Klavas 1989), and that taking this into account when trying to provide the best possible conditions for learning could well help to improve both learning achievement and attitudes.

A recent study of middle-school learners from differing ethnic backgrounds (Caucasian, African-American, Hispanic and Asian) found significant differences between groups on a number of variables with respect to learning preferences (Hickson *et al.* 1994). Hispanic and Asian learners were found to prefer more formally structured lessons in comparison with Caucasian and African-American learners. African-American and Hispanic learners both expressed a strong preference for food intake whilst learning in contrast to the Caucasian and Asian learners. As far as time of day was concerned, Asian and Hispanic learners expressed a preference for learning during the late morning. The African-American and Hispanic learners preferred to have sound present while they were learning, but Asian and Caucasian learners showed a preference for a quiet learning environment. The influence of others was demonstrated by the fact that Asian and Hispanic learners were greatly influenced by their parents' opinions whilst both Hispanic and African-American learners found that they worked better in the presence of an authority figure. The Asian learners registered as most responsible and conforming. Differences were also found between the groups with regard to their preferences for auditory (lecture-type) input and visual recall strategies, and to their kinesthetic (hands-on experience) involvement.

By making themselves aware of such cultural and individual differences, language teachers should be able to interact more profitably with their learners, who are frequently from a different cultural background to them. There is no need to go through the lengthy process of administering and scoring formalised tests, but a discussion with learners about whether they consider that they work better at certain times of day, whether they prefer structured or less structured environments, to work alone, in pairs or in groups and what external figures influence their motivation to learn is likely to produce fascinating and helpful information. Although it may not be possible to produce conditions that meet every individual's preferences, what it should do is to encourage a greater flexibility in teaching and classroom organisation. It should also make it clear that some learner behaviour previously interpreted as rude or disruptive may be no more than a reflection of cultural difference.

A related but somewhat different approach is taken by Pielstick (1988), who refers to four *domains* of learning environment – *physical, social, instructional* and *psychological*. With regard to the physical domain, Pielstick concludes from his overview of research that the physical aspects of the classroom learning environment are numerous and complex. Such factors as temperature, ventilation, light intensity and glare, noise level and acoustics all can play a significant contributory part in facilitating or hindering learning. Pielstick offers a useful checklist to aid in monitoring the environment (1988:121). It is important to emphasise at this point that it is the learners' perceptions and interpretations of their environments that will affect their learning rather than the actual physical characteristics of those environments. What to one group may appear to be physical barriers to learning (overheating, overcrowding, lack of resources, etc.) may be accepted as the norm by others.

9.4 Classroom structure

The term *classroom structure* has come to be used in a particular way by some researchers in this field. Here the emphasis has been upon the ways in which learning experiences have been organised and whether one form of organisation is necessarily any better than another. The main debate has been on whether learners learn better in *competitive, co-operative* or *individualistic* environments.

One currently available, structured method of identifying teacher, learner and parental preferences for different kinds of classroom structures emanates from Australia. *Learning Preference Scales* (Owens and Barnes 1992) are easy to read, complete and score, and, though as yet not widely used, they are beginning to provide interesting data on differences between learning structure preferences of males and females, and junior and secondary teachers (Owens 1983, 1985).

An excellent overview and analysis of this debate is provided by Carole Ames (1984), who suggests that as well as asking which kind of structure leads to greater achievement, we should also be investigating the meaning of success and failure to learners within different kinds of structures. An analysis of what is a common form of school and classroom organisation, one which is largely based on competitive reward structures, makes it clear that competition is only helpful to those who do well. The success of one person or group must always work to the detriment of the others, a situation which is exacerbated if rewards are only given for right answers. As Ames points out, this inevitably leads to a situation where learners become fearful of making mistakes and fail to see any value in doing so, a state which is not conducive to learning a language where learners need to feel able to try to communicate in the language. A further significant outcome in terms of learner attributions is that in competitive settings success and failure tend to be attributed to greater or lesser ability and self-esteem becomes dependent upon one's perception of one's own ability.

Within individualised or master-based structures where rewards are based on self-improvement, the emphasis is not on comparing oneself with others, but instead on comparing one's present level of performance with previous achievements (Covington and Beery 1976). Because in such settings learner achievements are independent of each other, everyone has an equal opportunity of gaining a reward of some kind. In such circumstances, success or failure is more likely to be attributed to effort. Another benefit of individualised learning is that it makes it possible to concentrate upon the learning process and to identify personal strategies that are likely to lead to successful learning of the language.

Within co-operative structures the learners become dependent upon each other in order to achieve success. Ways of organising groupwork in class vary enormously, but are generally based upon the five key principles of *positive interdependence, individual accountability, face-to-face positive interaction*, the development of *social skills*, and regular *group processing* (Johnson and Johnson 1989). Research appears to show that the group outcome of any task or activity has an effect upon individuals' perceptions of their own ability and their feelings of satisfaction and self-esteem. Group success can help to improve an individual's poor self-esteem, but equally, group failure can modify the positive self-perceptions of those who perform well individually. If you are a member of an unsuccessful group, you tend to feel less satisfied, even though you personally may have performed well. However, the strength of this effect is likely to be tempered by the strength of any individual's self-concept.

Ames goes on to suggest that competitive structures promote an egoistic or social comparison orientation in learners. Co-operative structures, on the other hand, elicit a moral orientation, that is, they motivate learners on the basis of an obligation to the rest of the group to try hard. Individualistic structures can be viewed as providing a form of self-competition, but differ from competitive structures in that they are essentially goal oriented and involve the development of self-awareness.

The importance of making such an analysis of the underlying assumptions behind the different structures is that it sheds light on long-term motivational and attributional consequences for learners. Organising learners into ability groupings in a language class or arranging a competitive learning atmosphere is likely to be effective in enabling some learners to pass examinations and achieve well. However, it will have the opposite effect on other learners and may also have negative long-term consequences for the high achievers. Co-operative groupwork, which is a popular way of working in language classes to allow learners to communicate, is likely to produce more positive general achievements across a broad range of learners but will not necessarily produce autonomous, self-directed learners. Individualised, 'mastery' learning structures which are used, for example, in self-access centres require a much greater knowledge and understanding by the teacher of every learner. A far greater amount of preparation and monitoring is required by the teacher, though learners should gradually take on both goal-setting and monitoring functions for themselves. A classroom which was run on totally individualised lines, however, would miss out on important aspects of social interaction and communication.

All three approaches have been employed effectively by language teachers. We would argue, however, that no one approach can ever be fully effective on its own. Each learner is an individual who must be helped to find his or her own way to become autonomous. Learners are also members of a social world and will need to be given opportunities to work co-operatively with others in order to be successful in such a world. At the same time, an element of healthy competition with oneself and between groups can be highly motivating in the short-term and can provide added zest to any classroom. The secret, therefore, must surely be to find ways of providing a flexible structure in the language classroom which effectively incorporates all three forms of organisation.

9.5   Group processes

It is clear that for a co-operative environment to be established, it is important to look into the nature of the interaction and processes that occur within groups of learners.

In an investigation into teachers' concerns in the classroom, Jill Hadfield and Angi Malderez (Hadfield 1992) found that teachers in language schools in the UK were more concerned about the atmosphere in the classroom and the chemistry of the group than problems of how to teach the language. Similarly, when they asked language learners to comment on their experience of learning in Britain they found that affective factors and group dynamics were an important concern. Hadfield argues:

> It seems to me that very little material exists to offer suggestions for practical things a teacher can do to improve relations and atmosphere within a group.
>
> (1992:10)

In language classrooms where pairwork and groupwork are used, it is particularly important to build up a co-operative group atmosphere both to enhance language learning and to develop the self-image and motivation of the group members.

Hadfield lists what she sees as characteristics of a successful group, some of which are listed below:

- Members have a definite sense of themselves as a group.
- There is a positive, supportive atmosphere: members have a positive self-image which is reinforced by the group, so that they feel secure enough to express their individuality.
- Members of the group listen to each other and take turns.
- The group is tolerant of all its members; members feel secure and accepted.
- Members co-operate in the performance of tasks and are able to work together productively.
- The members of the group trust each other.
- Group members are able to empathise with each other and understand each other's points of view even if they do not share them.

She then suggests a number of ways in which teachers can develop a supportive and co-operative group atmosphere.

9.6 Classroom climate

A fascinating, but still too little known literature on learners' and teachers' perceptions of classroom environments has grown up over the past twenty-five years, stimulated by Phillip Jackson's classic (1968) text, *Life in Class-rooms*. Most of the early work in this area was carried out in the USA under the direction, on the one hand, of Rudolf Moos, a psychiatrist, and, on the other, of Herbert Walberg, a social psychologist. Both were interested in the study of learning environments in the broadest sense, and each was instrumental in developing a variety of techniques for assessing such environments by obtaining the participants' perceptions.

An early attempt to examine the psycho-social environment of American junior high and high school classes by means of the participants' perceptions was the Classroom Environment Scale (Moos and Trickett 1974). The underlying premise of this scale was that classrooms are dynamic social systems. In contrast to more objective observer-based studies, the focus of this scale was on the sense that participants made of what happened in their classes rather than on the frequency, or even the content, of events.

Three domains were examined by the Classroom Environment Scale – *relationships*, which included feelings of involvement, affiliation and teacher support, *goal orientation*, which included task orientation and competitive-ness, and *aspects of system maintenance and change*, such as order and organisation, rule clarity, teacher control and innovation. The CES has been used extensively by Moos and others to provide helpful data on what kind of perceived classroom structures correspond best with different kinds of learning outcomes, even though it is long (90 items), somewhat unwieldy and time-consuming to administer, score and interpret. One intriguing finding arising out of Moos' work is that there is unlikely to be any such thing as an 'optimum' classroom environment. Different kinds of classroom organisation tend to give rise to different kinds of learning outcomes. Thus, the greatest all-round gains are likely to be made in reading and maths in classrooms that participants feel to be warm, task-oriented and systematic and orderly. However, greater willingness to work independently and better problem-solving skills are displayed in flexible classroom settings that provide more exploratory materials and allow more individual freedom. Comparisons of 'democratic' and 'formal' classroom environments, have tended to reveal that the former produce learners who are more satisfied and self-reliant and show more positive interpersonal relationships, while learners in formal classrooms usually score higher on measures of vocabulary, reading and mathematics achievement.

Four main conclusions arise out of these early studies:

- Classes oriented towards innovation and building relationships help to create learner satisfaction and interest in the subject matter. They enhance social and personal growth, but do less well in facilitating traditional achievement scores.

- Classes which emphasise task achievement at the expense of warmth often do foster high achievement, but fare far less well in facilitating learner interest, morale or creativity.

- Classes that are kept rigidly under the teacher's control are more likely to lead to dissatisfaction and alienation and do not facilitate personal, social or academic growth.

- The best results are likely to occur when there is a combination of warm and supportive relationships, an emphasis on specific academic tasks and accomplishments and a reasonably clear, orderly and well structured milieu.

Herbert Walberg is a contemporary of Moos who developed his own Learning Environment Inventory (LEI) quite independently as part of the evaluation of the Harvard Physics Project (Walberg 1968). Three principal domains – *instruction*, *aptitude* and *environment* – were identified as playing an interactive part in learning. The LEI consists of fifteen different scales, measuring such aspects of classroom organisation as cohesiveness, favouritism, democracy and competitiveness. Each scale is represented by seven items, thereby making the whole questionnaire extremely lengthy. However, a large number of studies have indicated that responses to the LEI can be effective in predicting learner achievement and positive attitudes towards science (Fraser 1989).

Both the CES and LEI scales are too lengthy and time-consuming to lend themselves to regular use by teachers, but the value of taking this kind of approach to examining classroom practice has been clearly demonstrated. A much more manageable set of scales was subsequently developed by the Australian science educator, Barry Fraser, who also took into account the conceptual and literacy level of younger and less able learners. Fraser (1986, 1989) has produced two questionnaires which can easily be applied, scored and interpreted by both junior and secondary school teachers. The My Class Inventory (MCI) consists of twenty-five easy-to-read items requiring yes/no answers. The answers are designed to assess five interrelated aspects of classroom environment – *satisfaction*, *friction*, *competitiveness*, *difficulty* and *cohesiveness*. Although the MCI has not as yet been widely used, recent research in Singapore has demonstrated that mathematics classes typified by satisfaction and cohesiveness are much more likely to produce positive attitudes and improved learning in that subject.

Fraser's other main scale, the Individualised Classroom Environment Questionnaire (ICEQ) has now been employed in a number of reported studies (Fraser 1986; Burden and Hornby 1988), mainly to investigate the effects of individualised or open classroom structures on learners' attitudes towards learning different subjects. The five domains of this particular scale which are investigated by a relatively brief questionnaire are – *personalisation, participation, independence, investigation* and *differentiation*.

Where Fraser differs from other researchers in this field is in his recognition that there might be a big gap between how an individual learner perceives his or her classroom to be organised and how he or she would like it to be. Fraser, therefore, produced both an *actual* and *preferred* version of his scale in order to make such a comparison possible. He also produced both teacher and learner versions so that further comparisons could be made between teachers' and learners' perceptions.

This particular aspect of Fraser's work is what lifts it from the realm of more conventional attitude studies onto a rather more complex conceptual level. What we have in any classroom is a multitude of perceptions: all the participants, teacher and learners, perceive what is happening in their own particular way. They also have an image of how they would like things to be, which more or less matches their perceptions of how things are. The greater the degree of concordance between one's *ideal* classroom and the *actual* classroom within which one finds oneself, the greater the degree of satisfaction there is likely to be. This sense of satisfaction is thereby likely also to increase one's liking for a subject and, by association, one's success at it. Alternatively, dissatisfaction and friction are likely to arise when there is a mismatch between how one would like things to be and how they actually appear to be, or if there is lack of agreement between teachers' perceptions and those of their learners.

Burden and Fraser (1993) report a study in which a grade 6 class demonstrated by means of the ICEQ considerable dissatisfaction with the way in which their lessons were organised. Interestingly, the teacher herself also expressed significant differences between her actual classroom practice and how she would like things to be. However, she was concerned that if she relaxed her strict, negative stance, the learners would take advantage of her. The ICEQ results were used as the basis for negotiation between the teacher and her learners. They agreed not to misbehave if she allowed them a greater degree of participation and individualised investigatory work. The teacher agreed also to provide more positive feedback and to personalise more her interactions with her learners. Six months later it was found that a more positive work attitude was being demonstrated in that class and that both the learners and the teacher were much more satisfied with its organisational structure.

In another study, a humanities teacher expressed her concern that she was too formal and didactic in her teaching style. She felt that she should be more open-ended in her verbal interactions and more flexible in her classroom organisation. However, her class indicated by means of their responses to the ICEQ that they did not agree with her. They knew that important examinations were forthcoming and considered, as a whole, that the teacher's interactive style was just right for preparing them optimally for these. Thus, we can see the importance of our perceptions of reality and how far they correspond between the participants in any learning enterprise.

Unfortunately, little of this work has yet been carried out in language classes, although in one informal study we found that prospective language teachers considered their own most helpful teachers to have operated in classrooms which were organised in an open manner. Exciting possibilities are provided for language teachers to explore more deeply the learning climate of their classrooms by means of the scales described here and by means of a slightly different approach to which we shall now turn.

9.7   Teacher behaviour as part of the learning environment

A somewhat different, but related aspect of the classroom environment which undoubtedly influences learners' learning outcomes is their interpretation of interpersonal teacher behaviour. The management of learners' learning, for example, is clearly linked to teachers' ability to set an appropriate tone and gain learner respect and co-operation in class. This has led many researchers into teacher effectiveness to emphasise that the creation and maintenance of a positive classroom climate is essential in producing optimum learning (Brophy and Good 1986; Doyle 1986).

A group of researchers in the Netherlands have made the helpful distinction between the *instructional-methodological* aspect of teacher behaviour, such as the selection of content and materials, methods, strategies and forms of assessment, and the *interpersonal* aspect which is social and emotional, and which concerns the creation and maintenance of a positive and warm classroom atmosphere conducive to learning (Wubbels, Creton and Hoomayers 1992).

By making this distinction and pointing out that teacher behaviour when viewed in this way is not only different from teacher personality, but also enables us to study the interactional and mutually influencing relationship between teachers and learners, Wubbels and his colleagues were able to embark on a series of studies into the association between learners' learning outcomes and their perceptions of their teachers' interpersonal behaviour (Wubbels, Brekelmans and Hermans 1987; Wubbels and Levy 1993).

In order to provide an instrument to assess teacher-learner relationships, Wubbels and his colleagues developed and validated a questionnaire based upon a model of interpersonal behaviour within a framework provided by systems communication theory. The Questionnaire on Teacher Interaction (QTI) examines eight teacher behaviour dimensions: Leadership, Helping/Friendly, Understanding, Student Responsibility/Freedom, Uncertain, Dissatisfied, Admonishing and Strict Behaviour.

199

Like similar questionnaires in this tradition, the QTI has parallel *Actual* and *Preferred* forms and separate versions for teachers and learners. Studies employing this approach in the Netherlands, the USA and Australia have found that interpersonal teacher behaviour is an important contributor to learner cognitive and affective outcomes. Teachers who demonstrated more leadership, as well as friendly and understanding behaviours in their interactions with learners were found to foster greater learner achievement and more positive attitudes towards their subjects. Teachers who showed more uncertain, dissatisfied and admonishing behaviour produced the reverse effect (Wubbels and Levy 1991; Wubbels 1993).

9.8 Individual perceptions of environments

What, then, can we say about language learning environments? We feel confident that the point has been made strongly here and elsewhere (Rutter *et al.* 1979; Mortimore *et al.* 1987; Galton *et al.* 1980; Good and Brophy 1986) that learning is greatly influenced by the environment in which it occurs. Where we differ, however, from most of the aforementioned writers is in our emphasis upon the *indirect* rather than the *direct* nature of this association. By this we mean that it is the way in which the participants in the teaching-learning process *make sense* of that process and of the environment in which it occurs which exerts the major influence on the learning outcomes.

A growing body of research has enabled us to identify factors within the physical environment, aspects of the social organisation and forms of teacher behaviour which seem most likely to enhance the learning climate of classrooms. However, it is the meaning that teachers and learners attribute to those factors and whether or not they construe them as helpful that makes the real difference. Quantitative research studies tend to indicate that we can make some fairly confident general predictions in this respect, but we can never take this for granted with regard to any individual learner.

The approach taken by Fraser, Wubbels and their co-workers in seeking ways of bringing together differing perspectives from both between and within learners and teachers, offers a potentially very useful way forward. However, there are many constructivists who would consider that even the creative use of structured questionnaires imposes unreal constraints upon individuals' examination of their personal constructions of reality.

Probably the most widely used method of tapping into people's personal constructs is George Kelly's Repertory Grid Technique (Beail 1985). Of particular interest and potential value to those interested in exploring the ways in which individuals make sense of social structures and organisational functioning, in the classroom and elsewhere, is the *personal resources dependency grid* (Davis 1985:319–32). This technique makes it possible to identify situations which individuals find problematical and the personal and social resources that they can call upon in dealing with those situations. As yet such techniques have mainly been used as aids to therapy but are by no means necessarily confined to such settings. Thomas and Harri-Augstein see the Repertory Grid as a means of carrying out a 'learning conversation' and have applied it to a wide variety of situations such as helping people to become more effective managers, to improve their teaching performance, to restructure the learning resources in a school, to obtain higher exam results, to explore personal change and to evaluate the effects of specific course work. Interested readers are referred to these authors' two books which describe in comprehensive detail their approach to constructing learning conversations (Thomas and Harri-Augstein 1985; Harri-Augstein and Thomas 1991).

A fascinating alternative is offered by Tobin (1991) who suggests that individuals often express their personal constructs in terms of *metaphors*. If our predominant metaphor for the classroom is 'the workplace', our expectations of what should take place there will be very different from those related to a 'prison' or a 'social club'. If a teacher employs the first metaphor but some of her learners' conceptions are more in line with the second or third metaphors, then a mismatch of expectations will undoubtedly occur. Tobin points out that most educators see the curriculum in terms of a transportable text or set of materials, which gives rise to certain expectations about what constitutes appropriate teaching and learning. If, on the other hand, the curriculum is construed as the entire set of learning experiences that are inextricably linked with the culture in which that learning occurs, or, in simple terms, 'everything that goes on around here', then a totally different set of expectations becomes possible.

Tobin has used the notion of metaphor in his work in getting teachers to change the way in which they organise their classrooms from traditional knowledge-transmission and role learning environments to places emphasising learning with understanding. A particular guiding force in this respect has been Habermas' (1972) theory of *knowledge-constitutive interests*. In line with this theory, teachers can be construed as representing one of three cognitive interests, the *technical*, where the basic orientation is toward control and management, the *practical*, where the basic orientation is toward understanding arising out of a consensual interpretation of meaning, and the *emancipatory*, where the orientation is toward empower-ment. Jakobowski and Tobin (1991) describe how teachers who work within Habermas' technical domain can be helped to change their orien-tation towards the practical and emancipatory by getting them to reflect on their metaphors and changing them from seeing themselves as dispensers and controllers of knowledge to facilitators. This in turn facilitates changes in the nature of their learning environments.

From a constructivist perspective, therefore, a learning environment is something a learner experiences in the process of learning. It can be seen as having personal and social components in that it is constructed out of the learner's own previous experiences, beliefs and values together with a shared set of beliefs, metaphors and meanings.

9.9   Conclusion

In this chapter we have discussed how any learning is always affected by the environment in which it takes place. The impact of the context on learning a language is considerable, both at the macro level of the culture in which the learning takes place or the educational system, and at the narrower level of the school or classroom ethos. By giving time and thought to providing learners with an environment that enhances motivation, and that considers learners' emotional, psychological and sociological preferences, teachers can greatly enhance the learning of a language. It is also clear that whether classrooms are organised according to individualised, competitive or co-operative principles will also have a substantial impact on the learning that occurs.

An important aspect of any investigation into classroom environment is the perceptions that learners have of the climate that prevails in their classroom, which frequently differ from the perceptions of their teachers. It is also important to consider the sense that learners make of the teacher-learner interactions that occur in the classroom.

Language classrooms in particular need to be places where learners are encouraged to use the new language to communicate, to try out new ways of expressing meanings, to negotiate, to make mistakes without fear, and to learn to learn from successes and failures. Emotionally, a suitable environment for language learning should be one that enhances the trust needed to communicate and which enhances confidence and self-esteem.

We have, however, argued that each individual will construct their own sense of the environment in which the language is learned, making it difficult to make any very sweeping statements about suitable contexts for learning. Even so, it would seem appropriate to suggest that asking learners about their own perceptions and discussing these with them must go a long way towards raising a teacher's awareness of the type of environment his or her learners would find most conducive for learning a language.

10   Putting it all together

We began this book with an historical overview of various ways in which psychology has been applied to education, particularly with regard to pedagogy. We emphasised what we saw as the need for a coherent theoretical framework within which the potentially valuable contributions of different theorists could be drawn together for the benefit of the practising language teacher. We selected one particular perspective, that of social interactionism, which we felt would best enable us to achieve this aim. Within the social interactionist framework we have also taken an essentially constructivist approach to learning. Our focus throughout has been on the sense that individuals make of the process of learning, within a social context.

In Chapter 2 we identified what we consider to be four key elements of this process: the learner, the teacher, the task and the context, and presented a model of the way in which these elements interact with each other in a dynamic way. In order to bring a clear system to the book, we then focussed on each of these in turn; however, our basic message is that no one aspect can be considered completely in isolation from the others.

Throughout the book we have returned several times to the same point, focussing on the learners' quest to make sense of their worlds and their learning situations. In order to do this, learners bring certain personal attributes to the learning situation. They come with particular feelings, attitudes and views of themselves in the world and as learners. They also possess a certain motivation which will incline them to make specific choices within the situation. In addition, they select certain strategies to use to enable them to learn in ways that are personal to them. These different aspects of *learners* were the focus of Chapters 5, 6 and 7.

In the learning context, learners meet other significant people: their teachers and their peers, all of whom will exert an influence on the choices they make about learning and the ways in which they view themselves. These teachers will also possess particular views, beliefs and attitudes, which will determine their own actions, and which in turn will have an influence on the actions of their learners. In Chapters 3 and 4 we focussed on the *teacher*. Chapter 3 considered the impact of teachers' attitudes and beliefs, while in Chapter 4 we presented a theory of mediation to account for the different ways in which teachers can enhance learning.

Teachers will, in addition, select certain types of tasks which they will present to their learners in particular ways that reflect their beliefs and values; but they are also interpreted by learners in ways that are personal to them. Thus in Chapter 8 *tasks* are seen as the interface between teachers and learners.

This in turn takes place within a particular context consisting of several variables, all of which affect the learning that takes place and the inter-actions that occur within the learning situation. The importance of the learning *context* is considered in Chapter 9.

We have throughout emphasised the complex and dynamic nature of the interactions between these separate elements. We shall now attempt to summarise some of the main points made in this book by presenting ten basic propositions that we consider to be crucial for language teachers.

1 There is a difference between learning and education

Our first proposition is one in which we have a strong belief, and one that underpins much of what this book is all about. This statement implies that in order to be of value, a learning experience should contribute to a person's whole education as well as to their learning of an aspect of the language. This is true whether the experience is an information-gap task, telling a story, acting out a situation, working out how a particular language form operates or discriminating between minimal pairs in pronunciation. In the first example, the information-gap task could be related to a topic that is relevant to the learners' lives, could help develop their co-operative skills (itself a life-skill), and could require a level of thinking that stretches them intellectually. In the second example, the story could provide an interesting trigger for discussion of life-issues, and could lead to a consideration of individuals' own viewpoints.

An important aspect of an educative experience is that the learners perceive the value of the task for themselves and their own development. Thus mediation plays a crucial role in helping individuals to see the signifi-cance to them of what it is they are required to do, as well as the value of the experience beyond the here and now.

There is possibly no situation in which the necessity of an educational value for learning experiences is so apparent as in schools. Too often children in schools are faced with a barrage of isolated learning tasks which they have no wish to do, cannot see the value of to them personally, and which do not to them add up to a coherent whole.

However, we would maintain that the same applies to adult learning. It could be argued by many teachers that the role of language schools providing courses for adults is to simply provide instruction for examinations such as IELTS or Cambridge Proficiency in English. However, we would argue that it is important for teachers also to incorporate aims of a more life-long nature such as learning to work as a group, learning to respect each other, learning about another's culture, or learning skills that will be of use for the future, if they are to attempt to incorporate educational value and principles into the process of learning a language. If the passing of an exam is seen as a short-term goal, but one that is embedded within longer-term goals and a more holistic attitude to learning involving the development of the whole person, then a more educational stance is being adopted.

2   Learners learn what is meaningful to them

A constructivist view of learning tells us that learners are engaged in actively making sense of the information provided to them. However, this is not necessarily always a conscious process. Each individual will construct a different message from the input provided. For language teachers it is important to be aware of the fact that whatever language input is provided, we cannot predict what each individual will learn, or how the learner's language system will develop.

Individuals will tend to learn what they think is worth learning, but this will also differ from one person to another. Some people will consider learning a particular language is valuable; others will see no value in it. At a narrower level, some language learners will consider it important to develop a wide vocabulary, whilst for others a more narrow technical vocabulary will be seen as far more valuable. Some will place great emphasis upon the quality of their accent, whilst others will see their priority as becoming conversationally fluent, no matter how poor their accent might be. Unless teachers have a sound grasp of what their learners see as important and meaningful, they will not possess all the information they need to make their courses truly motivational.

3   Learners learn in ways that are meaningful to them

One of our basic premises is that each learner is different, and will bring to the learning process a unique set of personal attributes, preferred ways of learning and learning strategies. Learners will make sense of the learning situation and learning tasks in ways that are personal and unique to them. A teacher, therefore, cannot assume that all the learners will go about any particular task in the same way. Teachers, therefore, need to provide a variety of language learning activities which allow for different learning styles and individual preferences and personalities: some visual, some auditory, some involving movement, some interactive and some analytic. It is also important that teachers realise the need to help learners to shape their learning strategies in ways that are meaningful to them, to encourage them to find their own style, to identify their own strengths, and to develop their own self-knowledge.

4 Learners learn better if they feel in control of what they are learning

Throughout this book we have stressed the importance of individuals making choices about what they do, of setting their own goals, of feeling that they can originate and be in control of their actions. For teachers, there is a need, therefore, to encourage learners to talk about their aims and set goals for themselves regarding learning the language, to help them to make choices and to encourage a sense of personal responsibility for actions. For language learners this might involve selecting books or texts to read, finding ways to record and learn vocabulary, seeking out opportunities to use and practise the language, making good use of grammar references, monitoring their own progress against their goals, or discussing their aims in learning the language.

5 Learning is closely linked to how people feel about themselves

An individual's self-concept will have considerable influence on the way in which he or she learns. If a person has a negative self-concept as a language learner, then it is likely that he or she will feel a sense of embarrassment at using the language and will avoid risk-taking situations or initiating conversations in the second language. If individuals feel positive about themselves, they are likely to set themselves more optimistic goals, to engage in situations which involve risks and to seek out opportunities to use the language. We have, however, pointed out the danger of an over-inflated or unrealistic self-concept.

6 Learning takes place in a social context through interaction with other people

If we take an interactionist view of learning, we see the nature of the interactions that take place as a key to learning. This is especially apparent in the case of learning a language, where using language is essentially a social activity, and interaction in the target language is an integral part of the learning process. Teachers need to be particularly aware of the impact of the interactions that occur in the classroom. These interactions can foster a sense of belonging, they can enhance sharing behaviour, they can encourage personal control and foster positive attributions. Particularly, the nature of the interaction in the target language will influence the quality of learning that language.

7 What teachers do in the classroom will reflect their own beliefs and attitudes

Teachers' actions in the classroom and their interactions with their learners will mirror, either implicitly or explicitly, their own beliefs about learning, their views of the world, their self-views, and their attitudes towards their subject and their learners. Thus, whatever methodology teachers purport to adopt, whatever coursebook or syllabus they are following, what goes on in their classrooms will be influenced by their beliefs about the learning process. Even if a country or an institution adopts a communicative syllabus and coursebooks, what actually goes on in the classroom will reflect a combination of teachers' and learners' beliefs about learning the language and the ultimate purpose of education, as well as the unique way in which a particular lesson is socially constructed by teacher and learners.

8 There is a significant role for the teacher as mediator in the language classroom

The role of the teacher in fostering language acquisition has frequently been in question, often limited to the provider of tasks that generate circumstances where interaction between two or more learners will occur. However, the theory of mediation presented in this book maintains that the teacher can play an important part in promoting effective learning in other significant ways. Rather than being peripheral, the teacher is vital in fostering the right climate for learning to take place, for confidence to develop, for people's individuality to be respected, for a sense of belonging to be nurtured, for developing appropriate learning strategies, and for moving towards learner autonomy.

9 Learning tasks represent an interface between teachers and learners

The learning activities that teachers select, and the way in which they present them, reflect their beliefs and values; learners in turn will interpret these activities in ways that are meaningful to them. Thus learning tasks represent an interface between teachers and learners. They are more than simply what is provided by the coursebook or the syllabus. Tasks are continuously reinterpreted by teachers and learners so as to render the making of any generalisation about different types of language learning tasks extremely difficult. Nevertheless, teachers need to be clear in their minds what their learning goals are, and attempt to implement these through the tasks they provide.

10 Learning is influenced by the situation in which it occurs

As we have seen, the whole context has a significant influence on any learning that takes place. This applies not only to the immediate context of the classroom, learning centre, or home where it is important to establish a supportive physical environment together with facilitative personal interactions. It applies also to the broader social, educational and political context within which language learning experiences are occurring. In addition, the cultural background of the learners will influence the sense they make of the learning situation, and their view of the culture to which the foreign language belongs.

There are undoubtedly many factors affecting the success with which languages are learned which have not been covered or even alluded to in this book. We have consciously not attempted to deal with all these factors. What we have tried to get to grips with here is how far a specific psychological approach (constructivism), when applied within a sophisticated social science framework (social interactionism) can be employed to make sense of and, ultimately, improve language learning and teaching. We have tried to present this approach with integrity, but we are aware that we have accomplished this more successfully in some sections than in others. If we have enabled our readers to reconstruct their practices in some small way critically as a result of our endeavours, then we would consider our journey to have been well worthwhile.

References

Adey, P. and M. Shayer. 1994. *Really Raising Standards: cognitive intervention and academic achievement*. London: Routledge.

Alexander, L. G. 1968. *Look, Listen and Learn*. London: Longman.

Aljaafreh, A. and J. P. Lantolf. 1994. Negative feedback as regulation and second language learning in the zone of proximal development. *The Modern Language Journal*, 78(4), 465–83.

Ames, C. 1984. Competitive, co-operative and individualistic goal structures: a motivational analysis. In R. Ames and C. Ames (Eds.) *Research on Motivation in Education*, vol. 1, 177–207. New York: Academic Press.

Ames, C. 1992. Classrooms: goals, structures and student motivation. *Journal of Educational Psychology*, 84(3), 261–71.

Ames, C. and R. E. Ames (Eds.). 1984. *Research on Motivation in Education*, vol. 1, *Student Motivation*. London: Academic Press.

Ames, C. and R. E. Ames (Eds.). 1985. *Research on Motivation in Education*, vol. 2, *The Classroom Milieu*. London: Academic Press.

Ames, C. and R. E. Ames (Eds.). 1989. *Research on Motivation in Education*, vol. 3, *Goals and Cognitions*. London: Academic Press.

Appel, G. and J. P. Lantolf. 1994. Speaking as mediation: a study of L1 and L2 test recall tasks. *The Modern Language Journal*, 78(4), 437–52.

Apter, S. J. 1978. *Troubled Children: troubled systems*. Oxford: Pergamon.

Argyris, C. and D. A. Schön. 1974. *Theory in Practice*. San Francisco: Jossey-Bass.

Argyris, C. and D. A. Schön. 1978. *Organizational Learning: a Theory of Action Perspective*. Reading, Mass: Addison-Wesley.

Arlin, M. and T. W. Whitley. 1978. Perceptions of self-managed learning opportunities and academic locus of control: a causal interpretation, *Journal of Educational Psychology*, 70(b), 988–92.

Ascione, F. R. and W. R. Berg. 1983. A teacher-training program to enhance mainstreamed handicapped pupil self-concepts. *Psychology in the Schools*, 12, 319–25.

Ashman, A. F. and R. N. Conway. 1989. *Cognitive Strategies for Special Education: process-based instruction*. London: Routledge.

Ashman, A. F. and R. N. Conway. 1993. *Using Cognitive Methods in the Classroom*. London: Routledge.

Ashton-Warner, S. 1980. *Teacher*, 2nd edn. London: Virago.

Atkinson, J. W. 1964. *An Introduction to Motivation*. Princeton, N.J.: Van Nostrand.

Atkinson, R. C. and R. M. Shiffrin. 1968. Human memory: a proposed system and its control processes. In W. K. Spence and J. T. Spence (Eds.) *The Psychology of Learning and Motivation: advances in research and theory*. New York: Academic Press.

Ausubel, D. 1968. *Educational Psychology – A Cognitive View*. New York: Holt, Rinehart and Winston.

Bachor, D. 1989. Do mentally handicapped adults transfer cognitive skills from the IE classroom to other situations or settings? *Mental Retardation and Learning Disability Bulletin*, 16(2), 14–28.

Bandura, A. R. 1977. Self-efficacy: toward a unifying theory of behavioural change. *Psychological Review*, 41, 191–215.

Bandura, A. R. 1986. *Social Foundations of Thought and Action: a social cognitive theory*. Englewood Cliffs, N.J.: Prentice Hall.

Bannister, D. and F. Fransella. 1986. *Inquiring Man: the psychology of personal constructs*, 3rd edn. London: Routledge.

Beail, N. (Ed.). 1985. *Repertory Grid Technique and Personal Constructs: applications in clinical and educational settings*. London: Croom Helm.

Bennett, N. 1976. *Teaching Styles and Pupil Progress*. London: Open Books.

Bennett, N. 1987. Changing perspectives on teaching-learning processes in the post-Plowden era. *Oxford Review of Education*, 13(1), 67–79.

Berlyne, D. E. 1960. *Conflict, Arousal and Curiosity*. New York: McGraw-Hill.

Berlyne, D. E. 1965. *Structure and Direction in Thinking*. New York: McGraw-Hill.

Best, J. B. 1986. *Cognitive Psychology*. St Paul, MN: West.

Biddle S. 1993. Attribution research and sport psychology. In R. N. Singer, M. Murphey and L. K. Tennant (Eds.) *Handbook of Research on Sport Psychology*, 437–64. New York: Macmillan.

Blagg, N. 1991. *Can We Teach Intelligence?* Hillsdale, N.J.: Erlbaum.

Blagg, N., M. Ballinger, R. Gardner, M. Petty and G. Williams. 1988. *Somerset Thinking Skills Course*. Oxford: Basil Blackwell.

Bligh, D. 1971. *What's the Use of Lectures?* London: Bligh.

Bolitho, R. and B. Tomlinson. 1980. *Discover English*. London: Heinemann.

Bornstein, M. H. and J. S. Bruner (Eds.). 1989. *Interaction in Human Development*. Hillsdale, N.J.: Erlbaum.

Boud, D., D. Keogh and D. Walker (Eds.). 1985. *Reflection: turning experience into learning*. London: Kogan Page.

Bransford, J. D. and M. Johnson. 1972. Contextual prerequisites for understanding: some investigations of comprehension and recall. *Journal of Verbal Learning and Verbal Recall*, 11, 717–26.

Brindley, G. 1987. Factors affecting task difficulty. In D. Nunan 1987, *Guidelines for the Development of Curriculum Resources*. Adelaide: National Curriculum Resource Centre.

Bronfenbrenner, U. 1979. *The Ecology of Human Development*. Cambridge, Mass.: Harvard University Press.

Brophy, J. E. and T. L. Good. 1986. Teacher behavior and student achievement. In M. C. Wittrock (Ed.), *Handbook of Research on Teaching*, 3rd edn, 328–75. New York: Macmillan.

Brown, A. L., J. D. Bransford, R. A. Ferrara and J. C. Campione. 1983. Learning, remembering and understanding. In P. Mussen (Ed.) *Handbook of Child Psychology: Cognitive Development*, vol. 3. New York: Wiley.

Brown, A. L. and J. C. Campione. 1986. Psychological theory and the study of learning disabilities. *American Psychologist*, 41(10), 1059–68.

Brown, G. and G. Yule. 1983. *Teaching the Spoken Language*. Cambridge: Cambridge University Press.

Brown, G. and C. Desforges. 1979. *Piaget's Theory: a psychological critique*. London: Routledge and Kegan Paul.

Brown, H. D. 1994. *Principles of Language Learning and Teaching*, 3rd edn. Englewood Cliffs, N.J.: Prentice Hall.

Brown, S. and D. McIntyre. 1983. *Making Sense of Teaching*. Buckingham: Open University Press.

Bruner, J. S. 1960. *The Process of Education*. Cambridge, Mass.: Harvard University Press.

Bruner, J. S. 1966. *Towards a Theory of Instruction*. Cambridge, Mass.: Harvard University Press.

Burden, R. L. 1981. Systems theory and its relevance to schools. In B. Gillham (Ed.) *Problem Behaviour in the Secondary School: A systems approach*. London: Croom Helm.

Burden, R. L. 1987. Feuerstein's Instrumental Enrichment Programme: important issues in research and evaluation. *European Journal of Psychology of Education*, 11(1), 3–16.

Burden, R. L. and B. J. Fraser. 1993. Use of classroom environment perspectives in school psychology: a British perspective. *Psychology in Schools*, 30(3), 232–40.

Burden, R. L. and T.-A. Hornby. 1988. Assessing classroom ethos: some recent promising developments for the systems oriented educational psychologist. *Educational Psychology in Practice*, 5(1), 17–22.

Burns, R. B. 1982. *Self-Concept Development and Education*. London: Holt, Rinehart and Winston.

Button, L. 1981 and 1982. *Group Tutoring for the Form Teacher*, vols. I and II. London: Hodder and Stoughton.

Caffyn, R. 1984. Rewards and punishments in schools. A study of their effectiveness as perceived by secondary school pupils and their teachers. MEd (unpublished) dissertation, University of Exeter.

Candlin, C. 1987. Toward task-based learning. In C. Candlin and D. Murphy (Eds.) *Language Learning Tasks.* Englewood Cliffs, N.J.: Prentice Hall.

Candlin, C. and D. Murphy (Eds.) 1987. *Language Learning Tasks.* Englewood Cliffs, N.J.: Prentice Hall.

Candlin, C. and D. Nunan. 1987. Revised Syllabus Specifications for the Omani School English Language Curriculum. Muscat: Ministry of Education and Youth.

Carraher, T., D. W. Carraher and A. D. Schliemann. 1985. Mathematics in the Streets and in Schools. *British Journal of Developmental Psychology*, 3, 21–9.

Carroll, J. B. and S. M. Sapon. 1959. *Modern Language Aptitude Test.* New York: The Psychological Corporation.

Chapelle, C. 1992. 'Disembedded figures in the landscape . . . '. An appraisal of Griffiths and Sheen's 'Reappraisal of L2 research on field dependence/ independence'. *Applied Linguistics*, 13(4), 375–84.

Chin, C. 1990. An Investigation into Teachers' Mediation with Primary Students' Learning English in Taiwan. Unpublished MEd dissertation. University of Exeter.

Clark, C. and P. Peterson. 1986. Teachers' thought processes. In M. Wittrock (Ed.) *Handbook of Research on Teaching*, 255–96. New York: Macmillan.

Cole, M. 1985. The zone of proximal development: where culture and cognition create each other. In J. V. Wertsch (Ed.) *Culture, Communication and Cognition: Vygotskian perspectives.* Cambridge: Cambridge University Press.

Coles, M. J. and W. D. Robinson. 1991. *Teaching Thinking, a Survey of Programmes in Education.* London: Bristol Classical Press.

Connell, J. P. and B. Ilardi. 1987. Self-system concomitants of discrepancies between children's and teachers' evaluations of academic competence. *Child Development*, 58(5), 1297–387.

Connelly, F. and D. Clandinin. 1990. Stories of experience and narrative inquiry. *Educational Researcher*, 19(4), 2–14.

Cooley, C. H. 1902. *Human Nature and the Social Order.* New York: Charles Scribner's Sons.

Coopersmith, S. A. 1967. *The Antecedents of Self-esteem.* San Francisco: W. H. Freeman.

Covington, M. V. 1992. *Making the Grade: a self-worth perspective on motivation and school reform.* Cambridge: Cambridge University Press.

Covington, M. V. and R. G. Beery. 1976. *Self-worth and School Learning.* New York: Holt, Rinehart and Winston.

Craske, M. L. 1988. Learned helplessness, self-worth motivation and attribution re-training for primary school children. *British Journal of Educational Psychology,* 58, 152–64.

Crookall, D. and R. Oxford. 1988. Review Essay. *Language Learning,* 31.1, 128–40.

Crookes, G. and S. M. Gass. 1993a. *Tasks in a Pedagogical Context.* Clevedon, UK: Multilingual Matters.

Crookes, G. and S. M. Gass. 1993b. *Tasks and Language Learning.* Clevedon, UK: Multilingual Matters.

Crookes, G. and R. Schmidt. 1991. Motivation: reopening the research agenda. *Language Learning,* 41.4, 469–512.

Csikszentmihalyi, M. and J. Nakamura. 1989. The Dynamics of Intrinsic Motivation: a study of adolescents. In C. Ames and R. E. Ames (Eds.) *Research on Motivation Education,* vol. 3, *Goals and Cognitions.* London: Academic Press.

Curran, C. 1972. *Counselling Learning: a whole person approach for education.* Apple River, Illinois: Apple River Press.

d'Anglejan, A. and C. Renaud. 1985. Learner characteristics and second language acquisition: a multivariate study of adult immigrants and some thoughts on methodology. *Language Learning,* 35, 1–19.

Damon, W. and D. Hart. 1982. The development of self-understanding from infancy through adolescence. *Child Development,* 53, 841–84.

Das, J. P., J. Kirby and R. F. Jarman. 1979. *Simultaneous and Successive Cognitive Processing.* New York: Academic Press.

Davis, B. D. 1985. Dependency Grids: an illustration of their use in an educational setting. In N. Beail (Ed.) *Repertory Grid Technique and Personal Constructs: applications in clinical and educational settings.* London: Croom Helm.

Deaux, K. 1985. Sex and gender. *Annual Review of Psychology,* 36, 49–81.

De Bono, E. 1977. *Lateral Thinking.* London: Penguin Books.

De Bono, E. 1979. *Future Positive.* London: Penguin Books.

De Bono, E. 1993. *Teach Your Child How To Think.* London: Penguin Books.

de Charms, R. 1984. Motivation enhancement in educational settings. In C. Ames and R. E. Ames (Eds.) *Research on Motivation in Education,* vol. 1, *Student Motivation.* New York: Academic Press.

Deci, E. L. 1975. *Intrinsic Motivation.* New York: Plenum.

Deci, E. L. 1980. *The Psychology of Self-Determination.* Lexington, MA: Heath.

Deci, E. L. and R. M. Ryan. 1985. *Intrinsic Motivation and Self-Determination in Human Behavior.* New York: Plenum Press.

De Guerrero, M. C. and O. S. Villamil. 1994. Social-cognitive dimensions of interaction in L2 peer revision. *The Modern Language Journal*, 78(4), 484–96.

Dickinson, L. 1987. *Self-instruction in Language Learning.* Cambridge: Cambridge University Press.

Donaldson, M. 1978. *Children's Minds.* London: Fontana.

Donaldson, M. 1992. *Human Minds: an exploration.* London: Penguin Books.

Donato, R. and D. McCormick. 1994. A sociocultural perspective on language learning strategies: the role of mediation. *The Modern Language Journal*, 78(4), 453–64.

Dörnyei, Z. 1994a. Motivation and motivating in the foreign language classroom. *The Modern Language Journal*, 78(3), 273–84.

Dörnyei, Z. 1994b. Understanding L2 motivation: on with the challenge! *The Modern Language Journal*, 78(4), 515–23.

Doyle, W. 1986. Classroom organization and management. In M. C. Wittrock (Ed.) *Handbook of Research on Teaching*, 3rd edn. New York: Macmillan.

Dreyer, P. J. 1994. Designing curricular identity interventions for secondary schools. In S. L. Archer (Ed.) *Interventions for Adolescent Identity Development.* London: Sage.

Dunn, R., J. S. Baudy and A. Klavas. 1989. Survey of research and learning styles. *Educational Leadership*, 46, 25–40.

Dunn, R., K. Dunn and G. Price. 1986. *Learning Style Inventory Manual.* Lawrence, K.S.: Price Systems.

Dunne, E. and N. Bennett. 1990. *Talking and Learning in Groups.* Basingstoke: Macmillan.

Dweck, C. S. and C. B. Wortman. 1982. Learned helplessness, anxiety and achievement motivation. In H. W. Krohne and L. Lanx (Eds.) *Achievement, Stress and Anxiety.* London: Hemisphere.

Dweck, C. S. 1985. Intrinsic motivation, perceived self-control and self-evaluation maintenance: an achievement goal analysis. In C. Ames and R. Ames (Eds.) *Research on Motivation in Education*, vol. 2, *The Classroom Milieu.* London: Academic Press.

Dweck, C. S. and E. L. Leggett. 1988. A social-cognitive approach to motivation and personality. *Psychological Review*, 95, 256–73.

Elkind, D. 1970. *Children and Adolescents.* London: Oxford University Press.

Ellis, G. and B. Sinclair. 1989. *Learning to Learn English: a course in learner training.* Cambridge: Cambridge University Press.

Ellis, G. 1991. Learning to Learn. In C. Brumfit, J. Moon and R. Tongue (Eds.) *Teaching English to Children*, 142–57. London: Collins.

Ellis, R. 1984. *Classroom Second Language Development.* Oxford: Pergamon.

Ellis, R. 1994. *The Study of Second Language Acquisition*. Oxford: Oxford University Press.

Ericksen, S. 1984. *The Essence of Good Teaching*. San Francisco: Jossey-Bass.

Erikson, E. H. 1963. *Childhood and Society*. New York: Norton.

Erikson, E. H. 1968. *Youth and Crisis*. New York: Norton.

Feuerstein, R., Y. Rand and M. Hoffman. 1979. *The Dynamic Assessment of Retarded Performers*. Glenview, Illinois: Scott Foresman.

Feuerstein, R., Y. Rand, M. Hoffman and R. Miller. 1980. *Instrumental Enrichment*. Glenview, Illinois: Scott Foresman.

Feuerstein, R., P. S. Klein and A. J. Tannenbaum. 1991. *Mediated Learning Experience: theoretical, psychological and learning implications*. London: Freund.

Findley, M. J. and H. M. Cooper. 1983. Locus of control and academic achievement: a literature review. *Journal of Personality and Social Psychology*, 44(2), 419–27.

Flavell, J. H. 1963. *The Developmental Psychology of Jean Piaget*. Princeton, N.J.: Van Nostrand.

Flavell, J. H. 1970. Developmental Studies of Mediated Memory. In H. W. Reese and L. P. Lipsitt (Eds.) *Advances in Children's Development and Behaviour*. New York: Academic Press.

Flavell, J. H. 1976. Metacognitive Aspects of Problem Solving. In L. B. Resnick (Ed.) *The Nature of Intelligence*. Hillsdale, N.J.: Erlbaum.

Flavell, J. H. 1981. Cognitive Monitoring. In W. P. Dickson (Ed.) *Children's Oral Communication Skills*. New York: Academic Press.

Flavell, J. H. 1985. *Cognitive Development*. Englewood Cliffs, N.J.: Prentice Hall.

Foley, J. 1991. A psycholinguistic framework for task-based approaches to language teaching. *Applied Linguistics*, 12(1), 62–75.

Fontana, D. 1988. *Psychology for Teachers*. Leicester: British Psychological Society.

Frankl, V. 1964. *Man's Search for Meaning*. London: Hodder and Stoughton.

Fraser, B. J. 1986. *Classroom Environment*. London: Croom Helm.

Fraser, B. J. 1989. Assessing and improving classroom environment. *What Research Says to the Science and Mathematics Teacher*, no. 2. Curtin University, Western Australia: The Key Centre for School Science and Mathematics.

Freire, P. 1970. *Pedagogy of the Oppressed*. New York: Continuum.

Gairns, R. and S. Redman. 1995. *True to Life*. Pre-Intermediate. Cambridge: Cambridge University Press.

Galbraith, V. and R. C. Gardner. 1988. *Individual Difference Correlates of Second Language Achievement: an annotated bibliography*. London, Ontario, UWO.

Galton, M., B. Simon and P. Croll. 1980. *Inside the Primary Classroom*. London: Routledge and Kegan Paul.

Gardner, H. 1983. *Frames of Mind*. New York: Basic Books.

Gardner, R. C. 1985. *Social Psychology and Language Learning: the role of attitudes and motivation*. London: Edward Arnold.

Gardner, R. C. and W. Lambert. 1972. *Attitudes and Motivation in Second Language Learning*. Rowley, Mass.: Newbury House Publishers.

Gardner, R. C. and P. D. MacIntyre. 1992. A student's contributions to second language learning, Part 1: cognitive variables. *Language Teaching*, 25, 211–30.

Gardner, R. C. and P. F. Tremblay. 1994a. On motivation, research agendas, and theoretical frameworks. *The Modern Language Journal*, 78(3), 359–68.

Gardner, R. C. and P. F. Tremblay. 1994b. On motivation, measurement and conceptual considerations. *The Modern Language Journal*, 78(4), 524–7.

Gattengo, C. 1972. *Teaching Foreign Languages in Schools: the silent way*. New York: Educational Solutions.

Glasser, W. 1969. *Schools without Failure*. New York: Harper and Row.

Good, T. L. and J. E. Brophy. 1986. School Effects. In M. Wittrock (Ed.) *Handbook of Research on Teaching*. New York: Wiley.

Gow, L. and D. Kember. 1993. Conceptions of teaching and their relationship to student learning. *British Journal of Educational Psychology*, 63, 20–33.

Gradman, H. and E. Hanania. 1991. Language learning background factors and ESL proficiency. *Modern Language Journal*, 75, 39–51.

Greenhalgh, P. 1994. *Emotional Growth and Learning*. London: Routledge.

Griffiths, R. and R. Sheen. 1992. Disembedded figures in the landscape: a reappraisal of L2 research on field dependence/independence. *Applied Linguistics*, 13(2), 133–48.

Griggs, S. A. and R. Dunn. 1989. Learning styles of multicultural groups and counseling implications. *Journal of Multicultural Counseling and Development*, 17, 146–55.

Gruneberg, M. M. 1987. *Linkword French, German, Spanish, Italian*. London: Corgi Books.

Gruneberg, M. M. and G. C. Jacobs. 1991. In defence of Linkword. *Language Learning Journal*, 3, 25–9.

Gurney, P. W. 1986. Self-esteem in the classroom: theoretical perspectives and assessment issues. *School Psychology International*, 8(1), 21–9.

Habermas, J. 1972. *Knowledge and Human Interests*, 2nd edn. London: Heinemann.

Hadfield, J. 1992. *Classroom Dynamics*. Oxford : Oxford University Press.

Halpern, D. F. (Ed.) 1992. *Enhancing Thinking Skills in the Sciences and Mathematics*. Hillsdale, N.J.: Erlbaum.

Hamachek, D. E. 1977. Humanistic Psychology: theoretical-philosophical framework and implications for teaching. In D. J. Treffinger, J. Davis and R. E. Ripple (Eds.) *Handbook on Teaching Educational Psychology*. New York: Academic Press.

Hamachek, D. E. 1988. Evaluating self-concept and ego development within Erikson's psycho-social framework: a formulation. *Journal of Counseling and Development*, April, 354–60.

Hamachek, D. E. 1992. *Encounters with the Self*. Orlando: Harcourt, Brace, Jovanovitch.

Handy, C. 1989. *The Age of Unreason*. Penguin.

Hanson, J. 1991. The Oxfordshire Skills Programme. In M. J. Coles and W. D. Robinson (Eds.) *Teaching Thinking, a Survey of Programmes in Education*. London: Bristol Classical Press.

Harri-Augstein, S. and L. Thomas. 1991. *Learning Conversations*. London: Routledge.

Harter, S. 1978. Effectance motivation reconsidered: toward a developmental model. *Human Development*, 1, 34–64.

Harter, S. 1981. A new self-report scale of intrinsic versus extrinsic orientations in the classroom: motivational and informational components. *Development Psychology*, 17(3), 300–12.

Hastings, N. J. 1992. Questions of motivation. *Support for Learning*, 7(3), 135–7.

Hastings, N. J. 1994. Enhancing motivation in the classroom: strategies for intervention. *Educational and Child Psychology*, 11.2, 48–55.

Hebb, D. O. 1959, 1966. *The Organisation of Behavior*. New York: Wiley.

Heider, F. 1944. Social perceptions and phenomenal causality. *Psychological Review*, 51, 358–74.

Heider, F. 1958. *The Psychology of Interpersonal Relations*. New York: Wiley.

Helmke, A., W. Schneider and F. E. Weinert. 1986. Quality of instruction and classroom learning outcomes: the German contribution to the I.E.A. classroom environment study. *Teaching and Teacher Education*, 2(1), 1–18.

Hewstone, M. 1989. *Causal Attribution: from cognitive processes to collective beliefs*. Oxford: Blackwell.

Hickson, J., A. J. Land and G. Aikman. 1994. Learning style differences in middle school pupils from four ethnic backgrounds. *School Psychology International*, 15(4), 349–60.

Higgins, E. T., D. N. Ruble and W. Hartup (Eds.) 1989. *Developmental Social Cognition: a social-cultural perspective*. Hillsdale, N.J.: Erlbaum.

Holt, J. 1964. *How Children Fail*. New York: Holt, Rinehart and Winston.

Holt, J. 1968. *How Children Learn*. New York: Dial.

Holt J. 1969. *The Underachieving School*. London: Penguin Books.

Holt, J. 1971. *What do I do Monday?* London: Pitman.

Horwitz, E. and D. J. Young. 1991. *Language Anxiety: from theory and research to classroom implications*. Englewood Cliffs, N.J.: Prentice Hall.

Huang, D. H. 1994. Social Comparison Information in the Classroom: a study of pupils and teachers in Taiwan Secondary Schools. Unpublished PhD thesis, University of Sheffield.

Hunt, J. McV. 1961. *Intelligence and Experience*. New York: Ronald Press.

Hunt, J. McV. 1965. Intrinsic motivation and its role in psychological development. In D. Levine (Ed.) *Nebraska Symposium on Motivation*, vol. 3. Lincoln: University of Nebraska Press.

Ishida, T. 1993. A Pilot Study of Communication Strategies Employed by Japanese Learners of English in the U.K. Unpublished MEd dissertation. University of Exeter.

Jackson, P. W. 1968. *Life in Classrooms*. New York: Holt, Rinehart and Winston.

Jacobowski, E. and K. Tobin. 1991. Teachers' personal epistemologies and classroom learning environments. In B. J. Fraser and H. J. Walberg (Eds.) *Educational Environments: evaluation, antecedents and consequences*. London: Pergamon.

John-Steiner, V. P. 1988. The road to competence in an alien land. A Vygotskian perspective on bilingualism. In J. Wertsch (Ed.) *Cognition: Vygotskian Perspectives*, 348–71. Cambridge: Cambridge University Press.

Johnson, D. W. and R. T. Johnson. 1987. *Learning Together and Alone*. Englewood Cliffs, N.J.: Prentice Hall.

Johnson, D. W. and R. T. Johnson. 1989. *Co-operation and Competition: theory and research*. Edina, M.N.: Interaction.

Jonas, B. S. and D. S. Martin. 1985. Cognitive improvement in hearing-impaired high-school students through instruction in Instrumental Enrichment. In D. S. Martin (Ed.) *Cognition, Education and Deafness*. Washington, D.C.: Gallandet College Press.

Jones, B., A. Palincsar, D. Ogle and E. Carr. 1987. Strategic teaching and learning: cognitive instruction in the content area. Alexandria, VA: Association of Supervision and Curriculum Development.

Kaiser, R. 1993. A change in focus . . . without losing sight of the child. *School Psychology International*, 14(1), 5–20.

Kaplan, P. S. 1990. *Educational Psychology for Tomorrow's Teacher*. St Paul, MN: West.

Kelly, G. 1955. *The Psychology of Personal Constructs*. New York: Norton.

Kemmis, S. 1985. Action Research and the Politics of Reflection. In D. Boud, D. Keogh and D. Walker (Eds.) *Reflection: turning experience into learning*, 139–64. London: Kogan Page.

Kirby, J. R. (Ed.) 1984. *Cognitive Strategies and Educational Performance*. London and New York: Academic Press.

Klatzky, R. L. 1980. *Human Memory: structure and processes*. San Francisco: W. H. Freeman.

Knowles, M. 1976. *The Modern Practice of Adult Education*. New York: Association Press.

Kornhaber, M. L. and H. Gardner. 1991. Critical thinking across multiple intelligences. In S. Maclure and P. Davies (Eds.) *Learning to Think – Thinking to Learn*. Oxford: Pergamon.

Kozulin, A. 1990. *Vygotsky's Psychology: a bibliography of ideas*. New York: Harvester-Wheatsheaf.

Krashen, S. 1981. *Second Language Acquisition and Second Language Learning*. Oxford: Pergamon.

Krashen, S. 1982. *Principles and Practice in Second Language Acquisition*. Oxford: Pergamon.

Kumaravadivelu, B. 1993. The name of the task and the task of naming: methodological aspects of task-based pedagogy. In G. Crookes and S. M. Gass (Eds.) *Tasks in a Pedagogical Context*. Cleveland, UK: Multilingual Matters.

Kynch, M. D., A. A. Norem-Hebeisen and K. Gergen (Eds.) 1981. *Self-concept: advances in theory and research*. Cambridge, Mass.: Ballinger.

Lawrence, D. 1973. *Improved Reading Through Counselling*. London: Ward Lock.

Lawrence, D. 1988. *Enhancing Self-Esteem in the Classroom*. London: Chapman.

Lawson, M. J. and D. N. Rice. 1987. Thinking aloud: analysing students' mathematics performance. *School Psychology International*, 84, 223–44.

Legutke, M. and H. Thomas. 1991. *Process and Experience in the Language Classroom*. Harlow: Longman.

Lepper, M. R., D. Greene and R. E. Nisbet. 1973. Undermining children's intrinsic interest in extrinsic reward: a test of the 'overjustification' hypothesis. *Journal of Personality and Social Psychology*, 28(1), 129–37.

Lepper, M. R. and D. Greene (Eds.) 1978. *The Hidden Costs of Reward*. Hillsdale, N.J.: Lawrence Erlbaum.

Lepper, M. R. and M. Hoddell. 1989. Intrinsic motivation in the classroom. In C. Ames and R. Ames (Eds.) *Research on Motivation in Education*, vol. 3, *Goals and Cognitions*. London: Academic Press.

Levi, P. 1979. *If This Is A Man*. London: Penguin Books.

Lidz, C. D. (Eds.) 1987. *Dynamic Assessment*. London: Guildford Press.

Lightbown, P. and N. Spada. 1993. *How Languages are Learned*. Oxford: Oxford University Press.

Lipman, M. 1988. *Philosophy Goes to School*. Philadelphia, PA: Temple University Press.

Lipman, M., A. M. Sharp and F. S. Oscanyan. 1980. *Philosophy in the Classroom*. Philadelphia, PA: Temple University Press.

Long, M. H. 1980. Inside the 'black box': methodological issues in classroom research on language learning. *Language Learning*, 30, 1–42.

Long, M. H. and G. Crookes. 1993. Units of Analysis in Syllabus Design: the case for the task. In G. Crookes and S. M. Gass (Eds.) *Tasks in a Pedagogical Context*. Clevedon: Multilingual Matters.

Louden, W. 1991. Collegiality, curriculum and educational change. *Curriculum Journal*, 2 (3), 361–73.

Lozanov, G. 1979. *Suggestology and Outlines of Suggestopedy*. New York: Gordon and Breach.

Lukmani, Y. 1972. Motivation to learn and learning proficiency. *Language Learning*, 22, 261–73.

McCormick, M. K. and J. H. Williams. 1974. Effects of a compensatory program on self-report, achievement and aspiration level of disadvantaged high-school students. *Journal of Negro Education*, 43, 47–52.

MacIntyre, P. D. and R. C. Gardner. 1989. Anxiety and second language learning: towards a theoretical clarification. *Language Learning*, 39, 251–75.

Maclure, S. and P. Davies (Eds.) 1991. *Learning to Think: Thinking to Learn*. Oxford: Pergamon.

Maehr, M. L. and J. G. Nicholls. 1980. Culture and achievement motivation: a second look. In N. Warren (Ed.) *Studies in Cross Cultural Psychology*, vol. II, 221–67. London: Academic Press.

Male, D. B. 1992. An investigation into the learning and memory processes of children with moderate learning difficulties. Unpublished PhD thesis: University of London.

Marcia, J., A. S. Waterman, D. R. Matteson, S. L. Archer and J. L. Orlofsky. 1993. *Ego Identity: a handbook for psychosocial research*. New York: Springer Verlag.

Marsh, H. W. 1990. A multidimensional, hierarchical model of self-concept; theoretical and empirical justification. *Educational Psychology Review*, 2, 77–172.

Marsh, H. W., J. Parker, and J. Barnes. 1985. Multidimensional adolescent self-concepts: their relationship to age, sex and academic measures. *American Educational Research Journal*, 22 (3), 422–44.

Marsh, H. W. and R. J. Shavelson. 1985. Self-concept: its multifaceted, hierarchical structure. *Educational Psychology*, 20, 107–23.

Maslow, A. H. 1968. *Toward a Psychology of Being*, 2nd edn. New York: Van Nostrand.

Maslow, A. H. 1970. *Motivation and Personality*, 2nd edn. New York: Harper and Row.

Meighan, R. and J. Meighan. 1990. Alternative roles for learners with particular reference to learners as democratic explorers in teacher education courses. *The School Field*, 1(1), 61–77.

Merrett, F. and K. Wheldall. 1990. *Positive Teaching in the Primary School*. London: Chapman.

Merry, R. 1980. The keyword method and children's vocabulary learning in the classroom. *British Journal of Educational Psychology*, 50(2), 123–36.

Moll, L. C. 1990. *Vygotsky and Education*. Cambridge: Cambridge University Press.

Molnar, A. and B. Lindquist. 1989. *Changing Problem Behavior in Schools*. San Francisco: Jossey-Bass.

Moos, R. H. and E. J. Trickett. 1974. *Classroom Environment Scale Manual*. Palo Alto, California: Consulting Psychologists Press.

Mortimore, P., P. Sammons, L. Stoll. D. Lewis and R. Ecob. 1987. *School Matters: the junior years*. Wells: Open Books.

Murray, H. A. 1938. *Explorations in Personality*. New York: Oxford University Press.

Neill, A. S. 1962. *Summerhill*. London: Gollancz.

Neill, A. S. 1967. *Talking of Summerhill*. London: Gollancz.

Nespor, J. 1987. The role of beliefs in the practice of teaching. *Journal of Curriculum Studies*, 19, 317–28.

Nicholls, J. G. 1979. Quality and equality in intellectual development: the role of motivation in education. *American Psychologist*, 34, 1071–84.

Niitsuma, H. 1992. A Study of the Motivation of Japanese Junior High School Students Towards Learning English as a Foreign Language. Unpublished MEd dissertation. University of Exeter.

Nisbet, J. and J. Shucksmith, 1991. *Learning Strategies*. New York: Routledge.

Nunan, D. 1989. *Designing Tasks for the Communicative Classroom*. Cambridge: Cambridge University Press.

Nunan, D. 1993. Task-based Syllabus Design: selecting, grading and sequencing tasks. In G. Crookes and S. M. Gass (Eds.) *Tasks in a Pedagogical Context*. Clevedon: Multilingual Matters.

O'Malley, J. and A. Chamot. 1990. *Language Learning Strategies*. Cambridge: Cambridge University Press.

O'Neill, R., R. Kingsbury and T. Yeadon. 1975. *Kernel Lessons Intermediate*. London: Longman.

Owens, L. 1983. With others, against others, and on your own: the learning preferences of teachers. *Journal of Education for Teaching*, 9, 131–49.

Owens, L. 1985. The learning preferences of students and teachers: an Australian-American comparison. *Teaching and Teacher Education*, 1, 229–41.

Owens, L. and J. Barnes. 1992. *Learning Preference Scales*. Hawthorn, Victoria: ACER.

Oxford, R. 1989. Use of language learning strategies: a synthesis of studies with implications for strategy training. *System*, 17(2), 235–47.

Oxford, R. 1990. *Language Learning Strategies: what every teacher should know*. New York: Newbury House.

Oxford, R. 1994. Where are we regarding language learning motivation? *The Modern Language Journal*, 78(iv), 512–14.

Oxford, R. and D. Crookall. 1989. Research on language learning strategies: methods, findings, and instructional issues. *The Modern Language Journal*, 73(iv), 404–19.

Oxford, R. and M. Ehrman. 1993. Second language research on individual differences. *Annual Review of Applied Linguistics*, 13, 188–205.

Oxford, R. and M. Nyikos. 1989. Variables affecting choice of language learning strategies by university students. *The Modern Language Journal*, 73(iii), 291–300.

Oxford, R. and J. Shearin. 1994. Language learning motivation: expanding the theoretical framework. *The Modern Language Journal*, 78(i), 12–28.

Pajares, M. F. 1992. Teachers' beliefs and educational research: clearing up a messy construct. *Review of Educational Research*, 62(3), 307–32.

Palincsar, A. S. and A. L. Brown. 1984. Reciprocal teaching of fostering and monitoring activities. *Cognition and Instruction*, 1(2), 117–75.

Perrott, E. 1982. *Effective Teaching*. London: Longman.

Piaget, J. 1966. *The Origins of Intelligence in Children*. New York: International Universities Press.

Piaget, J. 1972. *The Principles of Genetic Epistemology*. New York: Basic Books.

Piaget, J. 1974. *To Understand is to Invent*. New York: Viking Press.

Pielstick, N. L. 1988. Assessing the learning environment. *School Psychology International*, 9(2), 111–22.

Pienemann, M. 1989. Is language teachable? Psycholinguistic experiments and hypotheses. *Applied Linguistics*, 10(1), 52–79.

Pine, G. J. and A. V. Boy. 1977. *Learner Centred Teaching: a humanistic View*. Denver, Colorado: Love Publishing Co.

Plas, J. M. 1986. *Systems Psychology in the Schools*. New York: Pergamon.

The Plowden Report. 1967. *Children and Their Primary Schools*. London: HMSO.

Politzer, R. and M. McGroarty. 1985. An exploratory study of learning behaviours and their relationship to gains in linguistic and communicative competence. *TESOL Quarterly*, 19(1), 103–23.

Pope, M. L. and T. R. Keen. 1981. *Personal Construct, Psychology and Education*. London: Academic Press.

Poteet, J. A. 1973. *Behaviour Modification: a practical guide for teachers*. London: University of London Press.

Prabhu, N. S. 1987. *Second Language Pedagogy*. Oxford: Oxford University Press.

Pring, R. 1984. *Personal and Social Education in the Curriculum: concepts and content*. London: Hodder and Stoughton.

Purkey, W. W. and J. Novak. 1984. *Inviting School Success*. Belmont, California: Wadsworth.

Quicke, J. 1994. Megacognition, pupil empowerment and the school context. *School Psychology International*, 15, 3, 247–60.

Raugh, M. R. and R. C. Atkinson. 1975. A mnemonic method for learning a second language vocabulary. *Journal of Educational Psychology*, 67, 1–16.

Rees-Miller, J. 1993. A critical appraisal of learner training: theoretical bases and teaching implications. *TESOL Quarterly*, 27(4), 679–89.

Richards, J. and T. Rodgers. 1986. *Approaches and Methods in Language Teaching*. Cambridge: Cambridge University Press.

Rogers, C. R. 1969. *Freedom to Learn*. Columbus, Ohio: Charles Merrill.

Rogers, C. R. 1982. *Freedom to Learn for the 80s*. Columbus, Ohio: Charles Merrill.

Rogoff, B. and J. V. Wertsch (Eds.) 1984. Children's learning in the "zone of proximal development". *New Directions for Child Development*, 23. San Francisco: Jossey-Bass.

Rollett, B. A. 1987. Effort-avoidance and learning. In E. De Corte, H. Lodewijks, R. Parmentier and P. Span (Eds.) *Learning and Instruction: European Research in an International Context*, vol. 1. Leuven, Belgium: Pergamon Press.

Rose, A. 1978. The effects of self-instruction on the self-concept of children with learning problems. *Dissertation Abstracts International*, 39A(5), 2761.

Rosenberg, M. 1965. *Society and the Adolescent Self Image*. Princeton, N.J.: Princeton University Press.

Rosenshine, B. 1971. *Teaching Behaviour and Student Achievements*. London: NFER.

Rosenshine, B. and N. Furst. 1973. The use of direct observation to study teaching. In R. Travers (Ed.) *Second Handbook on Research on Teaching*, 122–83. Chicago: Rand McNally.

Rost, M. and S. Ross. 1991. Learner use of strategies in interaction: typology and teachability. *Language Learning*, 41, 235–73.

Rotter, J. B. 1954. *Social Learning and Clinical Psychology*. New York: Prentice Hall.

Rubin, J. 1981. The study of cognitive processes in second language learning. *Applied Linguistics*, 1, 117–31.

Rubin, J. 1987. Learner Strategies: theoretical assumptions, research history and typology. In A. Wenden and J. Rubin (Eds.) *Learner Strategies in language learning*. Hemel Hempstead: Prentice Hall.

Ruddock, J. 1984. Teaching as an art, teacher research and research-based teacher education. Second Annual Lawrence Stenhouse Memorial Lecture. University of East Anglia.

Rutter, M., B. Maughan, P. Mortimore and J. Oustan. 1979. *Fifteen Thousand Hours: secondary schools and their effects on children*. London: Open Books.

Salmon, P. 1988. *Psychology for Teachers: an alternative approach*. London: Hutchinson.

Savell, J. M., P. T. Twohig and D. L. Rackford. 1986. Empirical status of Feuerstein's Instrumental Enrichment techniques as a method of teaching thinking skills. *Review of Educational Research*, 56 (4), 381–409.

Schank, R. C. and R. P. Abelson. 1977. *Scripts, Plans, Goals and Understanding*. Hillsdale, N.J.: Erlbaum.

Schinke-Llano, L. 1993. On the value of a Vygotskian framework for SLA theory and research. *Language Learning*, 43(1), 121–9.

Schools Council. 1968. *Enquiry One: young school leavers*. London: HMSO.

Schön, D. A. 1983. *The Reflective Practitioner: how professionals think in action*. New York: Basic Books.

Schunk, D. H. 1989. Self-efficacy perspective on achievement behaviour. *Educational Psychologist*, 19, 48–58.

Seligman, M. E. P. 1975. *Helplessness: on depression, development, and death*. San Francisco: Freeman.

Sharron, H. 1987. *Changing Children's Minds*. London: Souvenir Press.

Sinclair, B. and G. Ellis. 1992. Survey: learner training in EFL course books. *ELT Journal*, 46(2), 209–27.

Skehan, P. 1989. *Individual Differences in Second Language Learning*. London: Arnold.

Skinner, B. F. 1957. *Verbal Behavior*. New York: Appleton.

Skinner, B. F. 1968. *The Technology of Teaching*. New York: Appleton-Century-Crofts.

Skinner, B. F. 1974. *About Behaviorism*. New York: Knopf.

Skinner, B. F. 1987. *Upon Further Reflection*. Englewood Cliffs, N.J.: Prentice Hall.

Smith, P., M. Boulton and H. Cowie. 1993. The impact of co-operative groupwork on ethnic relations in middle school. *School Psychology International*, 14(1), 21–42.

Smyth, J. 1991. *Teachers as Collaborative Learners*. Milton Keynes: Open University Press.

Stenhouse, L. 1975. *An Introduction to Curriculum Research and Development*. London: Heinemann.

Sternberg, R. J. 1983. Criteria for intellectual skills training. *Educational Researcher*, 12(2), 6–12.

Sternberg, R. J. 1984. A contextualist view of intelligence. In P. S. Fry (Ed.) *Changing Conceptions of Intelligence and Intellectual Functioning*. Amsterdam: Elsevier.

Sternberg, R. 1985. *Beyond IQ: a triarchic theory of human intelligence*. Cambridge: Cambridge University Press.

Stevick, E. 1976. *Memory, Meaning and Method. Some Psychological Perspectives on Language Learning*. Rowley, Mass.: Newbury House.

Stevick, E. 1980. *Teaching Languages: a way and ways*. Rowley, Mass.: Newbury House.

Sugden, D. (Ed.) 1989. *Cognitive Approaches in Special Education*. London: Falmer.

Suls, J. and A. G. Greenwald (Ed.) 1986. *Psychological Perspectives on the Self*, vol. 3. Hillsdale, N.J.: Erlbaum.

Sutherland, P. 1992. *Cognitive Development Today: Piaget and his critics*. London: Paul Chapman.

Tarone, E. 1977. Conscious Communication Strategies in Interlanguage. In H. D. Brown *et al.* (Eds.) *On TESOL 1977*. Washington: TESOL.

Thacker, J. and G. Feest. 1991. Groupwork in the Primary School. In G. Lindsay and A. Miller (Eds.) *Psychological Services for Primary Schools*.

Thomas, L. and S. Harri-Augstein. 1985. *Self-organised Learning: foundations of a conversational science for psychology*. London: Routledge and Kegan Paul.

Tobin, K. 1991. Constructivist perspectives on learning environments. Paper presented at the annual conference of the American Educational Research Association, Chicago, Illinois, 1991.

Toffler, A. 1970. *Future Shock*. London: Bodley Head.

Tran, T. V. 1988. Sex differences in English language acculturation and learning strategies among Vietnamese adults aged 40 and over in the United States. *Sex Roles*, 19, 747–58.

Vale, D. 1990. *Earlybird*. Cambridge: Cambridge University Press.

Vale, D., with A. Feunteun. 1995. *Teaching Children English*. Cambridge: Cambridge University Press.

van Werkhoven, W. 1990. The attunement strategy and spelling problems. In A. Van der Ley and K. J. Kappers (Eds.) *Dyslexia '90*. Lisse: Swets and Zeitlinger.

Vernon, P. E. 1964. The psychology of intelligence and 'g'. In J. Cohen (Ed.) *Readings in Psychology*. London: Allen and Unwin.

von Glasersfeld, E. 1995. *Radical Constructivism*. London: Falmer.

Vygotsky, L. S. 1962. *Thought and Language.* Cambridge, Mass.: MIT Press.

Vygotsky, L. S. 1978. *Mind in Society.* Cambridge, Mass.: MIT Press.

Walberg, H. J. 1968. Teacher personality and classroom climate. *Psychology in the Schools,* 5, 163–9.

Wang, M. 1983. Development and consequences of students' sense of personal control. In J. M. Levine and M. Wang (Eds.) *Teacher and Student Perceptions: Implications for learning.* Hillsdale, N.J.: LEA.

Warren, P. 1995. An Investigation into the Use of Tasks that Develop both Second Language Learning and Thinking Skills with Children. Unpublished MEd thesis. University of Exeter.

Weiner, B. 1979. A theory of motivation for some classroom experiences. *Journal of Educational Psychology,* 71, 3–25.

Weiner, B. 1980. *Human Motivation.* New York: Holt, Rinehart and Winston.

Weiner, B. 1986. *An Attributional Theory of Motivation and Emotion.* New York: Springer-Verlag.

Weinstein, C. S. 1989. Teacher education students' perceptions of teaching. *Journal of Teacher Education,* 40(2), 53–60.

Weller, K. and A. Craft. 1983. *Making Up Our Minds: an exploratory study of Instrumental Enrichment.* London: Schools Council.

Wenden, A. 1987a. Conceptual Background and Utility. In A. Wenden and J. Rubin (Eds.) *Learner Strategies in Language learning.* Hemel Hempstead: Prentice Hall.

Wenden, A. 1987b. Metacognition: an expanded view of the cognitive abilities of L2 learners. *Language Learning,* 37(4), 573–97.

Wenden, A. and J. Rubin (Eds.) 1987. *Learner Strategies in Language Learning.* Hemel Hempstead: Prentice Hall.

Whalley, M. J. 1991. Philosophy for Children. In M. J. Coles and W. D. Robinson (Eds.) *Teaching Thinking: a survey of programmes in education.* London: Bristol Classical Press.

Wheldall, K. and F. Merrett. 1987. What is the behavioural approach to teaching? In N. Hastings and J. Ackwieso (Eds.) *New Directions in Educational Psychology,* vol. 2, *Behaviour and Motivation.* Brighton: Falmer Press.

Wheldall, K. and F. Merrett. 1984. *Positive Teaching: the behavioural approach.* London: Allen and Unwin.

White, R. W. 1959. Motivation reconsidered: the concept of competence. *Psychological Review,* 66, 297–333.

White, R. 1988. *The ELT Curriculum, Design, Innovation and Management.* Oxford: Blackwell.

Williams, M. 1991. A framework for teaching English to young learners. In

C. Brumfit, J. Moon and R. Tongue (Eds.) *Teaching English to Children: from Practice to Principle*. London: Collins.

Williams, M. 1994. Motivation in foreign and second language learning: an interactive perspective. In R. L. Burden (Ed.) *Motivation: Recent Developments in Theory and Practice in the U.K. Educational and Child Psychology*, vol. 11, no. 2, 77–84.

Willis, J. and D. Willis. 1988. *Collins Cobuild English Course*. London: Collins.

Witkin, H. A., P. K. Oltman, E. Raskin and S. A. Karp. 1971. *Manual for the Embedded Figures Test*. Windsor: NFER-Nelson.

Wittrock, M. C. (Ed.) 1986. *Handbook of Research on Teaching*. New York: Wiley.

Wittrock, M. C. and F. Farley. 1989. *The Future of Educational Psychology*. Hillsdale, N.J.: Erlbaum.

Wubbels, T. 1993. Teacher-student relationships in science and mathematics classes. In B. J. Fraser (Ed.) *Research Implications for Science and Mathematics Teachers*, vol. 1. Perth: Curtin University of Technology.

Wubbels, T. and J. Levy. 1991. A comparison of interpersonal behaviour of Dutch and American teachers. *International Journal of Intercultural Relations*, 15, 1–18.

Wubbels, T. and J. Levy (Eds.) 1993. *Do You Know What You Look Like? Interpersonal Relations in Education*. Brighton: Falmer Press.

Wubbels, T., M. Brekelmans and J. J. Hermans. 1987. Teacher behaviour. An important aspect of the learning environment. In B. J. Fraser (Ed.) *The Study of Learning Environments*, vol. 3. Perth: Curtin University of Technology.

Wubbels, T., H. A. Creton and H. P. Hoomayers. 1992. Review of research on teacher communication styles with the use of the Leary model. *Journal of Classroom Interaction*, 27(1), 1–11.

Wylie, R. C. 1979. *The Self-concept*. Lincoln: University of Nebraska Press.

Zeeman, R. D. 1982. Creating change in academic self-concept and school behaviour in alienated secondary school students. *School Psychology Review*, 11, 459–61.

Subject index

ability, 105, 131
ability grouping, *see* streaming
accommodation, 22, 23
achievement motivation, *see* motivation
action research, 54
adaptation, 22
Adaptive Learning Environment Model
  (ALEM), 102–3
adolescence, 32, 98, 99, 102, 126
advance organisers, 17
affective factors, 37
  see also emotions
affective strategies, *see* strategies
agency, a sense of, 127–9
analytic learning style, 91
  see also learning style
anxiety, 37, 38, 94, 154
approach/avoidance ratio, 114
aptitude, 18, 58, 94
  see also Skehan, aptitude tests,
    Modern Language Aptitude Test
    (MLAT), intelligence
aptitude tests, 18
arousal, 120, 126–7
  see also optimal arousal, flow
assessment, 42
assimilation, 22–3
attention, 15–16
attitude, 115
Attitude/Motivation Test Battery
  (AMTB), 116
attribution theory, 104–7
attunement strategy, 132
audiolingual approach, *see*
  audiolingualism

audiolingualism, 10, 11, 12, 16
Australia, 192, 200
autonomy, 31, 68, 71, 75, 147
avoidance, *see* effort avoidance
awareness of change, 72, 75–6

Bangalore Project, 168
behaviour modification, 13
behaviourism, 8–13, 112–13, 134
belief in positive outcome, 72, 76–7
  see also mediation
beliefs
  about self, 28, 62–3, 131–2
  about learners, 28, 57–60
  about learning, 28, 60–2
  teachers', *see* teachers' beliefs
belonging; a sense of, 33, 35, 38, 44,
  69, 79
  see also mediation
Brazil, 131

Canada, 117
challenge, 25, 31–3, 35, 69, 75, 83,
  129
  see also goal setting, flow, mediation
change, 55, 61, 81, 96
change, awareness of, 69, 75–6
  see also mediation
choice, 36, 38, 119, 206
  see also motivation, cognitive view of
classical conditioning, *see* conditioning
classroom climate, 195–9
Classroom Environment Scale (CES),
  196
COBUILD, 13, 14

Author index

Author index

Author index